Challenging Austerity

This book analyses social movements and radical political parties' strategies in Spain, Greece, Portugal and Italy from 2008 to today. Events in 2011 such as the Arab Spring and the *indignados* movement in Spain initiated a new cycle of social protest. This book explores how the economic crisis and policies of austerity have transformed and continue to transform social movements, trade unions and radical political parties in Southern Europe.

The economic crisis has led to a rise in protest movements, which confront political institutions and conventional forms of democracy, and develop new spatial and organisational strategies. This book examines these cases, in addition to those groups who, contrastingly, have used institutional politics to achieve their aims, such as new political parties like Podemos in Spain or Movimento 5 Stelle in Italy.

Analysing the extent to which there has been a change in approach when it comes to contesting neo-liberal capitalism, this book makes an important contribution to the study of social movements and radical politics. With a comparative perspective and an emphasis on studying the largely unexplored recent social and political dynamics in the European periphery, this book is essential reading for students, scholars and activists interested in social movements, radical politics and European politics more generally.

Beltrán Roca is a Lecturer of Sociology at the University of Cadiz, Spain.

Emma Martín-Díaz is a Professor of Social Anthropology at the University of Seville, Spain.

Ibán Díaz-Parra is a Postdoctoral researcher at the University of Seville, Spain.

Routledge Studies in Radical History and Politics

www.routledge.com/Routledge-Studies-in-Radical-History-and-Politics/book-series/RSRHP

Series editors: Thomas Linehan
Brunel University
and
John Roberts
Brunel University

The series *Routledge Studies in Radical History and Politics* has two areas of interest. First, this series aims to publish books which focus on the history of movements of the radical Left. "Movement of the radical Left" is here interpreted in its broadest sense as encompassing those past movements for radical change which operated in the mainstream political arena as with political parties, and past movements for change which operated more outside the mainstream as with millenarian movements, anarchist groups, utopian socialist communities, and trade unions. Second, this series aims to publish books that focus on more contemporary expressions of radical left-wing politics. Recent years have been witness to the emergence of a multitude of new radical movements, adept at getting their voices in the public sphere. From those participating in the Arab Spring, the Occupy movement, community unionism, social media forums, independent media outlets, local voluntary organisations campaigning for progressive change, and so on, it seems to be the case that innovative networks of radicalism are being constructed in civil society that operate in different public forms.

The series very much welcomes titles with a British focus, but is not limited to any particular national context or region. The series will encourage scholars who contribute to this series to draw on perspectives and insights from other disciplines.

Titles include:

Challenging Austerity

Radical Left and Social Movements in
the South of Europe

**Edited by Beltrán Roca,
Emma Martín-Díaz and
Ibán Díaz-Parra**

LONDON AND NEW YORK

First published 2018
by Routledge
2 Park Square, Milton Park, Abingdon, Oxon OX14 4RN

and by Routledge
711 Third Avenue, New York, NY 10017

Routledge is an imprint of the Taylor & Francis Group, an informa business

British Library Cataloguing in Publication Data
A catalogue record for this book is available from the British Library

Library of Congress Cataloging in Publication Data
A catalog record for this book has been requested

ISBN: 978-1-138-21126-1 (hbk)
ISBN: 978-1-315-43809-2 (ebk)

Typeset in Times New Roman
by Wearset Ltd, Boldon, Tyne and Wear

MIX
Paper from
responsible sources
FSC
www.fsc.org   FSC® C013604

Printed and bound by CPI Group (UK) Ltd, Croydon, CR0 4YY

Contents

Illustrations

Figures

Tables

Contributors

Simone Castellani is a postdoctoral fellow at the University Institute of Lisbon (Portugal) for the UPWEB/NORFACE project. He holds a PhD in Social Anthropology (University of Seville) and in Migratory and Intercultural Processes (University of Genoa). He was visiting fellow at the Wellesley College (USA), University of Bielefeld and University of Freiburg (Germany), FLACSO Ecuador, University of Sussex (UK) and guest lecturer at University of Bielefeld. His topics of research focus on the correlation between youth and international migratory processes. In the last few years he has been studying the new Southern European migration flows towards Germany during the contemporary economic crisis.

Hermes Augusto Costa is a Sociologist Professor at the Faculty of Economics and researcher at the Center for Social Studies, University of Coimbra. He is co-coordinator of the PhD Program on "Labour Relations, Social Inequalities and Trade Unionism". He has published many articles and books on the issues of labour relations, trade unionism and European Works Councils. His most recent book is *Desigual e combinado. Precariedade e lutas sociais no Brasil e em Portugal* (co-edited with Ruy Braga and Elísio Estanque, 2016). www.ces.uc.pt/investigadores/cv/hermes_augusto_costa.php.

Elisabetta della Corte is Professor of Sociology of Labor and Economic Processes at the University of Calabria – Department of Social and Political Sciences. Her main research interests are related to the transformation of the capitalist system, globalisation, workers' movements, protest, and collective action. She teaches courses related to the sociology of work, migration and analysis of complex societies. She collaborates with blogs such as Esodoweb and online magazines; her latest articles on dockers' struggles were published on contropiano.org.

Ibán Díaz-Parra holds a PhD in Human Geography by the University of Seville. He has been a postdoctoral fellow in the National Autonomous University of Mexico, in the University of Buenos Aires and, currently, in the University of Seville. His work focus is on urban social geography, and he has developed, specifically, research in gentrification and socio-spatial segregation processes and urban conflicts and activism. Besides which, he has been involved in right-for-housing campaigns and social activism in Seville for nearly 15 years.

Elísio Estanque is a Professor at the Faculty of Economics and a senior researcher at the Centre for Social Sciences – University of Coimbra, Portugal. He has been visiting professor in different universities in Europe and Latin America, namely at USP and Unicamp, Brazil. As a "public sociologist" he has been studying and publishing on issues such as social movements and trade unions, labour relations, youth cultures and students movements. Recent books include *Praxe e Tradições Académicas* (2016) and *Classe Média e Lutas Sociais* (2015).

Dora Fonseca has a PhD in Sociology, with her thesis on "Social movements and trade unionism. The Portuguese case: alliances or latent tensions?" by the University of Coimbra (Portugal). She is a Post-Doctoral Researcher at the Center for Social Studies, in the research project "Rebuilding trade union power in the age of austerity: a review of three sectors". Her main publications include *Olas de indignación y su logica política: movimientos sociales y nuevas expresiones de radicalismo de clase media* (co-authored with Elísio Estanque, 2014) and *A mobilização de 12 de Março em Portugal: movimento social ou "explosão"?* (2012). Her research interests are mainly focused on trade unionism, collective action and social movements.

Kostas Kanellopoulos holds a PhD in Comparative Political Analysis from Panteion University (2009). Currently he is a research fellow at the University of Crete. He is the General Secretary of the Hellenic Political Science Association and an editor of the *Greek Political Science Review*. He has taught at the Higher Technological Institutes of Piraeus and Patras and at the University of Athens and the University of Crete. His work on social movements, globalization, and contentious politics has appeared in *Situations: Project of the Radical Imagination*, the *Greek Sociological Review*, *Social Movement Studies*, and in collective volumes in Greece and abroad.

Emma Martín-Díaz is Professor of Social Anthropology at the University of Seville. She is a specialist in migration, ethnic relationships and public policies. She obtained her MA Anthropology at the University of Seville in 1985, with a thesis on migrants returning from Western Europe to rural Andalusia. Her PhD thesis (1988) focused on Andalusian immigrants in Cataluña, inter-ethnic relationships and integration policies, and won the prize "Blas Infante" for the best original research on Social Studies in Andalusia in 1991. Since 1995 she has been carrying out research on "new immigration" in Spain. The topics include immigration, agriculture and labour markets in Mediterranean Spain (1999, 2004), immigration and citizenship (1999, 2003), immigration and domestic services (2002), immigration and prostitution (2004), migration and transnational social networks (2007) and the "second generation" (2009–today). She participates in several master's programmes and doctorates on migration, ethnicity, gender, development, citizenship and human rights at different universities from Europe and Latin America.

Julio Pérez Serrano is Associate Professor in Contemporary History and Head of the Grupo de Estudios de Historia Actual (GEHA) at the Universidad de Cádiz, where he coordinates the PhD programme in Arts and Humanities. He is President of the Association Historia Actual and leads the International Academic Network of Current History. He is editor-in-chief of the journals *Revista de Historia Actual* and *Historia Actual Online*, and editor of the collection *Historia Actual* of the publisher La Xara. He is currently Principal Investigator of the project "Del antifranquismo a la marginalidad: disidencias políticas y culturas en la transición española a la democracia" (HAR2016-79134-R), funded by the Ministry of Economy and Competitiveness of Spain. He has recently edited the book *La aportación de UGT Andalucía al medio rural andaluz* (2010), and is co-author, with Marie-Claude Chaput, of *Civilisation espagnole contemporaine, 1868–2011* (2011) and *La transición española. Nuevos enfoques para un viejo debate* (2015).

Luca Queirolo Palmas is Professor in Sociology of Migration and Visual Sociology at Genoa University. Co-director of Mondi Migranti, the Italian Review on International Migration, he also founded the Laboratory for Visual Sociology devoted to spreading visual forms of narrative and research in social sciences. He directed several European projects on gangs, youth cultures and migrations. He has been visiting professor in Barcelona, Quito, Paris and Tunis. During 2016 he led a filmic ethnography on youth after the Arab Spring in Tunisia. His most recent book is *After Revolution. Youth Landscape and Gender Gazes in Contemporary Tunisia* (2017).

Beltrán Roca is Assistant Professor of Sociology at the Department of General Economics, Universidad de Cádiz. He is member of the research group GEISA and Flacso-España, and has been visiting researcher at CONICET (Argentina), Yale (USA), LSE (UK) and Aix-Marseille Université (France). His research interests are trade unionism, migrations, third sector and collective action. His latest book is *Contrapoder Sindical* (*Trade Union Counterpower*) (2013). He has published in journals such as *American Anthropologist, Critical Sociology, Transfer, Anthropological Quarterly, Labour History* and *Anthropology of Work Review*.

Nikos Serdedakis is Assistant Professor of Sociology at the Department of Sociology, University of Crete. His main research interests include the sociology of social movements, collective behaviour, the sociology of collective action, political violence, and protest event analysis. His recent research and publications focus on collective action in post-war Greece. He is currently working on a protest event analysis research programme about collective action and protest dynamics during the years of the current crisis in Greece.

Markos Vogiatzoglou works as a Senior Adviser at the Greek Ministry of Digital Policy, Telecommunications and Media. Previously, he earned his living exercising a variety of professions, such as university lecturer, researcher – in several major international research projects – call-centre operator, leaflet distributor, advertising company executive. He also considers himself a trade union activist, having contributed to the founding and establishment of several grass-roots unions and collectives in the telecommunications and academic sectors. When not too busy disrupting employers, organizing strikes, and pretending to offer valuable advice to a government that pretends to be left-wing, Markos conducts research in social movements, trade union studies, and democratisation. He holds a PhD from the European University Institute (Florence, Italy) and a couple of Master's degrees.

Foreword

In the wake of the global financial crisis that erupted in 2008 and the subsequent government neo-liberal and austerity policies that were implemented across Europe, there was not only escalating social protests, street demonstrations and mass strike activity, but also the rise and growth of significant new political forces to the left of mainstream social democracy. Nowhere was this more apparent than in the four southern European countries of Spain, Portugal, Greece and Italy. It was here that the sheer scale of the social and economic impact of the crisis, combined with the widespread perception that the mainstream political parties and trade unions were an inadequate channel for social protection, stimulated a wide variety of innovative and inspirational social protest movements and radical-left formations.

In many respects, there have been two main surges of ideological and political radicalisation across Europe generally over the last 15–20 years. Between the late 1990s and mid-2000s some of the traditions of the early movements against neo-liberal globalisation combined with anger at the 1 per cent who sparked off but survived the financial crisis. Although these movements began to recede around 2005, there was a re-emergence of widespread social movement protest and radical-left influence with the stunning victory of the Syriza coalition in Greece, the spectacular growth of Podemos in Spain, and the huge support generated by the Left Bloc in Portugal. In reacting to, and filling the space left by, the rightward shift of conventional social democratic and socialist parties (such as PASOK in Greece and PSOE in Spain), such forces contained important underlying anti-austerity and anti-capitalist sentiment and potential, albeit with accompanying ultimately debilitating fault lines.

This book provides a new series of fascinating insights into the dynamics, trajectories and fortunes of such radical-left and social movement forces within Mediterranean Europe, celebrating their achievements but also providing a critical analysis of their limitations. In the process, it takes into account not only the *objective* material and *historical* context that provided the society-wide "opportunity structures" for such developments, but also the *subjective* role of leading actors and the specific strategic approaches that were adopted in respective countries. It does so not merely in terms of specific different *national* contexts with their inevitably diverse conditions, but also with a *comparative* dimension that makes a valuable contribution to our understanding of some common underlying dilemmas and challenges.

Notable in this respect is the complex and changing relationship between the different *social movements* (such as 15M in Spain) and the existing *political parties and trade unions*. Thus while social movements, that were defined by their radical democratic principles based on horizontal organisational structures and networks, often initially adopted an explicit rejection of parties and unions, they were later prepared to work together with some of these bodies, notably radical-left forces (such as SYRIZA in Greece) and more combative unions (such as CGT and CNT in Spain).

Another common feature was the shift from social *movement* to *party* politics. Thus while grass-roots mobilisation and protest was often autonomous of "old" institutional forms of political representation and state institutions, in turn, the new movements that developed in some countries (notably Greece, Spain and Portugal) gave birth to new forms of radical-left political organisation that effectively shifted the terrain much more towards the institutional, electoral and central political national arena.

At the same time, there is consideration of the way in which SYRIZA, Podemos and the Left Bloc attempted to strike the difficult balance between maintaining their left-wing principles and operating within the harsh contextual realities of a global capitalist economy and the EU's neo-liberal imperatives that placed enormous constraints on the autonomy of nation-state institutions. Such contradictory pressures contributed to the way in which the new radical-left forces tended to remain locked within the orbit of social democracy – with what were effectively a variety of different *left reformist* political outlooks. This was a process highlighted in graphic relief by the way in which *Rifondazione Comunista* in Italy was reduced to a marginal force following its disastrous participation in the centre-left government of 2004–2006, and the way in which SYRIZA capitulated to the European troika's neo-liberalist agenda in 2015. But in both cases the views and strategies that were adopted by the main radical-left *actors* also proved absolutely crucial to what one of the book's contributors refers to as a form of "political opportunism".

Another related feature explored is that, while the political radicalisation provided a highly significant alternative channel of resistance to the ravages of austerity, the main political beneficiary paradoxically was to be (however new their form) such left reformist forces rather than the more explicit and hard-line anti-capitalist and *revolutionary left* (such as the ANTARSYA – the coalition of the anti-capitalist left in Greece). No doubt this was because the former – whatever their ultimate limitations – were seen as a more credible opposition to the onslaughts on workers' and citizens' conditions in the face of powerful counter-forces. Moreover, despite the widespread questioning of the existing traditional institutions of the workers' movement, in some countries the still firmly embedded (but also left reformist orientated) communist parties in Greece (KKE) and Portugal PCP) retained an influential mobilising role.

Meanwhile, the accompanying ideological and political *polarisation* that occurred in countries such as Italy and Greece, in which the crisis not only stimulated collective resistance and political radicalisation, but also the growth of the *populist Right* (such as the Five Star Movement of satirist Beppe Grillo) and *fascist* forces (such as Golden Dawn), is also an uncomfortable, but important, feature that is explored with its wider potential implications.

However, notwithstanding the perceived tensions and limitations of the radical-left and social movements that developed in the southern EU countries, what also animates the pages of this edited collection is a highly sympathetic and thoughtful account and analysis that will be of immense value to both academics and activists alike. At the same time, it seems clear the radicalisation that such forces both reflected and produced has not gone away, which makes the experience of recent years a kind of political deposit that will be of enormous relevance for future battles.

Ralph Darlington
University of Salford

Introduction

Social movements and radical politics in the European periphery – a world-systems analysis

Beltrán Roca, Emma Martín-Díaz and Ibán Díaz-Parra

The economic crisis of 2008 has served as the perfect excuse for the establishment of a disciplinary system based on debt. Debt has been a step forward in the process of neo-liberalisation. While it is acknowledged that austerity policies are unable to place countries on a path of growth, employment and social welfare, economic and political powers have advocated for these types of measures. The hidden agenda of these powers, instead, is about dismantling social welfare, transferring private debt to the public sector, and generating profit to oligarchs. South European countries, such as Spain, Portugal, Italy and Greece, have been especially vulnerable to these harmful policies, suffering, as a result, from high levels of inequality, exclusion and injustice. These tendencies have been manifest in the semi-peripheral condition of the Mediterranean countries within the European Union (EU) and the World System.

Since austerity has dramatically damaged the conditions of the working class in South European countries, social conflict has skyrocketed in the last years. The economic crisis quickly turned into a representation or political crisis. Traditional actors, such as left political parties and trade unions, have played a key role in the response to austerity, however other new actors have entered the scene including new social movements and new political forces.

Consequently, the political landscape of southern EU countries has changed substantially. In general terms, the economic and political crises created an opportunity structure that has favoured the rise of the radical-left and vigorous social movements in such countries. From the 1970s, this kind of radicalism has not enjoyed such levels of social support and centrality. In Spain, the emergence of the 15M or *indignados* movement in 2011 and the subsequent creation of Podemos in 2014, exemplifies this process. In Portugal, the rise of autonomous anti-austerity protests and the electoral growth of *Bloco de Esquerda* are also symptoms of this tendency. In Greece, the escalating social protest and the victory of SYRIZA, and in Italy the emergence and growth of the Five Star Movement, are also expressions of these trends.

This book explores how the economic crisis and austerity policies are transforming social movements and radical political parties in southern Europe. Economic crisis has encouraged strong protest movements oriented, initially, towards strong confrontation with state apparatuses in the case of Greece, and the refusal of conventional democratic institutions in Spain. The autonomist character of the protests – oriented towards radical democracy, discrediting conventional political organisations and mistrusting any kind of instituted politics – was especially meaningful around the 2011 mobilisations, with a paradigmatic case in the Spanish *indignados*. This phase illustrates the development of particular spatial strategies and tactics, usually opposed or alternative to the spatial arrangements of the state territoriality (occupation of squares, squatted social centres, organisation of decentralised assemblies, and so on).

However, further evolution of the crisis, with the deepening of impoverishment and social cuts, showed the strong limitations of these perspectives. In the last years, the contestation to neo-liberalism and austerity seems to have turned towards statist and institutionalised politics. Thus, the creation of new political parties such as *Podemos* in Spain or *Movimento 5 Stelle* in Italy or the access to state political power of extreme left-wing parties such as SYRIZA in Greece or *Bloco de Esquerda* in Portugal, although extremely diverse, shows strong connections and answers to similar structural contexts. As a main thesis of this book, the aforementioned can be interpreted as a change in the frames and strategies of the contestation to neo-liberal capitalism.

The book explores such dynamics from different angles. The different chapters aim at responding to several questions:

- How has the economic crisis affected social protest in southern Europe?
- What role have trade unions played in social protest against austerity?
- What role have new social movements played?
- Has the representation crisis led to the emergence of new political subjectivities, discourses and practices?
- Have social movements incorporated new repertoires of action?
- How have radical left organisations, trade unions and new social movements interacted in a context of representation crisis?
- Is the growth of the radical left in the south of Europe a result of the semi-peripheral position of this region within the EU architecture?
- Can one speak about a Mediterranean or south European model of addressing economic and representation crises?
- What challenges emerge with the rise of the radical left regarding the project of the EU?

In order to respond to these questions, one must pay attention, first, to the context of the political economy of the European Mediterranean countries.

The articulation among European Mediterranean countries and northern European countries

The articulation among European Mediterranean countries and northern European countries can be analysed within the theoretical framework of the duality centre-periphery. This theory, developed by Latin American economists from the Economic Commission for Latin America and the Caribbean (ECLAC) (Furtado 1969), describes a world order formed by an industrial and hegemonic centre that establishes unequal economic transactions with an agrarian and sub-ordinated periphery. Mainly focused in the geographic area of Latin America, it was extended to a global scale by Wallerstein (1974) with his world-system model. It was later used and developed by Arrighi (1985) in his critical theory on economic cycles. The creation of an extroverted economy is one of the dimensions of the peripheral condition (Amin 1976). When we use the centre-periphery dualism for analysing the unequal relationship between the countries in Mediterranean Europe and the countries in central Europe, we opt to use the concept of the semi-periphery. The defining feature of semi-peripheries is that they share organisational characteristics with central and peripheral countries. In the European case, the concept comes from the relationship of dependence and the unequal development between the Mediterranean countries and central European countries, from the formation of the Economic Coal and Steel Community in 1951 and the Roma Agreements in 1957 (European Economic Community and Euratom) to the contemporary EU, which has as one of its main milestones, the Maastricht Agreement (1992).

Although this theory has often been criticised, particularly due to its ideological dimension, and by authors who shared opposing ideological positions, the main objection that can be formulated is that the most orthodox analysis defines the European Mediterranean countries as central countries. Nevertheless, we agree with the proposals of Gambarotto and Solari (2015), who, following Selwyn (1979), define periphery as:

> a region suffering from: 1) A lack of effective control over the use of resources; 2) a comparative lack of local innovation; 3) a weakness in internal linkages; 4) a weakness in information flows within the periphery and from the periphery to the center; and 5) migration outflows.
> (Gamabarotto and Solari 2015, 8)

According to these authors, the southern European countries suffer from these difficulties, which leads them to use the term "semi-periphery" as coined by Arrighi. From the perspective of the social sciences, the centre-periphery theory presents the problem of the economic reductionism of complex social processes that involves very diverse dimensions of social life. On the basis of these objections underlies a debate that has a central ontological and epistemological nature: the relationship between structural aspects and social agency aspects (Bakewell 2010). To avoid the positivist–realist bias that could derive from a methodological proposal focused on the analysis of economic realities among the European countries, we will combine this structuralist perspective with a subjectivist approach focused on the strategies of the social movements to implement their political projects.

This perspective implies that the different European states are under a centre-periphery relationship (Arrighi 1985; Gambarotto and Solari 2015), which is structural and, as such, remains, although with changing forms, despite the modernisation processes experienced by the peripheries. We consider that political strategies are designed in the context of specific economic models which act as windows of opportunities (Taylor 2014). However, these opportunities are at the same time the positive reverse of the negative situation created within political-administrative structures incapable of providing social coverage to citizenship in a context in which capital and work flows are determined by an unequal relationship between the centres and the peripheries of the system, conforming to the structural foundations of international relationships.

If the macroeconomic analysis helps to contextualise international relationships in the ambit of the fluxes of capital and labour, it is also true that this approach is excessively reductionist, blurring social subjects and ignoring the social, political and ideological aspects that operate in these processes. In other words, the emphasis on structural dimensions of the phenomenon should not hide agency elements. The emphasis on agency aspects, however, can overshadow the importance of structural factors by studying these networks and institutions as separate from the frame of circulation of work and capital flows.

European periphery, technological rent and financial-real estate circuit

Although structural, economic and geopolitical factors cannot explain everything, they are an unavoidable and decisive framework in which the complex political process that has defined the European Mediterranean during the last years must be located. A key element, which has triggered the protest movements and alternative political projects that are explored in this book, is the economic crisis of 2008. The financial crisis has affected the European countries in a remarkable and sustained way. As a result, eight years later they are far from economic recovery. Why has the crisis had a relative impact? What relation does this have with the semi-peripheral character of the European Mediterranean?

To address these questions, one must identify what types of economic and political relationships are beneath the particular situation of the Mediterranean region within Europe. It must be stated that there is not a static model capable of shedding light on all the domination and exploitation relationships among territories. Dependency theory can explain the relationship of economic exploitation among countries through the existence of unequal interchange. Contrary to the classical theory of Ricardo, international trade did not benefit all the participants but it ended up reproducing development on one side and underdevelopment on another (Furtado 1969). Within the international division of labour, those countries specialised in the production of raw materials transferred constant value towards those countries specialised in manufacturing high added value, allowing for the concentration of capital in those centres (Amin 1976). In addition, this value transfer implied an overexploitation of the working class in peripheral countries. The historical configuration of the European Mediterranean during the nineteenth and twentieth centuries, fits this dependency model. As Eric Wolf

(2005) suggested in his well-known work based on the World System Theory, Europe produced its own internal peripheries in its successive industrialisation processes. Territories within a State, which assume the role as providers of raw materials and labour, are characterised by a lack of industrialisation and a marked relative underdevelopment. This was the case, among others, of the Italian Mezziogiorno, the Spanish Andalusia, and Ireland within Great Britain. Putting aside the Irish case, the other two regions are still in a situation of relative poverty, sharing common features with some independent states, such as Greece and Portugal. However, this situation has changed notably. The European Mediterranean has passed from exporting an unskilled workforce and raw materials to becoming international tourist destinations, constructed by means of a high investment on physical and social infrastructure, financed mainly by EU structural cohesion funds. Of course, the 2008 crisis has shown the clear limits of a highly speculative model, which worked quite well in previous decades. What relationship does it have with the exploitation relationships between centre and periphery?

Echeverría (1998, 2005) stated that the key for the reproduction of exploitation relationships between the centre and the periphery was the growing relevance of technological rent, developed by central countries as a result of capital accumulation.[1] The concept of technological rent describes the extraordinary income favoured by control of the modernisation of cutting-edge technology, thanks to the monopoly that it allows over determinate dimensions of nature, unreachable for other economic agents. The use of the necessary technology for competing in a productive economy is only accessible by paying technological rent. This type of monopoly is a form of power, which became relevant during the second half of the twentieth century and especially the twenty-first century, making the protectionist and industrialist policies of the peripheral countries useless. The technological supremacy of central regions, based on the accumulative character of technological innovation, drove the periphery to a situation of permanent underdevelopment, whilst undermining the sovereignty of its Nation-state. The domination permitted by the control of technological rent rendered ineffective any kind of economic policy oriented to overcome the situation of subordination, implying the relative devaluation of natural products and contributing to the loss of sovereignty of Nation-states (subordination of rent of the land to the technological rent), leading to the emergence of a transnational quasi-state. Within the international market, the states with their national capital specialised in the exploitation of the rent of the land will always lose out against those specialised in the extraction of technological rent.[2]

If the EU is one of the most evident examples of this tendency to create transnational quasi-states, the domination relationships between the technological rent and the land rent take place clearly between northern and southern countries. The technological advantage attributed in general terms to Europe is located evidently in northern countries, especially in Germany. The other side of the coin is the development of an unproductive economy, based on land rent (through a tourism-real estate-construction complex) in the South as a result of

European spatial division of labour. Following capital flows among these spaces (from the central and northern countries to the Mediterranean countries) one can identify centre-periphery dynamics.

Harvey's Spatial Fix theory can be of interest here. Capitalism tends structurally to crises since competence forces technological innovation and drives the decline of the income rate, leading to the accumulation of idle capital in all its forms (stocks, unemployment, stopped machinery), which do not find opportunity for investment. This tendency can be eluded in different ways. Harvey (1983) argued for the centrality of the spatial solution, which consists of colonisation by the capital of new territories, which become storehouses of surpluses that otherwise would be destroyed. However, this strategy produces future competitors and future problems for colonisers. Another response to this problem is the investment in infrastructure and building, since because its long period of use and rotation, it is especially suitable within a context of capital surpluses and over-accumulation. Harvey (after Lefebvre) identified an economy progressively focused on space, in which a second circuit of accumulation is gaining weight at the expense of the circuit of production. The land becomes a form of fictitious capital, and the real estate market operates as a particular form of circulation of interest-bearing capital (Harvey 1983). In economic cycles, the reduction of the benefit rate is directly related to the creation of great amounts of fictitious capital, generating speculative bubbles. Thus, the secondary circuit of accumulation becomes a refuge before the drop in benefits. In the context of crisis, the capital does not find possibilities for reproduction on the circuit of production; consequently, it is directed towards non-productive sectors. The construction sector has several advantages in this sense, offering opportunities for employment and the formation of surplus value (Lefebvre 2013, 370; 1976, 102). Nonetheless, what Harvey calls a spatial solution to the crisis has serious limitations. Speculative investment on space acts as an interest-bearing capital, a fictitious capital that circulates without any material basis on goods or productive activities. This can only put off the problem, since future production will generate new capital, which, in turn, shall seek investment opportunities. Clearly, this type of massive investment is the one which has driven European integration in the Mediterranean, drawing ultimately on the economic activity of tourism mobilised by a particular type of monopolistic rent based on place.

Historically, construction has gained weight on an international scale as industry has declined. Harvey pointed out a political interest after the Second World War on the creation of a mass of housing owners, giving the construction sector a counter-cyclical role that promoted social stability (Harvey 1983, 28). After the crisis of the Keynesian model, the creation of house owners passed from being supported directly by the state to based on private indebtedness. The state privatisation of the sector took place at the same time with its rise within the formal economy; therefore, construction and speculation replaced the productive economy. With the extension of urbanisation and late capitalism, real estate stopped being a secondary circuit and turned into a central one.

This tendency contributes to what Lefebvre called urban neocolonialism. In peripheral territories, such as the European Mediterranean, real estate came to play a dominant role in the economy. Thus, the Mediterranean city became:

> a place of aesthetic pilgrimage and touristic consumption (…) the economy of this country depends primarily on this circuit: real-estate speculation, creation of capitals by this means, investment of these capitals on construction, and so on. This is a fragile circuit which can break down at any moment and which defines a type of urbanization without industrialization (…). The circuit maintains, thus, a fictitious prosperity.
>
> (Lefebvre 1969, 24)

The economic relationship among central and peripheral European countries does not consist only in the massive arrival of tourists from the central territories. The construction boom in the territories redefined as leisure spaces plays a refuge role for the surplus of capitals from the production centres, breeding highly speculative processes of space production. The risks of this type of economic model have been especially evident in the economic collapse of the European Mediterranean. Thus, the role of a secondary circuit of accumulation and ground rent in the Mediterranean can be understood as the other side of specialisation in the extraction of technological rent in northern Europe. Currently, this is a key factor for the reproduction of the centre-periphery dynamic within the EU.

Understanding social movements in the post-political era: materialism and the electoral arena

As Shefner *et al.* (2015) have highlighted, there is a close connection between World System dynamics and collective action. Although there are different paths to protests before similar material conditions, in all cases of anti-systemic protest, conditions of privation can be identified which affect large sectors of the population. The World System Theory has tended to focus on how social movements reflect transformations in global power relationships (Arrighi *et al.* 1989). Our approach, however, is more focused on the causes of the rise of new forms of mobilisation and collective action. It is about bringing back material conditions in the study of social protest (Shefner *et al.* 2015, 459; Roca and Díaz-Parra 2017).

For Touraine, the class polarisation and antagonism theorised by Marxism was the result of liberal-industrial capitalism of the nineteenth century in Western Europe, but it was not applicable to the reality of the twentieth century (Touraine 1973, 14–21). Similarly, it could be said that the idea of social movements – and, especially, those initially labelled as New Social Movements (NSMs) – popularised in the 1970s and developed two decades later, respond to a particular context and specific material conditions. The changes in capitalism and geopolitics since the 1970s entailed the progressive decline of the workers' movement and anti-capitalism in the countries of the global centre. The statistics about days not worked due to industrial action clearly shows this trend, but also the data on union density or demonstrations for labour issues. In the same way, industrial capital has moved to countries with lower salaries, displaced with labour conflict and worker mobilisation (Silver 2005).

The burst of NSMs in Europe coincides with the decline of the workers' movement. Political antagonism seems to move from class issues to other issues such as gender, race, sexuality, ecology or anti-militarism. These new forms of activism, together with the collapse of the URSS and its satellite countries, contributed towards shaping a new intellectual milieu in which Marxist and materialist explanations were set aside and came to stage new theorisations that put the emphasis on cultural, symbolic and identity dimensions (Barker and Dale 1998). It was argued that under a systemic change, defined under the rubric of "post-Fordism", "postmodern" society, "post-industrial" society, or "late modernity", the working class was no longer at the epicentre of social conflict, whilst numerous aspects of social life turned into fields of struggle.

In the European Mediterranean, the idea of social movements and NSMs gained importance against the classical workers' movement later and in a nuanced way than in the rest of Europe. Except for Italy, Mediterranean countries came from more or less prolonged military dictatorships between the end of the 1970s and beginning of the 1980s, a moment that began their integration into the EU. It was not until the late 1980s when NSMs gained relevance in the case of Spain, whereas in Greece and Portugal the workers' movement maintained its influence despite the burst of new antagonistic identities. Beyond this, the decline of workers' organisations came together with a process of growth and changes in the economic structure, among which the following stand out: "industrial restructuring" (a euphemism with which the EU technocrats referred to deindustrialisation), participation in real estate/financial bubbles, and the touristification of the Mediterranean coast. The economic success came with changes in the social and productive structures, which tended to undermine the power of labour organisations.

Nowadays, as recently suggested by Subirats (2015) in relation to the 15M, the term "social movement" has become a convention that is used without clear content, even within the academic field. The original definition of Touraine (1995) has very little to do with today's use, or even with the use of the French sociologist himself in a late stage of his career (this author evolved from the idea of social movement as a vehicle of class political capacities, to discard class society and the centrality of the category of class). The conditions attributed to urban social movements by his disciple Castells (1986) has been very extended, but generally they do not coincide with the current meaning given to the term, neither in its informal nor its academic forms. Two elements can be extremely useful to locate "social movements" in relation to classical or conventional political intervention. First, in contrast with the workers' movement, its post-materialist character can be underlined. Second, in contrast with political parties, its character in principle separated from party politics and state institutions.

These elements are present in most of the classical and contemporary analysis, and are generally identified with what is understood as social movements.

Reintroducing materialism in the study of social movements

In relation to post-materialist character, during a good part of the twentieth century most of the antagonist political discourses in the West came from the matrix of the workers' movement and, particularly, from Marxism, giving a central role to social classes. The critique of Marxist structuralism after the 1960s set the ground for new perspectives. Within the ambit of Marxism, in the work of Thompson (2012), social class began to be represented as a social construction, beyond objective determinants, and class struggle appeared as the result of cultural and ideological factors. Other authors, still within a discourse of social classes, moved the conflict from production relationships to the ambit of social reproduction (Lefebvre 2013; Bourdieu 2011). Beyond these arguments, after the 1970s a radical abandonment of Marxist positions and discourses based on social class took place, understood now as "essentialists" and "economicists" (Laclau and Mouffe 1985). Post-industrial society had then broken down the old social hierarchies to the extent that the materialism of the old pre-industrial, and even the industrial demands were replaced by a call to identity, to freedom and also to community. Therefore, the idea of the social class dissolved, whilst, on the contrary, the idea of movements grew stronger (Touraine 1995, 17). Thus, Melucci (1999) defended the existence of a post-materialist society in the West, where the conflict did not emerge from material needs or exploitation but from symbolic domination and the aspirations of recognition of subaltern identities.

Nevertheless, beyond the celebration of these characteristics of Western movements of the twenty-first century, they have also been called into question by several authors. In relation to the post-materialist character, in the context of anti-globalisation protests, some authors began to envisage a re-emergence of materialist motivations in response to the growing inequalities originated by neo-liberal capitalism (Della Porta 2005). In this context, initiatives appeared that identify the social subject opposed to neo-liberal capitalism in materialist terms. This is the case of the idea of *precariat* (Standing 2011) or *cognitariat*, referring to the rise of an intellectual stratum of precarious workers (Rodriguez and Sanchez 2004). In the realm of the refusal to participate or take the state, Harvey (2013, 152–153) pointed out recently the contradictions between the decentralisation associated with autonomist movements and the redistributive aspirations. Nicholls (2009) highlighted the difficulties of social movements to coordinate and develop strategies in the long term. In addition, Dean (2013, 261) warned that the refusal of conventional politics is identified in part with the incorporation of the ideological message about the unavoidability of neo-liberal capitalism. Finally, León (2011) underlined the existence of some sort of inversion of the fetish of the state in contemporary social movements, according to which they create an artificial separation between the state and society.

Movements and the electoral arena in the post-political context

The idea regarding the separation of social movements from political parties and state institutions is quite extended. Recent and echoed works, such as Nicholls (2007, 607), associate social movements with the pursuit of political objectives by non-traditional means (that is, outside political parties and state institutions). The reduction of politics to a single agent, the state, has characterised Western Modernity. Bolivar Echeverría (1998) pointed out the existence of a state fetishism, which he described as a formula by which politics is reduced to the pragmatic management of state institutions and professional politics. One of the innovations attributed to NSMSis the refusal of this state fetish, understood as the typical liberal separation between the state and civil society (De Sousa Santos 2001). Thus, before the classical objective of the take of the state, for Melucci (1999, 73) NSMs are oriented towards self-management goals and demands around alternative lifestyles and identities, thus movements acquire a "growing autonomy from political systems".

The NSMSperspective, typical of the 1980s, had continuity in the recent decades of the alter-globalisation protests. Calle (2005) characterised the "New Global Movements", emerging from the anti-globalisation protests, with similar features to the NSM: rejecting the participation or take of state institutions and oriented by objectives of radical democracy, although less focused on particular topics and with a global scope. In addition, there is a remarkable identification of these global movements with an autonomous perspective, defined by a horizontal and libertarian perspective on social organisation (Cuninghame 2010). In fact, one of the most popular slogans of these movements was the well-known "change the world without seizing power", used in the title of the referential books of that time (Holloway 2002). More recently, Jodi Dean (2013) characterised the movements from 2011 (Occupy, *indignados*, ...) as post-political,[3] since they share an explicit refusal of political organisation. These movements have also been associated with a middle-class radicalism, NSMSand demands of radical democracy.

Nonetheless, throughout the last decades, different political discourses and practices have refuted the separation between social movements and the state. First is the old proposal of the party-movement. Second is the project of radical democracy for social movements of Laclau and Mouffe. Finally, the populist paradigm proposed by late Laclau has had a clear impact on the recent political reality of Spain (Errejón 2015).

The idea of *party-movement* was initially coined by Herbert Kitschelt (1988) to refer to those new political parties promoted by left-libertarian and ecologist groups in Western Europe during the 1980s. In contrast to traditional communist parties, these parties were defined by their attempt to preserve some of the characteristics of social movements (horizontal organisational structure, and so on). The political cycle opened by the economic crisis of 2008 has driven some authors to rescue the concept of "party-movement" to explain the rise of new political formations born or invigorated by NSMs, such as SYRIZA in Greece,

Podemos in Spain, *Movimento 5 Stelle* in Italy or Bloco de Esquerda in Portugal (Subirats 2015). This debate has also been nourished by the experience of the progressive governments in Latin America. Nevertheless, the relation of these new formations with existing social movements is highly diverse, variable and sometimes contradictory.

In the context of NSMs, Laclau and Mouffe (1985) developed a critique to the supposed Marxist essentialism and the primordial role assigned to class struggle. They proposed a redefinition of the socialist project in terms of a radicalisation of democracy. Democracy should work in this project, articulating the irreducible multiplicity of struggles against different forms of subordination: class, sexual, racial, as well as those opposed by ecologist or antinuclear movements. Laclau and Mouffe privileged the political struggle for democracy, and all other struggles are ultimately the application of the principle of democracy to other domains: race, sex, religion, economy (understood as a discursive site of political struggles), and so on. The new task of the left is not to fight liberal-democracy ideology but just the opposite, to deepen and to expand it in the direction of a radicalised and plural democracy.

Later, Laclau (2005) moved from radical democracy to his particular definition of populism. For Laclau, populism is not a specific political movement, but the political at its purest, a neutral matrix of an open struggle, whose content and stakes are themselves defined by the contingent struggle for hegemony. Populism occurs when a series of particular democratic demands are enchained in a series of equivalences, and this enchainment produces people as the universal political subject. What characterises populism is the emergence of people as political subject, and all different particular struggles and antagonism appear as part of the struggle between the people and the Other (this content of us and them is not prescribed but the stake of the struggle for hegemony). In a context where hegemonic power cannot incorporate a series of popular demands, an antagonistic force would struggle for and banner some empty signifiers (democracy, justice, decency), which can incorporate the multiple unsatisfied demands of the people. This thesis has been highly influential in Argentina's left as well as in Podemos.

Diverse criticisms have been raised against the project of multiple identities and radical politics, as well as against Laclau's populist proposal. To begin with, for Žižek (2011, 226–228) as well as for Dean (2016), the postmodern identity politics, related to particular lifestyles, fits very well with the idea of a depoliticised society. The recent proliferation of cultural groups and lifestyles are only possible and thinkable in the context of capitalist globalisation. The only link that connects all these multiple identities is the capitalist market, always eager to satisfy its clients. Moreover, Žižek (2008, 95) criticised Laclau's defence of the "democratic invention" since in the very definition of political democracy there is a tendency to exclude the non-political, the (liberal) sphere of politics as separated from private life and the economy (state fetishisation, in Echeverria's words). On the other hand, Swyngedouw (2015, 177) blamed particularistic and local protests for representing a colonisation of the political by the social, rather than politicising the outer flanks of the political dimension, substituting the political by a proliferation of identity-based and fragmented communities.

The other key topic is the abandonment of the criticism of capitalism. Postmodernism has politicised aspects previously considered apolitical or private, but it has contributed to the de-politicisation of the economy and the naturalisation of capitalism. For Žižek (2008, 178) and Dean (2016, 54), the escape from Marxist essentialism drove Laclau and Mouffe to the acceptance of capitalism and the renunciation of any real attempt to overcome the existing social order. In a similar way, due to the necessary externalisation of the enemy into an intruder or an obstacle, from a populist perspective the cause of one's troubles is ultimately never the system as such, but the intruder who corrupted it (financial manipulators and not capitalists as such) (Žižek 2006). Thus, for Žižek and Dean, politicisation in the current neo-liberal context seems to unavoidably entail the politicisation of the economy.

The book

With these questions and the theoretical framework as a backdrop, Chapters 1 and 2 of this book provide a useful historical background for understanding the discourses and practices of the radical-left and the social movements in the austerity era in Portugal, Spain, Italy and Greece, which are described in the following chapters. The first chapter, "Radical left in Portugal and Spain (1960–2010)", written by Julio Pérez Serrano, reconstructs the evolution of radical-left political parties in Portugal and Spain, paying attention to the different ideologies, goals, leadership and organisational divisions and mergers. The second chapter, titled "Greece and Italy after the Second World War: contentious politics, cycles of protest and radical Left", written by Nikos Serdedakis, Elisabetta della Corte and Markos Vogiatzoglou, explores the historical background of the contemporary radical Left in Greece and Italy. Both countries have parallel and divergent tendencies. Although in the 1970s in both countries there was a vibrant radical Left, several factors led to the de-radicalisation and institutionalisation of the left during the two following decades. It has, with the new millennium and the alterglobalisation movement when a new generation of antagonism emerged, set the groundwork for the later anti-austerity cycle of contentious politics.

Chapter 3, "*Indignados*, municipalism and Podemos. Mobilisation and political cycle in Spain after the Great Recession", written by the editors, focuses on the evolution of social protest in Spain from 2008. The authors identify several stages: the first response from the trade union movements; the rise in 2011 of the *indignados* (as an NSM); the ulterior materialisation of the activists' frames; and finally, the emergence of Podemos and other political forces that operate in the institutional and electoral ambit.

The fourth chapter, "Political opportunities, threats and opportunism: Examining SYRIZA's rise in crisis-ridden Greek politics", written by Kostas Kanellopoulos, expounds the evolution of social protest and the radical Left in Greece. The author makes an essential distinction between opportunity structure and "opportunism". From his point of view, the latter behaviour explains the capitulation of SYRIZA to the pressures of the Troika, which constitutes a challenge for radical political forces of other countries that aim to counter austerity from the electoral arena.

The fifth chapter, titled "Building the 'Contraption': Anti-austerity movements and political alternative in Portugal", written by Elísio Estanque, Hermes Augusto Costa and Dora Fonseca, reflects on the recent Portuguese austerity experience, regarding the particularities of social struggles and the role of the radical Left in that country. In the recent context of the economic and financial crisis generated by austerity, a sociopolitical response was being built. Such a response was doubled-based. On the one hand, we witnessed signs of resignation and little consistency of anti-austerity movements. On the other hand, some spontaneous protest movements marked the public debate in crucial moments. The resistance in the left field was largely influenced by popular discontent but also by the presence of political forces organised with greater presence in the labour field (Communist Party) and among younger segments and a precarious workforce (*Bloco de Esquerda*). The austerity scenario and the Right government's stance during the rescue programme led to a defeat of the former governmental alliance between the PSD (Social Democrats) and the CDS (Christian Democrats), thus generating a scenario of necessity that forced an unexpected alliance between left-wing forces that support the PS (Socialists) government [called the "contraption"]. Unemployment, precariousness and the migration of thousands of young people weakened civil society, but the parties to the left (including the most "radical") responded with the desire to offer a political alternative opposed to austerity and replaced the usual counter-speech with a new compromise with the socialists. Consequently, the possibility of overcoming austerity generated legitimate expectations of the devolution of rights to citizens in general (especially public servants) and workers in particular, while increasing families' purchasing power. Portugal is still a country under scrutiny, however, trying to keep up in an uncertain and ambiguous way between a locked European dream and a modernisation project repeatedly postponed. Under these circumstances, the space of emancipation, alternative and radical democracy becomes increasingly narrow in the face of a Europe whose rules are not equal for all.

The sixth chapter, "When the spring is not coming. Radical left and social movements in Italy during the austerity era", written by Simone Castellani and Luca Queirolo Palmas, explores the Italian case. At the dawn of the new millennium, Italy experienced a rebirth and regrouping of left movements in the platforms against neo-liberal globalisation (such as the Global Social Forum, *No Dal Molin* and *No Tav*). The peak of this trend was the collective action and conflict during the G8 summit in Genoa in July 2001. Despite the critical mass, which the movements had in that moment, in less than a decade this political capital was wasted due to internal and external causes. In the middle of the economic crisis, the left did not take to the streets in Italy, whilst in many other countries of Southern Europe affected by crisis and austerity policies imposed by EU institutions, the so-called "European Springs" took place. In turn, the new party *Movimento 5 Stelle* was born. This chapter analyses the evolution of anti-globalisation movements in Italy and the reason why these forces did not massively join the anti-austerity protests in the south of Europe, leaving a political space empty which will be occupied by other historical subjects.

The final chapter, titled "Conclusion: learning from the economic crisis and the protest cycle in the South of Europe. Implications for social movements and the Left", written by the editors, provides some final conclusions from the different chapters of the book. In this part, the editors outline a set of lessons and reflections from the analysis of the responses of social movements, labour and left parties to austerity policies in Spain, Portugal, Greece and Italy.

The book contains partial results of several finished and ongoing research projects, however, the editors have been able to create the book by coordinating with the authors thanks to the project *Movilidades e inseguridad laboral como retos de las sociedades europeas* (Mobility and labour insecurity and challenges for European societies) [code EUIN2015–62600], funded by the Ministry of Economy and Science of Spain. The support of this agency made it possible to organise the Workshop titled *Civil Society and the "migrant and refugee crisis" in Europe: the multilevel governance of politics*, led by the Universidad de Sevilla (Department of Social Anthropology) and held in Seville on 10–11 November, where the authors could present and discuss their contributions during the first session.

Notes

1 Technological rent can be seen as the result of the circulation of capital in an alternative and not directly productive circuit of investment in technology, research, and development, including the funds for higher education, according to Harvey.
2 The loss of power from the land rent is more questionable than what can be inferred from the work of Echeverría. According to Harvey, the time–space compression favoured by telecommunications and transport has undermined the power of natural monopolies. Despite the neo-liberal rhetoric about free competence, monopolies are essential for the functioning of capitalism since they permit planning in the long term and the reduction of risks in investments. To some extent, all production is drawn from the monopoly of certain parts of the planet, thus, both innovation in the forms of intellectual property and other innovative forms of getting monopolistic rents over territory (such as urban marketing or touristic campaigns), respond to the need for generating monopolistic advantages in capitalism.
3 Post-politics has been defined as a situation in which the political is reduced to politics, to technocratic mechanisms and consensual procedures that operate within an unquestioned framework of representative democracy, free market economy, and cosmopolitan liberalism (Wilson and Swyngedouw 2015, 6).

References

Amin, Samir. 1976. *Unequal Development: An Essay on the Social Formations of Peripheral Capitalism*. New York: Monthly Review Press.
Arrighi, Giovanni. 1985. *Semiperipheral Development. The Politics of Southern Europe in the Twentieth Century*. London: Sage.

Arrighi, Giovanni, Terrence K. Hopkins and Immanuel Wallerstein. 1989. *Antisystemic Movements.* New York: Verso.

Bakewell, Oliver. 2010. "Some Reflections on Structure and Agency in Migration Theory". *Journal of Ethnic and Migration Studies* 36 (10): 1689–1708.

Barker, Colin and Gareth Dale. 1998. "Protest Waves in Western Europe: A Critique of 'New Social Movement' Theory". *Critical Sociology* 24 (1–2): 65–104.

Bourdieu, Pierre. 2011. *Las Estrategias de la Reproducción Social.* Buenos Aires: Siglo XXI.

Calle, Angel. 2005. *Nuevos Movimientos Globales. Hacia la Radicalidad Democrática.* Madrid: Popular.

Castells, Manuel. 1986. *La Ciudad y las Masas. Sociología de los Movimientos Sociales Urbanos.* Madrid: Alianza.

Cuninghame. Patrick G. 2010. "Autonomism as a Global Social Movement". *Working USA: The Journal of Labor & Society* 13 (14): 451–464.

Dean, Jodi. 2013. "After Post-Politics: Occupation and the Return of Communism". In *The Post-political and its Discontents. Spaces of Depoliticisation, Spectres of Radical Politics*, edited by Japhy Wilson and Erik Swyngedouw, 261–278. Edinburgh: Edinburgh University Press.

Dean, Jodi. 2016. *Crowds and Party.* New York: Verso.

Della Porta, Donatella. 2005. "Multiple Belongings, Tolerant Identities and the Construction of Another Politics". In *Transnational protest and global activism*, edited by Donatella della Porta and Sydney Tarrow. New York: Rowman and Littlefield.

De Sousa Santos, Boaventura. 2001. "Los nuevos movimientos sociales". *Osal* 5: 177–188.

Echeverría, Bolivar. 1998. *Valor de Uso y Utopía.* México: Silgo XXI.

Echeverría, Bolivar. 2005. "Renta Tecnológica y Capitalismo Histórico". *Mundo Siglo XXI* 2.

Errejón, Iñigo. 2015. "We the People. El 15M: Un Populismo Indignado?". *ACME: An International E-Journal for Critical Geographies* 14 (1): 124–156.

Furtado, Celso. 1969. *Teoria Política do Desenvolvimento.* Sao Paulo: Biblioteca Universitaria.

Gambarotto, Francesca and Stefano Solari. 2015. "The Peripheralization of Southern European Capitalism within the EMU". *Review of International Political Economy* 22 (4): 788–812. doi: 10.1080/09692290.2014.955518.

Harvey, David. 1983. *The Limits to Capital.* London: Verso.

Harvey, David. 2013. *Ciudades Rebeldes.* Madrid: Akal.

Holloway, John. 2002. *Changing the World Without Taking Power.* London: Pluto Press.

Laclau, Ernesto. 2005. *La Razón Populista.* México: Fondo de Cultura Económica.

Laclau, Ernesto and Chantal Mouffe. 1985. *Hegemony and Socialist Strategy.* London: Verso.

Lefebvre, Henry. 1969. *El Derecho a la Ciudad.* Barcelona: Península.

Lefebvre, Henry. 1976. *Espacio y Política.* Barcelona: Península.

Lefebvre, Henry. 2013. *La Producción del Espacio.* Madrid: Capitán Swing.

León, Efraín. 2011. "Geopolítica de la Lucha de Clases: Una perspectiva desde la reproducción social de Marx". Paper presented at the XII Encuentro Internacional de Geógrafos de América Latina, San José, Costa Rica, 25–29 July.

Melucci, Alberto. 1999. *Acción Colectiva, Vida Cotidiana y Democracia.* México: El Colegio de México.

Nicholls, Walter. 2007. "The Geographies of Social Movements". *Geography Compass* 1 (3): 607–622.

Nicholls, Walter. 2009. "Place, Networks, Space: Theorising the Geographies of Social Movements". *Transactions of the Institute of British Geographers* 34 (1): 78–93.

Roca, Beltrán and Ibán Díaz-Parra. 2017. "Blurring the Borders Between Old and New Social Movements: The M15 Movement and the Radical Unions in Spain". *Mediterránean Politics* 22 (2): 218–237.

Rodriguez Lopez, Emmanuel and Raúl Sanchez Cedillo. 2004. "Prólogo". In *Capitalismo Cognitivo, Propiedad Intelectual y Creación Colectiva*, edited by Olivier Blondeau, Nick Dyer Whiteford, Carlo Vercellone, Ariel Kyrou, Antonella Corsani, Enzo Rullani, Yann Moulier Boutang, and Maurizio Lazzarato, 13–28. Madrid: Traficantes de Sueños.

Selwyn, Percy. 1979. "Some Thoughts on Cores and Peripheries". In *Underdeveloped Europe: Studies in Core-Periphery Relations*, edited by Dudley Seers, Bernarde Schaffer, and Marja-Liisa Kiljunen, 35–44. Hassocks, Sussex: Harvester Press.

Shefner, Jon, Aaron Rowland and George Pasdirtz. 2015. "Austerity and Anti-Systemic Protest: Bringing Hardships Back In". *Journal of World-Systems Research* 21 (2): 460–494.

Silver, Beverly. 2005. Fuerzas del trabajo. Los movimientos obreros y la globalización desde 1870. Madrid: Akal.

Standing, Guy. 2011. *The Precariat*. London: Bloomsbury Academic.

Subirats, Joan. 2015. "Todo Se Mueve. Acción Colectiva, Acción Conectiva. Movimientos, Partidos e Instituciones". *RES* 24: 123–131.

Swyngedouw, Erik. 2015. "Insurgent Architects, Radical Cities and the Promise of the Political". In *The Post-Political and its Discontents. Spaces of Depoliticisation, Spectres of Radical Politics*, edited by Japhy Wilson and Erik Swyngedouw, 169–188. Edinburgh: Edinburgh University Press.

Taylor, Nick. 2014. "Theorising Capitalist Diversity: The Uneven and Combined Development of Labour Forms". *Capital & Class* 38 (1): 129–141.

Thompson, Edward P. 2012. *La Formación de la Clase Obrera en Inglaterra*. Madrid: Capitan Swing.

Touraine, Alain. 1973. *La Imagen Histórica de la Sociedad de Clases*. Buenos Aires: Nueva Visión.

Touraine. Alain. 1995. *La Producción de la Sociedad*. México DF: UNAM, IIS/IFA.

Wallerstein, Immanuel. 1974. *The Modern World System*. New York: Academic Press.

Wilson, Japhy and Erik Swyngedouw. 2015. *The Post-Political and its Discontents. Spaces of Depoliticisation, Spectres of Radical Politics*. Edinburgh: Edinburgh University Press.

Wolf, Eric. 2005. *Europa y la Gente sin Historia*. México: Fondo de Cultura Económica.

Žižek, Slavoj. 2006. "Against the Populist Temptation". *Critical Inquiry* 32 (3): 551–574.

Žižek, Slavoj. 2008. "Multiculturalismo o la Lógica Cultural del Capitalismo Multinacional". In *Estudios culturales. Reflexiones sobre el Multiculturalismo*, edited by Fredric Jameson and Slavoj Žižek. Buenos Aires: Paidos.

Žižek, Slavoj. 2011. *El Espinoso Sujeto. El Centro Ausente de la Ontología Política*. Buenos Aires: Paidos.

1 Radical Left in Portugal and Spain (1960–2010)

Julio Pérez Serrano

The Iberian transitions to democracy: intertwined processes

In the mid-1970s Portugal and Spain experienced change processes with remarkable similarities, as they affected authoritarian regimes installed during the interwar period in a context of parliamentarism crisis. Although analogies exist, what happened in Greece was very different, because the military dictatorship installed in 1967 was the result of the Cold War (Soto 2009, 12). During the 1960s, Iberian dictatorships had evolved in the same direction, taking advantage of international economic growth to implement liberalizing policies managed by technocrats trained under Opus Dei. In Spain, the enactment of the Organic Law of 1967 (*Ley Orgánica del Estado*) led to a certain political opening with the so-called "organic democracy", which coincided in Portugal with the *primavera marcelista* (Marcellist spring), a period of relative modernization and limited political liberalization promoted by Marcelo Caetano, after the withdrawal of Oliveira Salazar in 1968 (Rico 1974, 34–40). But neither the economic growth nor the timid *aperturismo* (policy of liberalization) avoided the wear and tear of the dictatorships. The internal division and the rise of social mobilization, encouraged by an increasingly active opposition, sharpened the crisis of both regimes in the early 1970s.

However, there are important differences between the two processes. In Spain the army, purged after the civil war, remained faithful to the regime, while in Portugal the Armed Forces became the determining agent of political change (Oliveira 1975). Thus, in Portugal the break came on April 25, 1974 by a military pronouncement known as the *Revolução dos Cravos* (Carnation Revolution), played by the middle cadres of the army (the "captains") with a democratic and socializing orientation (Sánchez Cervelló 1997). The military malaise, initially provoked by a corporate rejection to the new system of promotions, ended up promoting a democratic uprising with socialist borders that caused the dictatorship to fall. The opposition of the officers to the colonial war in Angola and Mozambique certainly contributed thereto (Campinos 1981, 173). In Spain, the conflict in Western Sahara, active in the same years, did not have the same effects, since the government, fearing that what happened in Portugal could be replicated in Spain, chose to hand over the territory to Morocco and Mauritania in the controversial Tripartite Agreement of Madrid, signed on November 14, 1975.

This proactive role of the Armed Forces made it possible for Portugal to materialize a democratic rupture, which is the fundamental difference with the so-called Spanish "transition" based on political reform (Pérez Serrano 2016). While in Portugal the legality of the dictatorship was abrogated and the elements committed to the regime were purged of the administration, in Spain the change allowed for the survival of Franco's legality (under the motto "from law to law") and continuity of the elites, institutions and symbols of the dictatorship. In Portugal the institutionalization of democracy was in the hands of a provisional government formed by the opposition, while in Spain the reins were always in the hands of Franco's heirs. As for the form of government, Portugal restored the Republic and Spain retained the monarchy that had been re-established after the death of Franco under the Act of Succession of 1947 and the Decree of 1969 in which Franco appointed successor to the then, "Prince" Juan Carlos de Borbón.

From April 1974 to November 1975 in Portugal there was a revolutionary crisis that coincided in Spain with an intense mobilization that was harshly repressed by the late Francoist government of Arias Navarro. Nevertheless, at the end of 1975, with the disappearance of Franco and the almost simultaneous fall of the pro-communist government of Vasco Gonçalves, who carried out the agrarian reform and the nationalization of the main means of production, both processes, so different in origin, ended up converging in a scenario of moderation and stability. In Spain, the negative image of the Portuguese revolution spread by the government acted as a vaccine to avoid contagion, while in Portugal the Spanish transition functioned as an antidote to re-establish social order (Sánchez Cervelló 1995). Between 1976 and 1978, the hardness of the economic crisis and the pressure of the Western powers, with the incentive of entry into the EEC, shaped a more docile citizenship, ready to accept the so-called "social costs" of modernization.

Renewed socialist parties reached the government by electoral means, pushing for deep liberalizing structural reforms, under the vigilant tutelage of the US and European Community institutions. Under the influence of the Socialist International and the SPD (Ortuño Anaya 2005), Iberian socialism was re-founded on the basis of pragmatism and moderation. The Portuguese PS was founded in 1973 in the German city of Bad Münstereifel, under the auspices of the SPD (Chilcote 2010, 223), and the PSOE was re-founded in 1974, in the Congress of Suresnes, turning towards the center-left, which made possible the alternation with the new center-right, emerged in both countries during regime change (Andrade Blanco 2012). All this forced the withdrawal of communist parties, hegemonic in the years of struggle against dictatorships, and marked the end of the revolutionary projects that emerged in the 1960s.

During the 1980s, the new international context that began to be seen with the crisis of the socialist system and the full insertion of China in the World system left no reference to radical organizations and promoted in them an intense debate. Some groups disappeared or were entrenched in the armed struggle, while others evolved, giving rise in the last decade of the century to new organizations that integrated ideals and values of the radical project with the experience of the new social movements. In the case of Portugal, this reconversion was reflected in the convergence of very heterogeneous parties (Maoists and Trotskyists) in the *Bloco de Esquerda* (Left Bloc), founded in 1999 (Soeiro 2009). In Spain, there was a first attempt of regrouping promoted by the PCE in 1986, with the creation of *Izquierda Unida* (United Left). Shortly afterwards, in 1991, the merger of former Maoists and Trotskyists led to the *Izquierda Alternativa* (Alternative Left), which was dissolved in 1993. With the revival of social movements in the heat of the 2008 crisis, new attempts have been made to rebuild the radical space around a new political force, *Podemos* (We can), created in 2014.

Radical projects in Spain and Portugal

After the Second World War there was a favorable political context for the spread of communist ideas. The renewed prestige of the USSR, due to its role in the victory over Nazi-fascism, was increased from 1949 by the dialectic between capitalism and socialism that would dominate the entire Cold War, and from 1959 by the powerful impetus of decolonization, animated in numerous occasions by socialist-inspired national-democratic movements supported by the USSR. This rise of communism also meant a reinforcement of its different tendencies, already existing in the inter-war period, mainly Marxism-Leninism, Trotskyism and Council Communism, to which new ones joined in the period of the Cold War. The main ones were Maoism and Guevarism (focalism or Castroism), which incorporated the experiences of the Chinese (1949) and Cuban (1959) revolutions; self-management based on Tito's Yugoslav model, and the Stalinism of the " Marxist-Leninist movement" inspired by Enver Hoxha, leader of the Party of Labour of Albania (PLA). This communist universe coexisted with another, inspired by libertarian ideas, equally fragmented, formed by old anarcho-syndicalist organizations,[1] already weakened and divided, and new anarcho-communist groups, in favour of workers' autonomy and direct action, including those who practiced revolutionary violence, such as the *Iberian Liberation Movement* (MIL) (Llecha 2014).

Since the late 1950s the European New Left had already distanced itself from the "old Left" and the Soviet model, criticizing the communist parties for their Stalinist heritage, their opportunism and bureaucracy. They demanded the libertarian legacy and traditions of revolutionary Marxism, like the workers' councils, encouraged by the success of the revolutions that were triumphing in peripheral countries like Cuba, Algeria or Vietnam, which made them put their trust in the Third World as an advance of the World revolution. These ideas were especially rooted in the young, promoting the student movement that began to emerge, in groups of intellectuals associated with the contestation and the counterculture, and sometimes also in Catholic circles influenced by Marxism.

Thus, between 1960 and 1974, anti-Americanism, anti-imperialism and Third Worldism penetrated strongly into the traditional communist imaginary, questioning the orthodoxy of "official" parties and their submission to the USSR's designs. Similarly, the Chinese Cultural Revolution (1966) and the 1968 Revolution, with different epicenters, encouraged Maoism and Trotskyism, the two main critical currents with the Soviet model and with the political line of the Communist Party of the Soviet Union (CPSU). From a very different angle, the rapprochement of some European Communist parties to reformist positions, which eventually led to "Eurocommunism" and the abandonment of the revolutionary socialist project, and the condemnation of these parties to the Soviet intervention in Czechoslovakia in 1968, inspired a new Marxist-Leninist dissent, in this case "orthodox" or pro-Soviet, in the communist movement.

Communist dissent, whatever its orientation, was thus articulated around claiming ideological positions of principle, linked to the interpretations that Lenin, Stalin, Trotsky, Mao Zedong, Gramsci or Rosa Luxemburg made of Marxism in the imperialist epoch. For most of the organizations opposed to the line of official communism, Leninist thought was the common core of the revolutionary program: anti-capitalism, anti-imperialism, rejection of bourgeois democracy, socialist revolution, vanguard party and workers' power. On this basis, interpreted according to the idiosyncrasy of each organization, very different analyses and proposals were generated, giving rise to a fragmented and unstable political space that also reflected the division within the international communist movement.

The crushing of the "Chilean way" to socialism, following Pinochet's coup in 1973, also meant for many militants the confirmation that socialism could only be achieved by using revolutionary violence, reinforcing strategies based on armed struggle. The *Brigate Rosse* (1969) in Italy, the Red Army Fraction (1970) in Germany and *Action Directe* in France (1977) were some of the best-known active groups in the mid-1970s (Sommier 1998, 2008). In Portugal and Spain, organizations also emerged that practiced the armed struggle as a strategy to trigger a revolutionary process. But most of the radical groups that emerged in the 1960s, although without renouncing the theory of violence, in practice developed exclusively political strategies.

Revolutionary currents in Portugal

Marxist-Leninist groups

In the Iberian peninsula, the first dissident groups appeared at the end of the 1950s, from the positions of the European *New Left*. But the great splits in the communist parties took place after the rupture between China and the USSR in 1962. Almost inmediately, in the Communist Party of Spain (PCE) and the Communist Party of Portugal (PCP) emerged criticisms to the "revisionist" line of the CPSU under the leadership of Nikita Kruschev. Advocates of the Stalinist orthodoxy and of the complete heritage of the Third International and influenced by the experience of the Chinese revolution, these groups gave birth in the Iberian peninsula to the " Marxist-Leninist" movements, promoted together, first, by the

China of Mao Zedong and the Albania of Enver Hoxha. The goal was to fight against "revisionism" within the official parties and, if this was not possible, to create new organizations with the aim of reconstituting the "authentic" communist party.

In the case of Portugal, " Marxist-Leninist" dissidence had three branches. The first was led by Francisco Martins Rodrigues (*Campos*), member of the Board of the PCP, who headed the first Maoist split. *Campos* and his followers created in 1964 the armed group, *Front for Popular Action* (FAP) and the *Portuguese Marxist-Leninist Committee* (CMLP), the germ of the party that would become the matrix of most of the Portuguese Maoist organizations (Cardina 2013, 128–131). The founding figures of this group were expelled in 1966 and in 1970 the CMLP turned into the *Communist Party of Portugal (Marxist-Leninist)* [PCP(m-l)], led by Heduíno Gomes (*Vilar*). However, dissident sectors from the CMLP, organized around the periodical *O Comunista* (The Communist), joined the group which published *O Grito do Povo* (The Scream of People), giving birth in 1972 to the *Portuguese Marxist-Leninist Communist Organization* (OCMLP). In 1974, a few months before the Revolution, the PCP(m-l) became divided into two factions, and one of them, led by Carlos Janeiro (*Mendes*), split, recovering the original name of CMLP in 1975. The biggest faction, led by *Vilar*, maintained the initials PCP(m-l) and launched its own front, the *Worker–Peasant Alliance* (AOC) that, in 1979, separated from a fading PCP(m-l), turned into the *Labour Party* (PT), and disappeared in 1983. Independently from this, in 1971 another former member of the FAP and the CMLP, Manuel Quirós, founder of *Edições Maria da Fonte*, an emblematic publisher who specialized in the dissemination of Marxist-Leninist books, created the *Communist Committee of Portugal* (CCP), mainly integrated by students. In 1973 he left it and, with former members of the OCMLP, founded the *Communist Union (Marxist-Leninist)* [UC(m-l)], which in September of 1975 joined the *Communist Union for the Reconstruction of the Marxist-Leninist Party* (UCRPML), created by the group José de Sousa, split from the periodical *O Comunista*. After the unfruitful attempt to join with other Maoist groups, the UCRPML ended up transforming in 1977 into the *Portuguese Communist (Marxist-Leninist) Party* [PC(m-l)P], which had a very short life.

The second branch rose in the student milieu and did not participate in any of the other unification processes of the other Maoist groups, preserving until today a different identity. Its origins come from *Student Democratic Left-Wing* (EDE), created in the University of Lisbon in 1968, where in 1970 appeared the *Reorganisation Movement of the Party* of the *Proletariat* (MRPP), under the leadership of the lawyer Arnaldo Matos, known by his followers as the "great educator of the working class". The singularity of the MRPP is that it did not have membership among either emigrants or the workers movement. This made this organization different to the rest of the Maoist groups, frequently led from outside. Its policy of alliances, inclined to collaborate with the PS, also differentiated it from other radical groups (Oliveira 1975, 147). It maintained an active student organization, the *Marxist-Leninist Students' Federation* (FEML), one of whose leaders was José Manuel Durão Barroso. In 1976, the MRPP adopted the name of *Portuguese Workers' Communist Party* (PCTP), with Luís Franco and António Garcia Pereira as leaders, although Arnaldo Matos continued as its most influential leader.

The tree of Maoism can be completed with three more groups which were also born outside the CMLP. The first, called *Revolutionary Communist Committees (Marxist-Leninist)* [CCR(m-l)] was created in January 1970 by João Bernardo (*Tiago*), who left the PCP in 1966 and exiled in Paris. According to a heterodox view on Marxist-Leninism ("libertarian Maoism") the CCR(m-l) had the duty of training the vanguard which would organize the future "mass" communist party.[2] Another group was the *Marxist-Leninist Revolutionary Unity* (URML), led by Joaquim Luciano and Artur Silva, split in 1971 from the *Electoral Democratic Commission* (CDE) which was created in 1969 by the opposition as a platform in order to participate in the "elections" of the *Estado Novo*. Until 1974 it was close to Trotskyite groups, although it finally identified with Maoism (Cardina 2011, 117–136). The third group was the *Committee for Support to the Reconstruction of the Party (Marxist-Leninist)* (CARP), founded in Italy in 1973 as a split from the *Marxist-Leninist Committee of Portugal* (*O Bolchevista*),[3] founded in 1969 by António Bento Vintém and Rui d'Espiney. It had very little presence in Portugal until April 25, 1974, when the recruited outstanding liberated political prisoners, such as *Campos*, who were freed after the Revolution.

The CCR(m-l), URML and the CARP created in December 1974 the *Popular Democratic Union* (UDP) as an electoral front for the constituent elections of 1975, achieving the only seat of the radical Left in the National Assembly. In April 1975, the three parties merged in the *Organization for the Reconstruction of the Communist Party (Marxist-Leninist)* [ORPC(m-l)]. In December, this organization joined the CMLP, founded again, as has been described, by the *Mendes* faction split from the PCP(m-l), creating the *Communist Party (Reconstructed)* [PC(R)], which in April 1976 would recruit most of the militancy of the OCMLP, although the rest preserved the name until its extinction in 1988. The new direction, led by José Caiao also included the charismatic *Campos*. From 1976, after the Chinese–Albanese breakdown, the PC(R) followed the thesis of Enver Hoxha and rejected Maoism as a new "revisionism", turning into the main reference of the pro-Albanese "Marxist-Leninist" movements (Pereira 1988). The UDP came to be the electoral front of the PC(R), preserving its seat in the successive elections until 1980, with a percentage of votes that surpassed the 2 percent in 1979 (Eleicoes.cne.pt 2017). Nonetheless, from 1983, the differences between the UDP and the PC(R) drove them to go separately to the elections of 1985 and 1987 and, consequently, leaving both forces out of the Assembly. They both disappeared in 1991. Finally, in 1992 the PC(R) turned into the *Communists for Democracy and Progress* (CDP), integrating as an association in the UDP in 1995.

Guevarist groups and armed struggle

The origin of the discussions about the unavoidability of armed struggle in Portugal can be found in the presidential elections of 1958, in which the opposition supported the General Humberto Delgado, who was victim of a great electoral fraud. Later, the epic Cuban revolution and the revolutionary movements of Latin America, and the anti-colonial wars in Algeria, Indochina, and the Portuguese colonies, from 1961, favoured the emergence of armed organizations with Guevarist orientation. These organizations, critical with the moderate line of the CPSU, also rejected Maoism due to its defense of Stalinism, refusing to consider the USSR as a "social-fascist" regime and to think of the PCP as the main enemy of the Portuguese people, as the PCP(m-l) had done. The armed struggle had in Portugal the double goal of fighting against the regime and of supporting the armed struggle of the colonial peoples. There existed a guerrilla group of the PCP, the *Armed Revolutionary Action* (ARA), which operated between 1970 and 1973, whose existence manifested the strategic differences between the PCP and the PCE (Serra 1999; Narciso 2000), but the main armed group consisted of radicals.

The *League of Revolutionary Unity and Action* (LUAR) was founded in 1967 in Paris by Hermínio da Palma Inácio (Bayo 1974, 91). The group undertook high impact armed actions, such as the assault to the Bank of Portugal in Figueira da Foz, and robberies of passports and stamps in Portuguese consulates overseas. After the Revolution it suspended its actions, adopting a position in favour of democratic consolidation and opposing the attempts to establish a communist regime (November 1975). It split off in 1976 and its leader joined the PS.

A second guerrilla group was born within the *Patriotic National Liberation Front* (FPLN), created in Rome in 1962 by the PCP and other anti-fascist groups. With its headquarters in Algiers, from 1964 it was controlled by the PCP, but in 1970 dissidents in favour of armed struggle took control of the Front and its radio broadcasting station *Voz da Liberdade* (Freedom's Voice). In 1971, they created a new organization, the *Revolutionary Brigades* (BR), which, in campaigning against colonial war gained influence among social movements, trade unions and catholic organizations (Martins and Loureiro 1980b). With this support, in 1973 they created their political arm, the *Revolutionary Party of the Proletariat* (PRP), led by Carlos Antunes (*André*) and Isabel do Carmo. The *Voz da Liberdade* adopted the name *Voz da Revolução* (The Voice of the Revolution).

Armed actions continued until April 25, 1974, a moment in which the BR joined the mass struggle of the PRP-BR, which became a legal organization. But the party kept on advocating for a socialist revolution. It participated in the land occupations in the South of the country and called for a boycott to the constituent elections of 1975, launching the *Revolutionary Councils of Workers, Soldiers and Sailors* (CRTSM), following the model of the soviets, and the movement *Soldiers United will Win* (SUV) (Robinson 1990, 109–112). In addition, the party supported the independence movements of Angola, Mozambique, Guinea

Bissau and East Timor. With the support of the COPCON[4] and its Major, Otelo Saraiva de Carvalho, the PRP joined the *Revolutionary Unity Front* (FUR) together with the LUAR, the *Internationalist Communist League* (LCI), the *Socialist Left Movement* (MES) and the *Popular Socialist Front* (FSP).

After the failed military uprising on November 25, 1975, the PRP and the MES, which had supported the attempt, bore the brunt of the State's repression. However, the party preserved its organizational structure and participated in the *Groups for the Dynamization of the People's Unity* (GDUPs), which supported the presidential candidature of Otelo Saraiva de Carvalho in 1976, whose defeat marked the end of the revolutionary process. In this context, the most radical faction splits, creating the *Workers' Unitary Organization* (OUT), legalized in 1980 as the *Popular Unity Force* (FUP), under the leadership of Saraiva de Carvalho. At the same time, repression continued and the main leaders, Carlos Antunes and Isabel do Carmo were sentenced to long prison terms in 1979. The sector that remained free expelled the imprisoned members and participated with the FUP in the creation of the armed group *Popular Forces 25 April* (FP-25) in 1980. The former leadership opposed the armed struggle and when in 1982 Carlos Antunes and Isabel do Carmo were finally freed, called a meeting and dissolved what remained of the party.[5] Some of them passed to the *Left Convergence*, with other revolutionary leftist parties, then to the Commission Pro-Amnesty of Otelo Saraiva de Calvalho, and finally to the *Ecologist and Alternative Forum* (FEA), founded in 1991.

Trotskyites groups

The different Trotskyites tendencies were also present in Portugal after 1969 in students' circles of Porto, Coimbra and Lisbon, although they never achieved the influence of the Maoist groups (Martins and Loureiro 1980a). The first Portuguese Trotskyite party, the *Internationalist Communist League* (LCI), was founded in 1973 as a section of the United Secretariat of the Fourth International (USFI), of Mandelist orientation. Its first secretary was João Cabral Fernandes. In 1978 merged with the *Workers' Revolutionary Party* (PRT), created in 1975 and also Trotskyite, but of Morenist[6] tendency, creating the *Revolutionary Socialist Party* (PSR). Although it suffered several splits and crises, the PSR, led by Francisco Louçã, survived, thanks to its connection with new social movements and to its political openness. Thus, in 1983 the PSR participated in the elections with the UDP, electoral front of the PC(R), and was one of the three forces, together with the ex-Maoist UDP and *Política XXI*, that constituted in 1999 the *Bloco de Esquerda* (BE). In 2006 it dissolved, turning into the *Revolutionary Socialist Political Association* (APSR) and became one of the currents within the BE.

Regarding the Morenist tendency, the rupture of its International reference, Nahuel Moreno, with the USFI in 1979, led the militancy from the PRT to leave the PSR. Thus in 1980, there appeared an ephemeral *Workers' Socialist Party* (PST), as a section of the Paritary Committee for the Reconstruction of the Fourth International, which gathered Lambertists and Morenists,[7] dissolved like this alliance in 1981. Most sections of the Morenist sector, including activists of the student movement, participated later in the creation of the *Workers' Socialist League* (LST), affiliated exclusively to the Bolshevist Fraction of Moreno. In 1989, the LST, led by Gil García, adopted the name of *Front of the Revolutionary Left* (FER), preserving its connections with Moreno and its current, the International Workers League-Fourth International (IWL-FI). In 2000, FER merged with the students movement *Ruptura* (Breach), giving birth to a *Ruptura-FER*, that in 2005 joined as a tendency to the *Bloco de Esquerda*.[8]

The International Committee of the Fourth International (ICFI) had its first expression in the *Liaison Committee of Portuguese Revolutionary Militants (for the Reconstruction of the Fourth International)* (CLMRP), born in 1969, which gathered mainly Lambertist militants. When in 1972 Lambert left the ICFI, followers of its leader, Gerry Healy, split from the party , creating in 1973 the *League for the Construction of the Revolutionary Party* (LCPR) which, until its disappearance in 1977, remained connected to the ICFI (Chilcote 2010, 40). Once the CLMRP disappeared, the Lambertist tendency, reborn through the initiative of Aires Rodrigues and Carmelinda Pereira, expelled from the PS, that in 1977 constituted the *Movement for Socialist Unity* (MUS). The group joined the *Organization of the Fourth International – Workers' Socialist Organization* (OST) in 1979, creating the *Workers' Party of Socialist Unity* (POUS). From the brief alliance between Lambert and Moreno, in 1980 the POUS participated in the elections in coalition with the PST. In 1994, the party adopted the name *Movement for the Unity of the Workers* (MUT), but went on to resume its former name in 1999.

The revolutionary socialist groups

Also born within the context of the Carnation Revolution were socialist groups with a revolutionary reading of Marxism. The first of these, founded in 1974, was the *Movement of Socialist Left* (MES), which grouped together trade unionists, Catholics, anti-colonialists, intellectuals and university students who had left the CDE in 1973. It also had a presence in the Armed Forces Movement (MFA) through young university militia officers (Oliveira 1975, 51–54). They created the Commission for the Independence of the Ancient Colonies (CIDAC). The MES suffered continuous divisions of the more moderate socialists and due to the little electoral success dissolved in 1981. The majority of its leaders, like Jorge Sampaio, went to the PS. In the same ideological sphere, the *Popular Socialist Front* (FSP), also created in 1974, was separated from the PS by the Marxist movement (*Popular Socialist Movement*) led by Manuel Serra (Bensaid et al. 1976, 201). Between 1976 and 1978 he was part of the *Electoral Front United People* (FEPU), with the PCP and the *Portuguese Democratic Movement* (MDP/CDE). It gradually declined until disappearing altogether.

The Bloco de Esquerda

During the last decade of the past century the end of the revolutionary project became evident. From the vast array of organizations that appeared from the end of the 1970s, but without parliamentary representation only a few of them survived due to its connection with social movements. This favoured a self-critique reflection that led to something that would have been impossible in the 1970s: the union on the same front as the main Maoist-like group, the UDP, with the Trotskyite PSR, including as a third partner to *Política XXI*, a party created in 1994 from the merger of the historical MDP/CDE and the group of the magazine *Manifiesto* (Lisi 2013). Thus emerged the *Bloco de Esquerda* in the elections of 1999, getting two seats and 132,000 votes (2.44 percent). From that time and for the decade that followed, its weight grew dramatically, getting almost 560,000 votes (9.82 percent) in the elections of 2009, in which it got 16 seats, one more than the *Unitary Democratic Coalition* (CDU), led buy the PCP (Eleicoes.cne.pt, 2017).

Revolutionary currents in Spain

The origin of the Spanish radical Left is in the so-called Front Organizations, created in the late 1950s with the aim of merging all the tendencies of revolutionary Marxism located outside the PCE. The *Popular Liberation Front* (FLP), the *Workers Front of Catalunya* (FOC) and *Euskadiko Sozialisten Batasuna* (Basque Country Socialist Union) (ESBA), known generically as *Felipe*, shaped the confluence of the new European Left with traditions heterodox of the Spanish revolution. Its axes were the defense of revolutionary Marxism, the condemnation of Stalinism and confidence in the Third World first protagonists of a world revolution. They were rooted in the student movement and Catholic circles influenced by Marxism, which criticized the PCE for its Stalinist heritage, its opportunism, its reformism and its submission to the USSR (García Alcalá 2001). Its evolution was short and rugged. In only a decade it was dismantled four times, it suffered continuous divisions and changes of direction until, after intense repression after the events of 1968, it disintegrated in 1969. Thus the unitary force of the Spanish New Left of the 1950s disappeared, although its polymorph inheritance will continue on in the radical parties that were born from their ashes.

Marxist-Leninist groups

In the Spanish case, the criticism to "revisionism" also began in the exile. In 1964, several groups of dissident with the PCE created in Paris the *Communist Party of Spain (Marxist-Leninist)* [PCE(m-l)], led by Benita Ganuza (*Elena Ódena*) and Julio Manuel Fernández (*Raúl Marco*). The party adopted Marxism-Leninism-Mao Zedong Thought, proclaiming itself as successor of the PCE. It suffered continuous splits and an intense police pressure, but it survived because its leadership was out of Spain. Its situation became more complicated after 1968 as a result of the improvement of the relationships between the Communist Party of China (CPC) and the PCE, after separating from the CPSU, and due to the melting of goodwill between China and the USA. In 1970, China stopped helping the PCE(m-l) and it separated from Maoism and sided with Albanian Stalinism, that rejected the theory of the three worlds of Mao Zedong. In 1971, the party promoted the *Revolutionary Anti-fascist Patriotic Front* (FRAP), with a program that included armed struggle against the dictatorship and Yankee imperialism in order to impose a popular democracy (Castro Moral 2009, 44–45). In 1974, they constituted the FRAP in order to counter the Democratic Junta of Spain, created by the PCE, and in the summer of 1975 they began the armed actions. The regime responded by executing three militants of the FRAP and two of ETA on September 27, 1975. After this, the organization withdrew, maintaining its activity outside of Spain. In 1976, the PCE(m-l) renounced to the armed struggle and launched the *Republican Convention of the Peoples of Spain* (CRPE), alternative to the platform of the moderate opposition, Democratic Coordination (or *Platajunta*). Legalized in 1981, it declined until becoming dissolved in 1992.[9] In Portugal, its brother party was the PC(R), also Stalinist and pro Albanian.

In 1968, also out of the country, other Maoist and Guevarist groups created the *Organization of Marxist-Leninist of Spain* (OMLE). In its beginning it was limited to the ambit of emigration, prevailing Third World perspectives and support for the Cultural Revolution. Although it shared with the PCE(m-l) a project based on the armed struggle, the OMLE viewed Spain not as a Yankee colony, but as a developed capitalist country, consequently the objective should be the dictatorship of the proletariat and not a popular democracy. After 1970, its membership swelled with an influx of returned emigrants and in 1971 the leadership was assumed by Manuel Pérez Martínez (*Arenas*), who began the conversion of the OMLE into a centralized party of professional revolutionaries, whose rise drove the creation in 1975 of the *Communist Party of Spain (Reconstituted)* [PCE(r)] and, its armed branch, the *First of October Anti-fascist Resistance Groups* (GRAPO), led by Enrique Cerdán Calixto. Similar to the PCE(m-l), the GRAPO thought in the summer of 1975 that it was the time for armed struggle, and on October 1 they began their actions as a response to the executions by firing squad of September 27. They were able to commit attacks of great impact, but in the 1980s, police pressure and its political isolation ended up strangling the organization that survived in the margins, committing robberies and kidnappings as means of subsistence (Roldán Barbero 2008).

After the Cultural Revolution, the dogmatic and violent Maoism of these parties gave way to a new Maoism that attempted to link the party with the needs and wishes of the people. This was the case of the group *Unity*, founded in Barcelona in 1967 by dissidents of the *Unified Socialist Party of Catalonia* (PSUC), who were upset about the agreements policy of the PCE. In 1969, led by Manuel Valverde, a former leader of the PSUC, they founded the *Communist Party of Spain (international)* [PCE(i)] and the *Revolutionary Workers' Commissions* (COR), apart from CCOO which were related to the PCE. In 1970, Valverde was arrested and expelled from his party and in 1972 the new leadership began a shift in policy in order to strengthen links with society, what gave in 1973 the leadership to Eladio García Castro (*Ramón Lobato*). The party adopted the masses line, and came back to CCOO, adopting in 1975 the name the *Party of Labour of Spain* (PTE). This contributed to its take-off in the main industrial centers of the country and in the day-labourer communities of Andalusia (Martín Ramos 2011). From 1973 it took part in the Assembly of Catalonia and joined the Democratic Junta of Spain in 1975. The PTE came to be the most influential force at the Left of the PCE, with mass organizations such as the *Democratic Association of Women* (ADM) and the *Democratic Union of Soldiers* (UDS), and their own union, the *Workers Unitary Trade Union Confederation* (CSUT), split from CCOO in 1977. In the elections of 1977 it joined the coalition *Left of Catalonia*, which gained one seat.[10] The PTE became gradually more moderated, and in 1978 it called for a supportive vote to the Constitution. In 1979, it did not achieve representation in the Parliament, something that favoured the merger with the *Revolutionary Organization of the Workers* (ORT), creating the *Workers Party* (PT), which disappeared in 1980 due to the disagreements between both sectors (Wilhelmi 2016, 263–270). The debts contracted during the electoral campaigns influenced decisively its evolution.

From the group *Unity*, created in 1968, appeared the *Union of Revolutionary Students* (UER), opposed to the Leftism of the prevailing sector that founded the PCE(i). They were joined by former PSUC militants, such as Jordi Solé Tura, thus creating in 1969 the *Communist Organization (Red Flag)* [OC(BR)]. They defined themselves as Leninist, but they had eclectic positions influenced by the French May, Mao Zedong, Althusser or Poulantzas. From 1970, the party entered into university, working-class and neighborhood ambits, recruiting Christian activists such as Alfonso Carlos Comín, and further expanded throughout the country. In 1973 they adopted the name *Communist Organization of Spain (Red Flag)* [OCE(BR)], defining themselves as Marxist-Leninist and with the Russian, Chinese and Vietnamese revolutions as a model; advocated, as other Maoist groups, for a revolution by stages; and proposed a democratic-popular democracy. In 1974, the group of the "intellectuals", headed by Jordi Solé Tura, Jordi Borja and Alfonso Carlos Comín, returned to the PSUC (Pala 2011). The working-class sector, led by Ignasi Faura (*José Sierra*) remained in the OCE(BR), suffered a new split and in 1976 the *Communist Party (Red Unity)* [PC(UR)] emerged but was not long-lasting. After this crisis the OCE(BR) lost strength. It was not legalized, like all the radical Left, until after the 1977 elections, to which they called for a boycott addressing that the great Capital was using it to perpetuate its domination. They also opposed the Constitution of 1978, calling for abstention in the referendum, and for the integration of Spain into the European Economic Community (EEC) and the North Atlantic Treaty Organization (NATO), advocating for an Agrarian Reform, the nationalization of the bank and the retirement of foreign military bases. The bad electoral results and the lack of allies drove the OCE(BR) closer to the PCE, and which they eventually joined in 1989.

Other groups emerged from the progressive Catholicism. It was the case of the union *Workers' Trade Union Action* (AST), constituted in the early 1970s by groups of working-class Catholics influenced by the Second Vatican Council.[11] Due to its links with CCOO and the parties of opposition in the hidden struggle against the dictatorship, in 1966 AST defined itself as anti-capitalist and revolutionary, something that attracted dissidents of the PCE. As a result of these influences in 1969 AST transformed into the *Workers' Revolutionary Organization* (ORT), defining itself as a Marxist and class organization in 1971 (Treglia 2013). Within the ORT there were three tendencies: a communist one, a syndicalist one, and a Trotskyite-like one, formed by former militants of the FLP, and that soon vanished. The communist faction, the biggest one, strengthened with the recruitment of Maoist students, such as José Sanroma (*Intxausti*), among others. Consolidated and spread throughout the country, in 1972 the ORT adopted Marxism-Leninism-Mao Zedong Thought and pointed to the objective of a Popular-Democratic Republic as a transition stage to socialism. For this purpose, they assumed the need of "mass" revolutionary violence, but not individual terrorism. They defended the Unique Front of the proletariat in order to promote the leading role of the working class in the revolutionary process. They thought that CCOO was that front, and understood that union as a tool of the workers to seize political power and not as a mere labour union limited to the economic struggle. After 1974, the ORT assumed the democratic rupture and moderated its political line, in a similar vein to its Portuguese homologue, the PCP(m-l). Thus, in 1975 it joined the Democratic Convergence Platform (PCD), promoted by the PSOE, and in 1976 the Democratic Coordination. As with the PTE, they left CCOO and launched in 1977 their own union, the *Unitary Trade Union* (SU) and supported the Constitution of 1978 in order to "consolidate democracy". This orientation drove it to an ephemeral merger with the PTE, dissolved in 1980. After the elections of 1982 its leader, José Sanroma, and other cadres began to collaborate with the PSOE.

There was also a Maoist group that was born in the Basque *New Left* by Catholic university students and radical workers, led by Patxi Iturrioz and Eugenio del Río. In 1965, they joined ETA, the main opposition force in the Basque Country, where they created a Marxist and workerist tendency. In 1966, this sector was expelled by the nationalist mayority, and in 1967 created the New ETA (*ETA Berri*), inspired by Leninism and the Cuban Revolution. In 1969, they adopted the name *Komunistak* (The Communists), and then *Euskadiko Mugimendu Komunista* (Basque Communist Movement) [EMK], with a Maoist line and a Third World perspective, and together with other related organizations from other territories, created in 1972 the *Communist Movement of Spain* (MCE), advocate of Marxism-Leninism-Mao Zedong Thought, but opposed to the armed struggle. The MCE aimed at achieving socialism by means of two stages: a national-democratic revolution, which gave the power to popular classes, and a dictatorship of the proletariat toward socialism and communism. The tool for this was a peasant-worker front, allied to the anti-fascist bourgeoisie in a national democratic front. They also defended a federal republic that recognized the right of self-determination of oppressed nations, and connected popular democracy with national independence, consequently they rejected the treaties with the USA and demanded the exit of the troops from the Spanish territory. In 1975, they left Maoism and defended the idea of democratic rupture, so they joined the PCD and, later, Democratic Coordination (Cucó i Giner 2008). In 1976, they adopted the name *Communist Movement* (MC), reinforcing their federal character. In the elections of 1977 they participated in the coalition *Euskadiko Ezkerra* (Basque Country Left), which obtained one seat.[12] Its evolution towards an eclectic Marxism and the common campaign against the Constitution in 1978, calling for abstention in the referendum, favored its merger with the *Organization of Communist Left* (OIC) in 1979. In the 1980s, the MC converged with the LCR in social movements. Both groups merged in 1991 in *Alternative Left* (IA), which was dissolved in 1993. The MC faction reoriented its line towards civil society without going back to the electoral arena.

Another branch of the Marxist-Leninist Left comprised those who defended the USSR against the reformism of the PCE and "Maoist Leftism". These groups did not rise in Portugal, since the PCP always had good relationships with the CPSU. But the PCE suffered several pro-Soviet splits due to its condemnation of the intervention of the Warsaw Pact in Czechoslovakia in 1968. The first split led to the formation of the *Communist Party of Spain (VIII–IX Congress)* in 1969. From it appeared in 1973 the *Spanish Communist Workers' Party* (PCOE), founded by the historical leader Enrique Líster. Apart from those parties, although also in line with the USSR, after 1973 there were several groups within the PCE that attempted to counter the Euro-communist line of the PCE leader Carrillo (Pérez Serrano 2013, 271–273). The most outstanding ones were the *Left Opposition of PCE* (OPI), led by Carlos Delgado (*Carlos Tuya*) that, in 1976, turned into the *Workers' Communist Party* (PCT), and the *Communist Cells* (CC), strong in the Canary Islands, where Fernando Sagaseta achieved one seat in 1979 with the coalition *Canarian People's Union* (UPC). With the crisis of the PCE, these forces began to gather. In 1980, the PCE(VIII-IX) and the PCT merge in the *Unified Communist Party of Spain* (PCEU). In 1982, the pro-Soviet faction of the PSUC founded the *Party of the Communists of Catalonia* [PCC], led by Pere Ardiaca and Juan Ramos, with strong links to the workers movement. In 1983 PCEU, CC, PCC and two other small groups launched the *State Commission for Communist Unity* (CEUC), forming in 1984 the *Communist Party of the Peoples of Spain* (PCPE), led by Ignacio Gallego. The PCPE participated in 1989 in the foundation of the *United Left* (IU), with which Gallego became a member of Parliament. In 1989, Gallego's party and a part of its leadership came back to the PCE, and the PCPE was excluded from IU, although it still survived, led by Juan Ramos.

Revolutionary Marxist groups

From the implosion of the FLP in 1969, council communist and Trotskyite groups also emerged. They all rejected reformism, interclass alliances and the authoritarian and bureaucratic behaviour of both the PCE and Marxism-Leninism. They defended direct democracy and the power of workers councils. But there were differences among them: before Trotskyites, whose key reference was the ideas of Leon Trotsky, council communists, influenced by Rosa Luxemburg, Rühle or Pannekoek, rejected the leading role of the party in the revolution, which should be as a result of the workers themselves and not of any vanguard (Pérez Serrano 2015, 104).

The first council communist group was *Communist Action* (AC), a split from the FLP in 1965, after the expulsion of its Foreign Federation, which advocated for leaving the frontist strategy and for creating a revolutionary Marxist party. The group articulated around the magazine *Communist Action*, directed in Paris by Carlos Semprún. Their ideology combined libertarian Marxist, Luxemburgist, Leninist and Trotskyites influences, without a clear adscription to any of them. They aimed at building a party that integrated all revolutionary Marxists. With that purpose, they participated in the candidature of the *Front for Workers Unity* (FUT), together with the LCR, the OIC and the POUM for the elections of 1977. In 1978 they attempted to merge with the POUM and the *Collective for Marxist Unification* (CUM), a split from the OIC after its turn toward the MC (Roca 1994, 57). But the process failed and the AC disappeared. The Trotskyite sector joined the LCR, others passed to the POUM, and libertarian Marxists joined the CNT.

The historical *Workers' Party of Marxist Unification* (POUM) almost vanished during the dictatorship, and its leadership in the exile was divided. In 1974 young socialists tried to recover the party in Catalonia as an anti-Stalinist reference and as an influence for the rest of the revolutionary Left. After the death of Franco, a sector of its veteran militancy, around Enric Adroher (*Gironella*), reconstituted the leadership of the POUM in Catalonia, joining the process of socialist unity that in 1978 ended in the creation of the *Party of the Socialists of Catalonia* (PSC). In the exile, Wilebaldo Solano took the leadership, advocating for a party open from the left to Trotskyism, democratic rupture, self-determination of nationalities and a constituent process (Pagés 1998). Young people, opposed to taking part in the elections of 1977, split demanding the establishment of the Republic. The POUM took part in those elections in the FUT, and after that attempted without success, as mentioned earlier, to achieve unity with AC and CUM. They then focused on opposition to the Constitution in the 1978 referendum, but in 1979, aware of their weaknesses, did not participate in the elections and the militancy began to move to other parties. The Catalonian group was the most resistant, but it vanished in 1981.

A sector split from the *Workers' Front of Catalonia* (FOC), the Catalonian branch of the FLP, founded in 1969 the *Cadres Training Circles* (CFC), opposed to the political control of the PSUC and the FOC over the union CCOO. They advocated for worker autonomy and refused the guardianship of the intellectuals and the idea of a vanguard party. The CFC aimed at training the workers in an autonomous way, apart from the parties, and setting the ground for the creation of a true worker party. Thus, they promoted the *Workers Commissions of Enterprises* (COE), not controlled by the PSUC and articulated into *Platforms*, which should elaborate the revolutionary theory from the workers' struggles. The group collapsed in 1970 when most of its members, led by Dídac Fábregas, proposed to assume Leninism. They gave birth to the *Communist Workers Circles* (COC) in 1971 and in 1974 to the *Organisation of Communist Left of Spain* (OICE), when the COC merged with the *Communist Workers Nuclei* (NOC), which operated in the Basque Country under a very similar basis. The new party preserved the *Anticapitalist Workers Commissions* (COA) and the *Anticapitalist Platforms*, from where they attempted to promote an independent and democratic union, the *United Center of Workers* (Estebaranz 2011, 76–77). After 1976, the OIC evolved towards an eclectic Marxist-Leninism that combined Leninist, Trotskyite and Gramscian references. This did not impede them in participating in the 1977 elections with the FUT. But several months after, it was legalized as the *Organisation of Communist Left* (OIC), adopting a federal structure as self-declared Marxist-Leninist, and leading to the split of the revolutionary Marxist sector, the CUM, described earlier. In 1978, the OIC decided to merge with the MC, a decision that triggered Fábregas's departure from the party. The merger took place in 1979. Eugenio del Río, leader of the MC, was elected general secretary. The new party preserved the name MC and in the labor arena they adopted the strategy of working within CCOO.

Trotskyite groups

Although Trotskyite organizations are also self-defined revolutionary Marxists, they differ from the rest for their defense of the legacy of Trotsky: the transition program and the theory of the permanent revolution. Opposed to Stalinism and Maoism, they were divided by their adscription to different international currents of Trotskyism. In Spain, the minority Fourth International Posadist already constituted in 1962 the *Revolutionary Workers' Party (Trotskyist)* [POR(T)], which participated in 1971 in the foundation of the Assembly of Catalonia (Iniesta 2003, 18). But the real origin of these groups can be found in the Trotskyite tendency of the FLP and the FOC. Split in 1969 after a great repression of the student movement in 1968, it created in Barcelona the group *Communism*. In 1971 it divided, due to differences over the international affiliation. The majority sector founded the *Revolutionary Communist League* (LCR), connected to the United Secretariat of the Fourth International (USFI), and the minority founded *Trotskyist Fraction* (FT), linked to the other big current of the Fourth International, the International Committee (ICFI). In 1972 appeared two tendencies in the LCR. The first, with majority, joined the Mandelist current of the USFI whilst the second created in 1973 the *Communist League* (LC) – more radical, affiliated to the Lenin Trotsky Tendency (TLT) and inspired by Nahuel Moreno and the USA *Workers' Socialist Party*. In 1973, the LCR joined the workerist sector of ETA, the Sixth Assembly, giving birth to the LCR-ETA(VI). The unified party consolidated, integrating other Trotskyist groups.[13] In 1976, it took again the name LCR, with the exception of the Basque Country, where it took the name of *Liga Komunista Iraultzailea* (LKI). During the Transition, the LCR refused the alliances with the bourgeoisie promoted by PCE and PSOE and launched the United Front of the workers for advancing toward socialism (Caussa and Martínez 2014). In the elections of 1977, the LC called for a boycott, whilst the LCR launched the FUT. In 1978, most of the LC came back to the LCR, campaigning against the Constitution. But the bad results in the elections and the loss of militancy drove the LCR to focus on social movements, working together with the MC. Both forces created the Current of Union Left in CCOO and developed a great work within feminist, student and pacifist movements, especially in the campaign against NATO in 1986. In 1991, LCR and MC merged to become the IA, which left the Fourth International. The marriage, however, did not last long and in 1993 it was dissolved.

The FT, on its behalf, was suddenly affected by the dissensions in the ICFI. In 1973, after the split of Lambert, which had created in 1972 the Organising Committee for the Reconstruction of the Fourth International (OCRFI), it split from the *Trotskyite Organization* (OT). The rest of the FT remained with the ICFI, led by Gerry Healy, founding that year the *Communist Workers League* (LOC). The OT was affected by the divisions between the two leaders of OCRFI, Pierre Lambert and Michel Varga, which ended with the exit of the latter and the creation of the International League for the Reconstruction of the Fourth International (ILRFI). The OT joined the ILRFI, and in 1974 transformed into the *Revolutionary Workers' Party of Spain* (PORE). The new party, led by Arturo Van den Eynde (*Aníbal Ramos*), mobilized without success in favor of a revolutionary general strike in 1976, and in 1977 called for a boycott of the elections (Iniesta 2003, 28). The party was not legalized until 1983 and in 1984, the it broke with Varga and promoted in 1995 the merger of ILRFI with the Revolutionary International Current in the International Workers' Unity–Fourth International (IWU-FI), and in 1992, adopted the name *Revolutionary Workers' Party* (POR), with presence virtually limited to Catalonia.[14]

With the integration of the OT into the ILRFI, Lambertism disappeared in Spain until 1976, when a sector of the OT constituted the *Fourth International Organization* (OCI), the Spanish section of the OCRFI. In 1977, dissidents from the PORE joined them, and in 1978 a sector of the LC, opposed to the merger with the LCR, did the same. In 1980 the OCI converged with the *Workers Coordination of Socialist Groups* (COAS), formed by Marxists expelled from the PSOE in 1979, and with Trotskyites of the POUM, together creating the *Internationalist Socialist Workers' Party* (POSI), to which they joined dissident factions of the LC and the LCR. In 1982, the POSI supported the transformation of the OCRFI in the Fourth International-International Centre of Reconstruction (FI-CIR). From the end of the 1980s they moderated their positions, working in the UGT and supporting the International Agreement of the Workers and the People (AIT) created by Lambert in 1991.

The Morenist current, in favour of the thesis of Nahuel Moreno, has its origins in Spain in the Revolutionary Socialist Tendency of the LC, which left the party in 1976 and created the *Socialist Revolutionary League* (LSR). In 1977, the LSR divided into two groups: the majority joined the PSOE as a tendency, the other joined the LCR. In 1979, the first left the PSOE and joined the LCR, but in November, after the breakdown of Moreno with the SU, Morenists also left the LCR and created their own party, the *Workers' Socialist Party* (PST), affiliated to the Bolshevist Faction (FB) of Moreno (Pérez Serrano 2013, 284–285). In 1981, the convergence between Moreno and Lambert drove PST and POSI to have contacts for a possible merger, but it was aborted several months later due to the breakdown of both international tendencies. In 1982, the PSR joined the International Workers League–Fourth International (IWL-FI), constituted by Moreno from the FB. In 1993, the PST split. The biggest sector, *Contra Corriente* (Counter Current), abandoned Trotskyism and focused on social movements; the minority current, *The Socialist Truth*, joined the dissidents of the POSI, giving birth in 1994 to the *Workers' Revolutionary Party* (PRT), which merged in 2002 with the *Revolutionary Left* (IR) in the PRT-IR (today *Red Current*).

From the other Trotskyite currents, the one led by the British revolutionary, Ted Grant, *The Militant*, integrated since 1974 in the Committee for a Workers' International (CWI) and led by Allan Woods, is the only that had a certain presence in Spain. It was introduced in 1976 within the Socialist Youth (*Juventudes Socialistas*), the youth branch of the PSOE, controlling the periodical *Nuevo Claridad*. They were expelled from the PSOE and the UGT in 1978, forming *Youth for Socialism* (JPS). They founded, in 1986, the influential Students Union (*Sindicato de Estudiantes*), but in the 1990s the divisions within the CWI fragmented the Spanish organization, which split into several small groups.

Radical Left nationalist groups

Unlike Portugal, the existence in Spain of an unresolved national question, exacerbated by Francoist repression, explains that there are also nationalist revolutionary groups in some historical communities of the Spanish State (Rubiralta 1997). The most emblematic of them is ETA, *Euskadi Ta Askatasuna* (Basque Fatherland and Liberty), created in 1959 by young dissidents of the *Basque Nationalist Party* (PNV). The armed struggle began against the Franco dictatorship in 1968. In the 1960s, ETA suffered, as has been seen, two workers' divisions – ETA Berri and ETA (VI) – that gave rise to Marxist parties, but the majority sector remained faithful to nationalism. In 1973, it was divided into two branches, military (ETA-m) and the workers' front. From the second emerged new Marxist organizations, such as the *Revolutionary Patriot Workers' Party* (LAIA) and, shortly thereafter, *ETA political-military* (ETA-pm), which in 1977 created *Euskal Iraultzarako Alderdia* (Party for the Basque Revolution, EIA) to participate in the elections through *Euskadiko Ezkerra* (Basque Country Left). In 1982, ETA-pm was dissolved and integrated into EE. Earlier, ETA-pm, LAIA and other groups of the Left-wing nationalist (*abertzale*)[15] had created, in 1976, the *Patriot Socialist Coordinator* (KAS), whose political program, the KAS Alternative, was the origin of *Herri Batasuna* (Popular Unity, HB). Created in 1978, HB was the main force of radical nationalism in Spain, with extensive parliamentary, autonomous and municipal representation since 1979 (Infoelec-toral.mir.es, 2017). From 1998 it promoted unity with other Basque radical forces in *Euskal Herritarrok* (Basque Citizens, EH) and, in 2001, it was trans-formed into *Batasuna* (*Unity*), which was outlawed in 2003[16] (Fernández Sol-devila and López Romo 2012).

In Catalonia, the main radical nationalist group is the *Socialist Party of National Liberation of the Catalan Countries* (PSAN), split in 1969 from the *National Front of Catalonia* (FNC). In 1973, the most radical sector, mainly formed by young people, was separated, giving a place in 1974 to PSAN-Provisional, partisan of the armed struggle and allied of ETA (Bassa et al. 1985) that, in 1979, transformed into *Independentists of the Catalan Countries* (IPC) (Buch i Ros 1995). Other dissidents from the PSAN, together with former members of armed groups such as the *Popular Catalan Army* (EPOCA) and the *Catalan Liberation Front* (FAC), founded in 1978 *Terra Lliure* (Free Land, TLL), the main Catalan armed organization (Fernández Calvet 1986; Sastre et al. 2012). In 1984, the PSAN and IPC promoted the *Movement for Defence of the Land* (MDT), which acted as the political branch of *Terra Lliure* until its dis-solution in 1991. Since 1987, the *Popular Unity Candidacy* (CUP) was on the MDT list in the municipal elections.

In Galicia, the most important group was the *Galician People's Union* (UPG), created in 1964, promoters of Marxist-Leninist ideology and partisans of inde-pendence (Rubiralta 1998). Its expansion was due to the action of *Galician Revolutionary Students* (ERGA), who were very active between 1972 and 1988. Initially it had a strong relationship with PSAN-Provisional, ETA-pm, the IRA (Irish Republican Army) and Portuguese armed groups like LUAR and PRP-BR (Loff 2004, 24). Nevertheless, in the Transition, it ended up opting for the polit-ical route, promoting the *Galician National-Popular Assembly* (AN-PG), with which it appeared in the elections of 1977 as *Galician National-Popular Bloc* (BN-PG), and transformed in 1982 into the *Galician Nationalist Bloc* (BNG). The moderation of the BNG led to two divisions in the UPG in 1986: on the one hand the *Communist Party of National Liberation* (PCLN) emerged, which shortly afterwards gave rise to the *Galician Popular Front* (FPG), while others participated in the creation of the *Guerrilla Army of the Free Galician People* (EGPGC), which carried out armed actions between 1986 and 1991, with the *United People's Assembly* (APU) as its political arm.

Conclusions and reflections

This chapter has demonstrated that the cycle of the revolutionary Left in Portu-gal and Spain was closely linked to the international context and the process of political change in both countries. As a result of a long-term historical wave that began in 1917 and ended in the collapse of the USSR in 1991, during the second half of the twentieth century the evolution of radical organizations was con-nected to the logic of the Cold War, the result of which determined their fate. The paradigm of the socialist revolution touched the ceiling in Europe in 1968, with the French May and the Prague Spring, but it remained alive due to the influence of Maoism and Trotskyism until the end of the 1970s. Under regression in other countries, revolutionary discourse persisted for a further decade in the Iberian Peninsula, due to the duration of the dictatorships.

The change of regime in Portugal and Spain can be inserted with great precision within the critical moment of the Cold War. In Spain and, above all, in Portugal, the strategies of the socialist revolution and capitalist modernization confronted each other openly and with a clear result. It was the revolutionaries who lost the battle in all of its stages and scenarios (De la Torre and Sánchez Cervelló 1992, 252–259). Capitalism, dissociated from the burden of both dictatorships, could continue its development in a liberalized context that allowed for integration into the EEC and for achieving a certain level of internationalization. Both in Portugal and in Spain, once the uncertainty of 1974–1976 was overcome, most of the population endorsed, with their votes, both the procedures and the goals of the moderated governments, committed with the order and stability demanded by both the factual powers and the Western powers. Consequently, the revolutionary Left was soon delegitimized and excluded from the system (Pérez Serrano 2016, 77).

The participation of most radical forces in the elections of 1975 in Portugal, and 1977 in Spain, meant the implicit acknowledgment that representative democracy had won, and it marked the beginning of their decline. During the 1980s, the radical Left put up its last battle in the Iberian peninsula, which resulted in the integration of both countries in the EEC in 1986 and the continuity of Spain in NATO, to which Portugal was a member from its origins in 1949. After 1986, having achieved the most ambitious objectives of the political transitions, the radical organizations began to weaken and virtually disappeared at the beginning of the 1990s.

The peak of activity of the revolutionary Left coincided with the rise of class struggle in the Iberian dictatorships, from the beginning of the economic liberalization until the consolidation of representative democracy, with the enforcement of the Constitutions of 1976 and 1978 and the governments of Mario Soares and Felipe González. From then on, the decline of the radical Left and the withdrawal and institutionalization of social movements coincided in both countries with the consolidation of the political system, the economic boom, the integration into Europe and the end of the Cold War.

Despite its strong symbolic impact, the life of radical organizations was not long. Some were assimilated or simply disappeared altogether during the 1970s. Those that did last longer felt exhausted under the rubble of the Berlin Wall, or survived but were reduced to marginality. Their development was limited by the dynamic of political "normalization", which discriminated against the revolutionary Left by several means or forced it to make essential renunciations. The pacts between the forces of center-right and center-left built up a bipartisan model that excluded radicals. It also acted against them in the practice of the "useful vote" to the PS and the PSOE, and the co-optation of their leaders in exchange for organic responsibilities and public positions, or as union-paid officials. For these reasons, with the exception of the Basque radical Left, only the Portuguese UDP and the pro-Soviet Spanish parties had seats in Parliament before 1999.[17]

The repression over the radicals continued after the dictatorships, although in a more selective and less evident form. A good number of militants were victims of the violence of the police and the far Right, in some cases to the death, during the change of regime. They were exhausted from the struggle against the dictatorship and later from the unpleasant task of putting into question the reformist discourses. The progressive subordination of politics to the mass media contributed decisively to the dissemination of these illusions, fostering consumerism, pragmatism, depolitization and other postmodern stereotypes.

The great problem, most probably, of the radical Left was the confidence – without empirical evidence – in the transformation potential of the working class of the 1970s, trumpeting it to the category of revolutionary subject. The goal of socialism, which oriented all of their political agendas, depended on the capacity of the national proletariat, be it alone or allied with other subaltern classes, to seize power. Thus, revolutionaries repeated as a mantra that the working class could put an end to capitalist domination. The problem was that, neither in Portugal nor in Spain, was the working class ready for assuming this task, and after decades of repression and indoctrination, did not have the courage nor the will to do it.

It is true that workers mobilized from the end of the 1950s, but most of the time in an autonomous way or under the hegemony of the communist parties. Before the reformist and social-democratic parties, the revolutionary Left lost the battle without exception. In addition, it was extremely difficult to know to what extent mobilizations and protests were launched in order to achieve immediate goals or they contained deeper demands. This uncertainty also affected the political parties, which in fact disagreed on what kind of capitalism existed in the Iberian countries from the middle of the 1960s, agreement being essential in order to create class alliances, political strategies and the type of revolution to pursue. All of this was decided with not much objective data, because the dictatorships did not promote nor publish trustworthy analyses and statistics.

The forms of struggle of the radical Left did not succeed either. Armed struggle was always defeated. Violence, with the exception of the Basque case, where it had the support of certain social sectors and was connected to a national project, was never understood by the workers. In Spain particularly, violence was much more present than what was usually reported, and the Left paid a high price for feeding the violence (Baby 2013). Both victim and executioner of violent actions, the left became discredited before those who were supposed to support its actions and, condemned by the media, it was equal to the far Right in the collective imaginary. Those who opted for integration into the system by means of suffrage realized how difficult it was to overcome the fear that the dictatorships had injected into society. In Spain, no radical group became legal before the decisive elections of 1977, from which emerged the Parliament that passed the Constitution of 1978. In other words, they were allowed to participate once the rules of the game were fixed. On the other hand, as the ideological profiles became blurred, the techniques of electoral publicity expressed in big-money campaigns that depended on credit from the banks – something unreachable for radical parties, which had to resort to personal debt to fund their propaganda – gained weight.

To sum up, the working class was not up to the task of carrying out the historical mission to which it was called. The militancy did not always respond to the self-proclaimed stereotype of "revolutionary vanguard" either. The leaders frequently used a rhetorical and dogmatic style that many times hid a profound ignorance about the reality, applying Marxism in an unseasonable way and without the minimal conditions to yield fruit. Sectarianism, authoritarianism and demagogy were weapons that were all used at the service of the superior proposed goal. When the electoral results or the police repression confirmed the unviability of the project, messianism, heroism and total dedication were substituted by possibilism and pragmatism (Pérez Serrano 2015, 115–121). Many confused self-critique with opportunism and with the same scarce fundament with which they defended the revolution they passed to defend the excellences of liberalism. The main benefit of the diaspora of radical cadres and militants was, as has been said, the moderated Left, although there were also some leaders that went to Right parties. In the end, if politics was a professional activity, something that many learnt in their own Leninist practice, the great parties of the system offered the most effective channel to perform it.

Of course, many persons, both in the rank-and-file and in the leadership of the radical parties struggled in an honest, selfless and aware way for a socialist society, using to define it the theoretical references and the empirical models of their time. The revolution was not yet discredited as a political goal and was reinforced by the experience of anti-colonial struggles, the Chinese Cultural Revolution and the guerrilla war. In these battles were forged many of the political and social cadres of the first generation of the new Iberian democracies. The radical Left also promoted attitudes and values of a modern citizenship, such as the exercise of the critique and protest in the public space, the defense of the environment, gender equality, anti-nuclear awareness, anti-colonialism, pacifism, or minority rights, contributing to the articulation of a civil society (Pérez Serrano 2012). They helped to secularize society and to democratize the political practice. With their revelry they opened crevices in the established systems of values and challenged traditional authority structures, putting into question socialization rituals imposed by the dictatorship (football, feasts and religious celebrations). In their struggle, they organized and gave voice to those who had none: young people, students, soldiers, artists, people of the neighborhoods, homosexuals or migrants, and offered to women channels for political intervention, at the same time defending their social, labour and reproductive rights.

In the symbolic realm, the radical Left was pioneer vindicating the anti-fascist memory and rehabilitating the victims of the repression, coming early to the current debate on historical memory. They were also groundbreaking, detecting and denouncing firmly the – real, hidden and potential – vices of the system that was coming into the world: the privilege of the elite, bureaucratism, control of the major parties, submission of the judicial power, autonomy of the lobbies and factual powers, threats of coups, opacity, financial and urban speculation, international guardianship, opportunity inequality, etc. (Morán 2015), and attempted, without success, to mobilize the society to confront them. They dreamt of socialism and many of them promoted Iberian federalism in order to solve both social problems and the national issue. The evolution of the events vanquished some of those proposals, but it has also exposed the risks, weaknesses and profound contradictions of a consolidated system (Wilhelmi 2016, 380). These pages can shed some light on a time of change, in which the aspirations that today are emerging again seem possible, and contain abundant evidence of why they were aborted.

Acknowledgment

This chapter is the result of the research projects "Sindicalismo y nuevos movimientos sociales en la construcción de la democracia: España, 1976–2012" (HAR2012-38837) and "Del antifranquismo a la marginalidad: disidencias políticas y culturales en la Transición española a la democracia" (HAR2016-79134-R), funded by the Ministry of Economy and Competitiveness of Spain.

Glossary of radical Left political organizations and movements in Portugal and Spain

AC	Acción Comunista
ADM	Asociación Democrática de la Mujer
AN-PG	Asemblea Nacional-Popular Galega
AOC	Aliança Operário-Camponesa
APSR	Associação Política Socialista Revolucionária
APU	Assembleia do Povo Unido
ARA	Acção Revolucionária Armada
AST	Acción Sindical de Trabajadores
Batasuna	(Unity)
BE	Bloco de Esquerda
BN-PG	Bloque Nacional-Popular Galego
BNG	Bloque Nacionalista Galego
BR	Brigadas Revolucionárias
CARP	Comité de Apoio à Reconstrução do Partido (marxista-leninista)
CC	Células Comunistas
CCOO	Comisiones Obreras
CCP	Comité Comunista de Portugal
CCR(m-l)	Comités Comunistas Revolucionarios Marxistas-Leninistas
CDE	Comissão Democrática Eleitoral
CdE	Convergência de Esquerda,
CDP	Comunistas pela Democracia e Progresso
CDU	Coalição Democrática Unitaria

CEUC	Comisión Estatal de Unidad Comunista
CFC	Círculos de Formación de Cuadros
CIDAC	Comissão para a Independência das Antigas Colónias
CLMRP	Comité de Ligação dos Militantes Revolucionários Portugueses (para a Reconstrução da IV Internacional)
CMLdP	Comité Marxista-Leninista de Portugal (O Bolchevista)
CMLP	Comité Marxista-Leninista Português
CNT	Confederación Nacional del Trabajo
COA	Comisiones Obreras Anticapitalistas
COAS	Coordinadora Obrera de Agrupaciones Socialistas
COC	Círculos Obreros Comunistas
COE	Comisiones Obreras de Empresa
COPCON	Comando Operacional do Continente
COR	Comisiones Obreras Revolucionarias
CPAO	Comissão Pró-Amnistia de Otelo
CRPE	Convención Republicana de los Pueblos de España
CRTSM	Conselhos Revolucionários de Trabalhadores, Soldados e Marinheiros
CSUT	Confederación de Sindicatos Unitarios de Trabajadores
CUM	Colectivo por la Unificación Marxista
CUP	Candidatura d'Unitat Popular
EdC	Esquerra de Catalunya
EDE	Esquerda Democrática Estudiantil
EE	Euskadiko Ezkerra (Basque Country Left)
EGPGC	Exército Guerrilheiro do Povo Galego Ceive
EH	Euskal Herritarrok (Basque Citizens)
EH Bildu	Euskal Herria Bildu (Euskal Herria unida)
EIA	Euskal Iraultzarako Alderdia (Party for the Basque Revolution)
EMK	Euskadiko Mugimendu Komunista (Communist Movement of Euskadi)
EPOCA	Exèrcit Popular Català
ERC	Esquerra Republicana de Catalunya
ERGA	Estudantes Revolucionarios Galegos
ESBA	Euskadiko Sozialisten Batasuna (Basque Country Socialist Union)
ETA	Euskadi Ta Askatasuna (Basque Fatherland and Liberty)
ETA-m	ETA-militar
ETA-pm	ETA-political military
ETA(VI)	ETA (VI Asamblea)
FAC	Front d'Alliberament Català
FAP	Frente de Acção Popular
FB-L	Fracción Bolchevique-Leninista
FEA	Fórum Ecologista e Alternativo
FEML	Federação dos Estudantes Marxistas-Leninistas
FEPU	Frente Eleitoral Povo Unido

FER	Frente da Esquerda Revolucionária
FLP	Frente de Liberación Popular
FNC	Front Nacional de Catalunya
FOC	Front Obrer de Catalunya
FP-25	Forças Populares 25 de Abril
FPG	Front Popular Galega
FPLN	Frente Patriótica de Libertação Nacional
FRAP	Frente Revolucionario Antifascista y Patriota
FSP	Frente Socialista Popular
FT	Fracción Trotskista
FUP	Força de Unidade Popular
FUR	Frente de Unidade Revolucionária
FUT	Frente por la Unidad de los Trabajadores
GDUPs	Grupos Dinamizadores de Unidade Popular (GDUPs)
GRAPO	Grupos de Resistencia Antifascista Primero de Octubre
HB	Herri Batasuna (Popular Unity)
IA	Izquierda Alternativa
IPC	Independentistes dels Països Catalans
IR	Izquierda Revolucionaria
IU	Izquierda Unida
JDE	Junta Democrática de España
JPS	Jóvenes por el Socialismo
KAS	Koordinadora Abertzale Sozialista (Patriot Socialist Coordinator)
LAIA	Langile Abertzale Iraultzaileen Alderdia (Revolutionary Patriot Workers' Party)
LC	Liga Comunista
LCI	Liga Comunista Internacionalista
LCPR	Liga para a Construção do Partido Revolucionário
LCR	Liga Comunista Revolucionaria
LKI	Liga Komunista Iraultzailea (Revolutionary Communist League)
LOC	Liga Obrera Comunista
LSR	Liga Socialista Revolucionaria
LST	Liga Socialista dos Trabalhadores
LUAR	Liga de União e de Acção Revolucionária
MAS	Movimento Alternativa Socialista
MC	Movimiento Comunista
MCE	Movimiento Comunista de España
MDP/CDE	Movimento Democrático Português/Comissão Democrática Eleitoral
MDT	Moviment de Defensa de la Terra
MES	Movimento de Esquerda Socialista
MFA	Movimento das Forças Armadas
MIL	Movimiento Ibérico de Liberación
MRPCE	Movimiento de Recuperación del (PCE)
MRPP	Movimento Reorganizativo do Partido do Proletariado (MRPP)

MRUP	Movimiento de Recuperación y Unificación del PC
MSP	Movimento Socialista Popular
MUS	Movimento para a Unidade Socialista
MUT	Movimento para a Unidade dos Trabalhadores
NOC	Núcleos Obreros Comunistas
OC(BR)	Organización Comunista Bandera Roja
OCE(BR)	Organización Comunista de España (Bandera Roja)
OCI	Organización Cuarta Internacional
OCMLP	Organização Comunista Marxista-Leninista Portuguesa
OIC	Organización de Izquierda Comunista
OICE	Organización de Izquierda Comunista de España
OMLE	Organización de Marxistas-Leninistas de España
OPI	Oposición de Izquierda del PCE
ORPC(m-l)	Organização para a Reconstrução do Partido Comunista (marxista-leninista)
ORT	Organización Revolucionaria de Trabajadores
OST	Organização da IV Internacional – Organização Socialista dos Trabalhadores
OT	Organización Trotskista
OUT	Organização Unitária de Trabalhadores
PA	Plataformas Anticapitalistas
PC(R)	Partido Comunista (Reconstruído) (Portugal)
PC(UR)	Partido Comunista (Unidad Roja)
PCC	Partit dels Comunistes de Catalunya
PCD	Plataforma de Convergencia Democrática
PCE(i)	Partido Comunista de España (internacional)
PCE(m-l)	Partido Comunista de España (marxista-leninista)
PCE(r)	Partido Comunista de España (reconstituido)
PCE(VIII-IX)	Partido Comunista de España (VIII-IX Congresos)
PCE	Partido Comunista de España
PCEU	Partido Comunista de España Unificado
PCOE	Partido Comunista Obrero Español
PCP(m-l)	Partido Comunista de Portugal (marxista-leninista)
PCP	Partido Comunista Português
PCPE	Partido Comunista de los Pueblos de España
PCT	Partido Comunista de los Trabajadores
PCTP	Partido Comunista de los Trabalhadores Portugueses
Podemos	(We Can)
PXXI	Política XXI (Politics XXI)
POR	Partido Obrero Revolucionario
PORE	Partido Obrero Revolucionario de España
POSI	Partido Obrero Socialista Internacionalista
POUM	Partido Obrero de Unificación Marxista
POUS	Partido Operário de Unidade Socialista
PRP	Partido Revolucionário do Proletariado

PRT	Partido Revolucionario de los Trabajadores (España)
PRT	Partido Revolucionário dos Trabalhadores (Portugal)
PS	Partido Socialista (Portugal)
PSAN	Partit Socialista d'Alliberament Nacional dels Països Catalans
PSC	Partit dels Socialistes de Catalunya
PSOE	Partido Socialista Obrero Español
PSR	Partido Socialista Revolucionário
PST	Partido Socialista de los Trabajadores (España)
PST	Partido Socialista dos Trabalhadores (Portugal)
PSUC	Partido Socialista Unificado de Cataluña
PT	Partido de los Trabajadores (España)
PT	Partido Trabalhista (Portugal)
PTE	Partido del Trabajo de España
Ruptura	(Breach)
Ruptura-FER	(Breach-FER)
SdE	Sindicato de Estudiantes
SU	Sindicato Unitario
SUV	Soldados Unidos Vencerão
TLL	Terra Lliure
UC(m-l)	União Comunista (marxista-leninista)
UCRPML	União Comunista para a Reconstrução do Partido Marxista-Leninista PC(m-l)P Partido Comunista (marxista-leninista) Português
UDP	União Democrática Popular
UDS	Unión Democrática de Soldados
UER	Unión de Estudiantes Revolucionarios
UGT	Unión General de Trabajadores
UPC	Unión del Pueblo Canario
UPG	Unión do Povo Galego
URML	Unidade Revolucionária Marxista-Leninista

Notes

1 The *National Confederation of Labour* (CNT), founded in 1910, and the Anarchist Federation of Portuguese Region (FARP), created in 1932.
2 In his search for a radical and self-managed communism, *Tiago* broke with his own original Leninism, and ended up leaving the CCR(m-l) in 1974.
3 This organization should not be confused with the Portuguese Marxist-Leninist Committee of Portugal can be denominated with the name of its periodical *O Bolchevista* (The Bolshevik).
4 *Comando Operacional do Continente*, created in July 1974 by the *Movimento das Forças Armadas* in the period after April 25. It was formed by special forces of revolutionary soldiers.
5 The PRP was rebuilt by former militants in 2002.
6 The PRT was affiliated to the Trotskyite Leninist Tendency, led by Nahuel Moreno, a minority within the Unified Secretariat of the Fourth International.
7 The Paritary Committee for the Reconstruction of the Fourth International joined

the Bolshevist Fraction (BFC), led by Nahuel Moreno, and the Committee for the Reconstruction of the Fourth International (OCRFI), led by Pierre Lambert. In 1980, it adopted the name of Fourth International (International Committee) [FI(IC)].

8 In 2011, the current *Ruptura-FER* left the *Bloco de Esquerda* and created a new party, the *Alternative Socialist Movement* (MAS), legalized in 2013, which maintains a relationship to the IWL-FI.

9 The PCE(m-l) was recreated in 2006 regrouping regional and local organizations that came from the former party.

10 The coalition was formed by the PTE and *Republican Left of Catalonia* (ERC). The elected member of the parliament was Heribert Barrera, leader of ERC.

11 These groups were the Workers Brotherhood of Catholic Action (HOAC) and Youth Worker Vanguard (VOJ), created by the Jesuits in the 1950s as a branch of the Social Worker Vanguard (VOS).

12 The coalition was formed by the MC and *Euskal Iraultzarako Alderdia* (Partido para la Revolución Vasca, EIA), the political branch of ETA-political-military. The coalition obtained one representative, Francisco Letamendía, and one senator, Juan María Bandrés, both from EIA. Patxi Iturrioz became a representative for several months after the withdrawal of Letamendía in 1978.

13 In 1974 the LCR integrated the *Bolshevist-Leninist Fraction* (FB-L), a split from the FT, and the *Leninist Fraction* of ETA(VI) ("minos"), that did not participate in the merger LCR-ETA(VI).

14 In 2013, the POR adopted the name of *La Aurora – Organización Marxista* (The Dawn-Marxist Organisation).

15 The *Coordinadora KAS* was formed by ETA-pm, LAIA, *Euskal Herriko Alderdi Sozialista* (Socialist Party of Euskal Herría, EHAS) and the centrals *Langile Abertzale Komiteak* (Patriot Workers' Committees, LAK) and *Langile Abertzaleen Batzordeak* (Patriot Workers' Commissions, LAB). Later the EIA and *Abertzale Sozialista Komiteak* (Patriot Socialist Committees, ASK) were added. ETA-m was not integrated, but it accepted the KAS Alternative, while LAK and a part of LAIA left the Coordinator for disagreements with this political program.

16 The abertzale Left, reborn in 2011 with the creation of *Sortu*, which together with *Aralar*, collects the inheritance *of HB* in the coalition *Euskal Herria Bildu* (Euskal Herria together, EH Bildu) and Amaiur.

17 With the exception of the short period of two months in which Patxi Iturrioz (MC) held his seat in Euskadiko Ezkerra at the end of 1978.

References

Andrade Blanco, Juan Antonio. 2012. *El PCE y el PSOE en (la) Transición: La Evolución Ideológica de la Izquierda durante el Proceso de Cambio Político.* Madrid: Siglo XXI.

Baby, Sophie. 2013. *Le Mythe de la Transition Pacifique. Violence et Politique en Espagne (1975–1982).* Madrid: Casa de Velázquez.

Bassa, David, Carles Benítez, Carles Castellanos, and Raimon Soler. 1985. *L'independentisme Català, 1979–1984.* Barcelona: Llibres de l'Index.

Bayo, Eliseo. 1974. *Portugal: Rn Libertad Condicional.* Barcelona: Dirosa.

Bensaid, Daniel, Carlos Rossi, and Charles-André Udry. 1976. *Lecciones de Abril: Análisis Políticos de la Experiencia Portuguesa.* Barcelona: Mandrágora.

Buch i Ros R. 1995. *El Partit Socialista d'Alliberament Nacional dels Països Catalans (1974–1980).* Barcelona: ICPS.

Campinos, Jorge. 1981. "La Transición del Autoritarismo a la Democracia en la Europa del Sur: el Ejemplo Português". In *Transición a la Democracia en el Sur de Europa y América Latina*, edited by Julián Santamaría, 151–197. Madrid: CIS.

Cardina, Miguel. 2011. *Margem de Certa Maneira. O Maoismo em Portugal, 1964–1974.* Lisboa: Tinta-da-China.

Cardina, Miguel. 2013. "Génesis, Estructuración e Identidad del Fenómeno Maoísta en Portugal (1964–1974)". *Ayer* 92 (4): 123–146.

Castro Moral, Lorenzo. 2009. "El Terrorismo Revolucionario Marxista-Leninista em España". *Historia del Presente* 14 (2): 39–56.

Caussa, Martí and Ricard Martínez, eds. 2014. *Historia de la Liga Comunista Revolucionaria (1970–1991)*. Madrid: La Oveja Roja.

Chilcote, Ronald H. 2010. *The Portuguese Revolution: State and Class in the Transition to Democracy.* Lanham, MD: Rowman & Littlefield Publishers.

Cucó i Giner, Josepa. 2008. "Recuperando una Memoria en la Penumbra. El Movimiento Comunista y las Transformaciones de la Extrema Izquierda Española". *Historia y Política* 20 (2): 73–96.

De la Torre, Hipólito. and Josep Sánchez Cervelló. 1992. *Portugal en el siglo XX.* Madrid: Istmo.

Eleicoes.cne.pt. 2017. Comissão Nacional de Eleições (CNE) Resultados. Available at: http://eleicoes.cne.pt/sel_eleicoes.cfm?m=vector (accessed 2 January 2017).

Estebaranz, Juantxo. 2011. "La Eclosión de la Corriente Asamblearia (1969–1975)". *Viento Sur* 115: 72–78.

Fernández Calvet, Jaume. 1986. *Terra Lliure, 1979–1985*. Barcelona: Llamp.

Fernández Soldevilla, Gaizka, and Raúl López Romo. 2012. *Sangre, Votos, Manifestaciones. ETA y el Nacionalismo Vasco Radical (1958–2011)*. Madrid: Tecnos.

García Alcalá, Julio Antonio. 2001. *Historia del "Felipe" (FLP, FOC y ESBA): de Julio Cerón a la Liga Comunista Revolucionaria*. Madrid: Centro de Estudios Políticos y Constitucionales.

Infoelectoral.mir.es. 2017. Consulta de resultados electorales. Ministerio del Interior. Available at: www.infoelectoral.mir.es/min/ (accessed 4 January 2017).

Iniesta, Rafael. 2003. *La Premsa Trotskista (1939–2000): Catàleg de les Publicacions Troskistes a les Biblioteques Catalanes.* Barcelona: Servei de Publicacions UAB.

Lisi, Marco. 2013. "Rediscovering Civil Society? Renewal and Continuity in the Portuguese Radical Left". *South European Society and Politics* 18 (1): 1–19.

Llecha, Canela. 2014. *Le Movimiento Ibérico de Liberación (MIL) et ses Représentations dans la Presse: Mythes et Mystifications* (Doctoral dissertation). Paris: Université Paris Ouest Nanterre La Défense.

Loff, Manuel. 2004. "Revolución versus Transición? Visiones de España desde el Portugal Revolucionario y Posrevolucionario". *Gerónimo de Ustáriz* 20: 17–44.

Martín Ramos, José Luis, ed. 2011. *Pan, Trabajo y Libertad. Historia del Partido del Trabajo de España*. Barcelona: El Viejo Topo.

Martins, João Paulo, and Ruio Loureiro. 1980a. "A Extrema-Esquerda em Portugal (1960–1974): Os Marxistas Leninistas e os Trotskistas". *Historia* 17 (3): 8–23.

Martins, João Paulo, and Ruio Loureiro. 1980b. "As Organizaçoes Armadas em Portugal de 1967 a 1974". *Historia* 18 (4): 4–26.

Morán, G. 2015. *El precio de la Transición*. Madrid: Akal.

Narciso, Raimundo. 2000. *A.R.A. Acção Revolucionaria Armada: A História Secreta do Braço Armado do PCP*. Lisboa: Publicações Dom Quixote.

Oliveira, César. 1975. *MFA y Revolución Socialista.* Barcelona: Anagrama.

Ortuño Anaya, Pilar. 2005. *Los Socialistas Europeos y la Transición Española (1959–1977)*. Madrid: Marcial Pons.

Pagés, Pelai. 1998. *El Partit Obrer d'Unificació Marxista durant la transició democràtica (1974–1981)*. Barcelona: Institut de Ciènces Potitiques i Socials, Working Paper n. 156.

Pala, Giaime. 2011. "Una Semilla de Discordia. La Entrada de Bandera Roja en el PSUC". *Revista HMiC: Història Moderna i Contemporània* IX: 140–162.

Pereira, Jose Pacheco. 1988. "El Partido Comunista Portugués y la Izquierda Revolucionaria". *Revista de Estudios Políticos (nueva época)* 60–61: 69–100.

Pérez Serrano, Julio. 2012. "Democracia y Feminismos. La Lucha por la Liberación de la Mujer en la Transición Española, 1975–1983". In *Masculin/féminin en transition. Espagne – 1970–1986*, edited by Marie Claude Chaput, 11–24. Paris: Université ParisOouest Nanterre-La Défense.

Pérez Serrano, Julio. 2013. "Orto y Ocaso de la Izquierda Revolucionaria en España (1959–1994)". In *Los Partidos en la Transición. Las Organizaciones Políticas en la Construcción de la Democracia en España*, edited by Rafael Quirosa-Cheyrouze, 249–289. Madrid: Biblioteca Nueva.

Pérez Serrano, Julio. 2015. "Estrategias de la Izquierda Radical en el Segundo Franquismo y la Transición (1956–1982)". In *La Transición Española: Nuevos Enfoques para un Viejo Debate*, edited by Marie-Claude Chaput and Julio Pérez Serrano, 95–125. Madrid: Biblioteca Nueva.

Pérez Serrano, Julio. 2016. "Funcionalidad y Límites de la Transición a la Democracia como Paradigma Historiográfico". In *La Transición Sentimental. Literatura y Cultura desde los Años Setenta*, edited by Maria Ángeles Naval and Zoraida Carandell, 67–89. Madrid: Visor Libros.

Rico, Eduardo G. 1974. *La Caída del Fascismo Portugués*. Bilbao: Zero.

Robinson, Peter Forbes. 1990. *Workers' Councils in Portugal 1974–1975* (MPhil Thesis). The Open University

Roca, José Manuel. 1994. "Una Aproximación Sociológica, Política e Ideológica a la Izquierda Comunista Revolucionaria en España". In *El proyecto radical. Auge y declive de la izquierda revolucionaria en España (1964–1992)*, edited by José Manuel Roca, 33–68. Madrid: Los Libros de la Catarata.

Roldán Barbero, Horacio. 2008. *Los GRAPO: Un Estudio Criminológico*. Granada: Comares.

Rubiralta, Fermí. 1997. *El Nuevo Nacionalismo Radical. Los Casos Gallego, Catalán y Vasco (1959–1973)*. San Sebastián: Tercera Prensa.

Rubiralta, Fermí. 1998. *De Castelao a Mao. O Novo Nacionalismo Radical Galego (1959–1974). Orixes, Configuración e Desenvolvemento Inicial da UPG*. Santiago de Compostela: Laiovento.

Sánchez Cervelló, Josep. 1995. *La Revolución Portuguesa y su Influencia en la Transición Española (1961–1976)*. Madrid: Nerea.

Sánchez Cervelló, Josep. 1997. *La Revolución de los Claveles en Portugal*. Madrid: Arco Libros.

Sastre, Carles, Carles Benitez, Pep Musté and Joan Rocamora. 2012. *Terra Lliure. Punto de Partida 1979–1995. Una Biografía Autorizada*. Barcelona: Txalaparta.

Serra, Jaime. 1999. *As Explosões que Abalaram o Fascismo: O que foi a ARA (Acção Revolucionária Armada)*. Lisboa: Editorial Avante.

Soeiro, Jose. 2009. "The 'Bloco de Esquerda' and the Founding of a New Left in Portugal". In *The Left in Europe. Political Parties and Party Alliances between Norway and Turkey*, edited by Cornelia Hildebrandt and Birgit Daiber, 176–183. Brussels: Rosa Luxemburg Foundation.

Sommier, Isabelle. 1998. *La Violence Politique et son Deuil: l'après 68 en France et en Italie*. Rennes: Presses Universitaires de Rennes.

Sommier, Isabelle. 2008. *La Violence Révolutionnaire*. Paris: Presses de Sciences Po.

Soto, Alvaro. 2009. "La Transición a la Democracia en el Sur de Europa. La Historia como Instrumento para su Comparación". *Estudios Internacionales* 162: 7–30.

Treglia, Emanuele. 2013. Izquierda Comunista y Cambio Político: El Caso de la ORT. *Ayer* 92 (4): 47–71.

Wilhelmi, Gonzalo. 2016. *Romper el Consenso. La Izquierda Radical en la Transición Española (1975–1982)*. Madrid: Siglo XXI de España.

2 Greece and Italy after the Second World War

Contentious politics, cycles of protest and radical Left

Nikos Serdedakis, Elisabetta della Corte and Markos Vogiatzoglou

Introduction

The radical Left in post-war Greece and Italy, after the end of the anti-Nazi national liberation struggles, initially followed different paths due to clear differentiations in the construction of their political systems. In Italy, the major anti-fascist armed movements were absorbed in the two major Left parties, PCI and PSI, which opted for a parliamentary and institutionalised course to promote the democratisation of Italian society and safeguard the civil rights of the working classes. In Greece, the defeat of the communist forces in the civil war (1947–1949) and the constitution of a nationalist anti-communist state of emergency created negative political opportunities for collective action until the mid-1960s. During that period, massive movements erupted, claiming the democratisation of Greek society. The coup d'état of April 1967 can be analysed as the final stage of the post-civil war period, leading after the fall of the dictatorship to the formation of a pluralist parliamentary political system in Greece.

In the meantime, in Italy the juvenile contestation and protest gave significant space for the creation of a vast leftist area with significant penetration in diverse social strata and social milieu. The intensification of contentious politics in Italy led to severe repression of the social movement organisations, radicalising a large number of activists, who adopted violent means in their confrontation with state apparatuses and the political establishment.

Both in Greece and Italy, during the 1980s and 1990s, new social movements emerged, especially feminist, environmental and civil rights movements. As a general trend described by the theorists of the political process perspective in the study of social movements, we can argue that, in both countries, strong tendencies towards the de-radicalisation and the institutionalisation of the new social movements were present. Despite these tendencies, towards the end of the 1990s, and in the aftermath of "the battle of Seattle", the meetings of the World Social Forum in Porto Alegre and the creation of the European Social Forum, as well as the violent confrontations in the G8 summit in Genova 2001, left radical social movements reinvigorated as a consequence of severe social inequalities and economic crisis, resulting from the implementation of core neo-liberal policies in the South of Europe.

Civil war and the constitution of the "cachectic democracy" in Greece

The liberation of Greece (1944), following the defeat and capitulation of the Nazi regime, found the Greek society deeply wounded and divided. During the occupation, several distinct centres of political power were established: the king was settled in London; in Cairo – recognised by the Allies – a government was formed; while in the occupied territories a government collaborating with German forces was fighting against the National Liberation Front, dominated by the Communist Party of Greece (KKE). During the early months of liberation, a new political cleavage was crystallised between the communist left and the nationalist right, gradually leading to the civil war of 1947–1949. After the defeat of the communist forces, a typical representative political system was formed, excluding and intensively oppressing any instance of dissent. Under these circumstances, no space was left for the expression of social grievances and the public articulation of the interests and demands of those groups and social categories were unrepresented and excluded from the decision-making centres.

In the post-civil war decades, the political and the party system, the overall nexus of power, were constructed around the declared aim of constant vigilance and repression of the defeated Left, which is acclaimed as the "internal enemy" that has to be suppressed at all costs. This precondition for the new informal constitution of the Greek polity found its legitimisation in the post-war polarisation of the Cold War. In this environment, despite the acute character of the economic crisis, intensified by counter-inflation austerity policies, producing deprivation and extreme poverty, there were few protests or collective efforts to promote the demands of the powerless for the advancement of their living conditions. Indicatively, during the 1950s, due to the tight control of trade unions by the Right-wing governments and the surveillance performed systematically by the security forces, hardly any disruptive protest events in the field of labour relations and demands can be found (Serdedakis 2015). Adversely, social grievances did erupt in the context of the Cyprus crisis and the formal and informal initiatives of the Greek Right-wing governments (1952–1959) to achieve the unification of Cyprus with Greece. Initially, the Church of Greece and nationalist associations of Cypriot and Greek students organised mass rallies, aiming to strengthen the efforts of the Greek government to secure favourable decisions by the UN. These mass gatherings rapidly escalated beyond control. Spontaneous violent attacks against the British diplomatic mission and street clashes with police forces unveiled a hidden dynamic of grievance amongst Greek youth. Additionally, young Left activists were successful in their effort to diffuse a counter-collective action frame: in their view, the struggle for the union of Cyprus with Greece was substantially an anti-imperialist, anti-colonial struggle, a continuation of the national liberation struggles of the Left against the German Nazis and their indigenous nationalist collaborators. The Cyprus issue created those necessary preconditions of legitimisation for the reappearance of Left organisations in the public realm and especially in the Greek universities.

The student movement was strengthened, exploiting the structure of political opportunities created by the intense political crisis that followed the elections of 1961. A decade after the conclusion of the civil war, the winners were seriously divided. The newly formed coalition by democratic leaders and parties, named Union of the Centre (UC), argued that the electoral outcome was a result of fraud, organised by then-Prime Minister Karamanlis (the leader of the Right-wing party National Radical Union), the army and police apparatuses. This new cleavage between the nationalist Right and the democratic progressive political forces gave birth to concerted efforts undertaken by excluded social groups and social categories to express their grievances and claims, opting for the democratisation of Greek society and economy. As recent research has pointed out, this unexpected cycle of protest produced significant outcomes in the realm of institutional politics, collective perceptions, feelings and collective action (Seferiadis 2008). Left and progressive syndicalist cadres formed a wide network of labour organisations and unions undertaking important strike struggles. Students engaged in several campaigns for the democratisation of the Greek polity to ensure equal opportunities for poor students in higher education, and for the respect of the Greek Constitution by the ruling class. The most significant institutional outcome was reflected in the electoral victory of Georgios Papandreou (leader of UC) in the consecutive elections of November 1963 and February 1964. In contrast with the austerity policies implemented by Right-wing governments since the end of civil war, the new government adopted a redistributive economic agenda in favour of popular strata and carried out major institutional reforms. The government's overthrow by King Konstantinos and the fracture within the UC parliamentary group introduced the country to a period of intense turmoil. From July to September 1965, despite strong police repression, thousands of protesters engaged in daily, often riotous, manifestations. Finally, in April 1967, a group of junior army officers organised a successful *coup d'état*, a pre-emptive response to a potential victory of the centre-left in the forthcoming elections of May. The projected victory of the centre-left would have meant the definitive end of the post-civil war emergency state, undermining the predominant role of the army, the King and the ultra-nationalist political elite. Practically, the military junta brutally ended the gradual democratisation process of the country, leading to more radical changes after its fall in July 1974, mainly due to the particular characteristics of the anti-dictatorial struggle.

Despite the massive arrests of political cadres from different political areas, during the seven years under military rule, various forms of resistance emerged. Young militants of the left who had escaped imprisonment formed small resistance groups, engaging in various acts of dissent. While the official leaders of the Left were expecting a rapid fall of the dictatorship, putting pressure on public opinion in European countries to weaken the military regime, the new organisations of the

Left opted in favour of a violent repertoire to urge the population to undertake concrete forms of active resistance. The first recorded act of this kind occurred in July 1967 and was carried out by the leftist organisation Democratic Committees of Resistance. From the centre-left spectrum, the most important group was Democratic Defence. The members of those groups were young intellectuals, as well as military officers, politicised during the sixties, and radicalised after the coup. In summary, the anti-dictatorial movement of "dynamic resistance" constituted a continuation of the pre-junta democratisation movement. At the same time, it can be considered as the starting point for the birth of the radical Left in Greece, formed under the strong influence of the guerrilla groups in Latin America and the various movements of dissent and contestation which erupted in Europe and the USA (Serdedakis 2007).

Dynamic resistance as a privileged means of resistance soon faded away, due to the severe repression of the underground militant groups. After 1971, the emerging students movement expressed its opposition to the dictatorship adopting public semi-legal and illegal forms of collective action (Kornetis 2015). This shift in the repertoire of action was caused by the opening of limited political opportunities, as the junta attempted to convince Western governments and international public opinion that the dictatorial regime was liberalising. Students' action against dictatorship reached its peak during the occupation of the Athens Law School and the Athens Polytechnic School in 1973, with the latter being violently repressed by the hardliners of the dictatorial regime. This fact marked the severe suppression of every public protest until the fall of the junta, caused by its inability to stop the Turkish invasion of the Republic of Cyprus in July 1974. The fall of the junta signalled the end of the post-civil war political regime, "liberating" new social and political forces.

Social movements and collective action in the Third Hellenic Republic (1974–2000)

Studies on dictatorship in Greece and the democratic shift of 1974 are a part of wider comparative research in South European and Latin American countries, which shared similar political experiences. However, as Giannis Voulgaris pointed out (2001, 25), the transitional process in Greece presented radical differences compared to other countries' experiences: the transition towards democracy in Greece was "velvet-smooth and instantaneous". It occurred peacefully, directly, and without turbulent internal tensions. Immediately after the return of Karamanlis from his exile in Paris and the constitution of a government of "national unity", concrete decisions preconfigured the coming of the Third Hellenic Republic, founded on genuine democratic representative institutions: (a) the monarchy was abolished, (b) the army was limited to its institutional role, and (c) the activity of the communist left, for the first time after the end of the civil war, was legalised.

The abolition of the monarchy, the limitation of military officers to their institutional duties, and the removal of any barrier concerning the political activity of leftist parties and political organisations reflect a wider ideological transformation. The anti-communist ideology of the post-civil war state, the division between nationalists and communists, and the identification of the Greek nation with the Orthodox Church and religion, suddenly vanished. The political field was organised under a new collective spirit that emphasised anti-fascism (as national resistance during the Second World War was linked to collective action against the dictatorship), democracy and popular sovereignty (Voulgaris 2001, 29). The post-junta society was predominantly "[...] a society of mobilised masses and increased expectations" (Voulgaris 2001, 71). In other words, the intense collective action undertaken from 1974 until PASOK came to power in 1981 is attributed to the increased discontent by a great part of the population – those who, for decades, had been living in a state of exclusion and marginalisation. In the post-junta period, such experiences were converted into expectations regarding the redistribution of income and the upward social mobility of the low-waged strata. However, to verify this interpretation, further evidence must be considered. As research and theory on social movements has concluded, discontent and rising expectations do not transform automatically into collective action without the interference of other factors. In Greece, in a context of rather limited political opportunities, collective action was inspired by the feeling that the struggle against the dictatorship had not ended. This master frame for the deepening of democracy and for the redistribution of wealth in favour of the subaltern classes combined with the organisational growth of the radical Left, especially in youth and labour milieus, gave rise to a robust strike wave in the mid-1970s.

As earlier research (Serdedakis 2007) has shown, strikes as a form of claim-making were privileged between the strata of wage earners. Wildcat strikes and factory occupations, lasting more than two weeks, were usually organised by factory workers' councils in the private industrial sector. More massive strikes, with less intensity and duration, were proclaimed by the larger established trade unions, mainly operating in the public sector. Despite their fighting spirit and their engagement in long-term disputes, the industrial labour movement gradually declined as strike struggles organised by factory councils met fierce reaction from the employers, the state repression mechanisms, but also by established trade unions, even those under the influence of the traditional left. In the absence of support from other more institutionalised actors, and gaining only small concessions from their opponents unable to fabricate a wider solidarity network, most of the movements' radical activists found themselves marginalised and persecuted, especially due to their ideological-political stance, influenced by the Italian paradigm of Potere Operaio and Autonomia Operaia.

In a quiet parallel fashion, turbulence started to reappear in Greek universities. After the junta's collapse, the student movement was portrayed as the guardian of democratic values and of the recent anti-dictatorship struggle. From 1975 to 1978, students were absorbed in their collective efforts to expel all the university professors who had backed the military regime and actively participated in the repression of the anti-dictatorial movement. Furthermore, party youth organisations engaged in intense competition within the ranks of student associ-ations, especially of the Left, to secure their supremacy in the National Student Association, as a way to reaffirm their protagonist role in the Polytechnic insur-gency of 1973 and as proof of their militant spirit, character and authenticity. In 1979, government initiatives to pass a new bill on higher education led to a wave of occupations in all major faculties of Athens and in other university campuses across the country. Newly-formed student groups, nominating themselves as "anarcho-autonomous", became the protagonists in this wave of protest, contest-ing (and finally disappearing) the dominant culture which, until then, had pre-vailed in the organisations of the parliamentary and extra-parliamentary communist Left. The conflict between students and government reached its peak in December 1979, when massive demonstrations and street clashes in Athens forced PM Karamanlis to step back and repeal the contested law. The student movement culminated in November 1980 during the celebration of the Poly-technic insurgency. The government's decision to prohibit the conclusion of the annual march in front of the American Embassy of Athens led to violent clashes resulting in two deaths caused by special police anti-riot units.

Labour and student unrest can be considered as indicative of more deeply underlying strains in Greek society, exacerbated by deepening economic stagna-tion, due to the successive international oil crises during the 1970s, in conjunc-tion with other endogenous factors. In the arena of economic policy, the first seven years of the Third Hellenic Republic are strongly reminiscent of the post-civil war cleavages. Right-wing governments steadily pursued monetary stability, as a prerequisite of disinflation, striving to lower the cost of labour and attract foreign investments to foster economic growth (Kazakos 2001). On the other hand, centre-left and Left parties were inclined to support more redistribu-tive policies with the aim to reinforce the welfare state and the consuming capa-bility of popular strata. This alternative course towards economic growth found its archetypical depiction in the figure of Andreas Papandreou, leader of the newly formed (1974) socialist party (Panhellenic Socialist Movement, PASOK). As a truly charismatic leader, Papandreou was successful in bringing together politically and ideologically dissimilar groups: traditional style politicians origi-nating from the fragmented area of the former UC and young activists, of Marxist orientation, emerging from the anti-dictatorial struggles (Spourdalakis 1988). In a steady manner, PASOK successfully incorporated popular expecta-tions and demands, presenting itself as radical, but also a viable, political altern-ative option, capable of opening a new chapter in Greek history, after almost 30 years of right-wing domination.

PASOK's electoral victory in the elections of 1981, among other things, reflected its ability to articulate, in a coherent programme, various interests and claims, initially represented by the communist left. The recognition of the "National Resistance" and of the active role played by the communists against the German occupation, the guarantee of equal rights between women and men, the right to vote for young people aged 18 years, and other significant pro-labour reforms, found in PASOK's electoral programme a privileged position tied with issues regarding Greece's status in the Western world. Rhetorically, A. Papandreou promised to pull Greece out of NATO and the European Community, to shut down all American military bases installed in the Greek territory, to reinforce the collaboration with the socialist countries and the anti-imperialist/anti-colonial movements and regimes of the Third World. On the other hand, during this period, the traditional communist left proved unable to overcome its internal divisions and politically recompose underlying grievances expressed in multiple radical social struggles. The above-mentioned features in the systemic and traditional Left created the necessary space for the emergence of political subjects connected to the European New Left. In the next two decades, from 1981 to 2001, under the "electoral regime" (the concept from McAdam and Tarrow 2010, 2013) of the centre-left, we can distinguish different trends regarding the emergence of social movements in Greece.

On the one hand, we can individuate a current related to the European new social movements, especially the formation of green-political networks and the intensification of feminist activism. Autonomous feminist groups were formed in the aftermath of university occupations (1979) by young women, former members of youth communist organisations. Until 1980, 24 such small groups were formed, putting forward the "second wave", a feminist frame that "the personal is political". Young feminists were claiming equal rights in all social realms, sexual self-determination, rigid laws against rape, male violence and abuse, and finally the legalisation of abortion, as significant steps along a path leading to the recognition of actual male domination (Repousis 2014, 624). Emergent autonomous feminism faced severe opposition inside the male-dominated left organisations, as well as strong antagonists in the so-called women's movement, which was dominated by stronger women party organisations. In 1983, PASOK's law guaranteed social gender equal rights leaving little room for radical feminist protest and action. Many of the above-mentioned groups were dissolved while others followed a course of gradual incorporation inside newly formed institutions (Varika 1992; Repousis 2014).

Environmental and social ecology organisations followed the same pattern. The origins of modern Greek ecological movement can be traced back to the mid-seventies, when significant mobilisations regarding fears of environmental degradation were recorded (Louloudis 1987). All of them had a local character and mobilised small communities in protest activity aiming to prevent the building of new industrial installations, perceived as calamitous for the local natural environment. In 1987, 82 ecological/environmental organisations of all kinds were recorded while environmental periodicals, newspapers and literature were also flourishing. Thus, Greek environmentalism in the late 1980s was in a trajectory towards a social movement. After three unsuccessful attempts to create a unified political organisation, in 1989 a federation of more than 100 groups and associations was set up, under the title Federation of Ecological and Alternative Organisations. Following the break-up of the Federation and the failure of the ecologists' attempt to establish an autonomous political presence, the groups with an exclusive environmentalist orientation became dominant and imprinted their green paradigm on the Greek environmental movement (Alexandropoulos *et al.* 2007). The political ecology groups were marginalised, and certain leaders were absorbed by traditional political parties. Indicative of this shift is the fact that many environmental organisations came to define themselves as NGOs, rather than participants of a broader environmental movement. Throughout the 1990s, a prominent role was played by the environmentalist organisations, especially those that functioned as local chapters of the big international environmental organisations (Botetzagias 2001; Kousis 2003). A key characteristic of these organisations continues to be their shift towards professionalisation that focuses on "effectiveness" thus "sacrificing" the social movement aspect of broadening their organisational basis (Alexandropoulos *et al.* 2007).

On the other hand, in addition to new social movement organisations, the radical Left, especially after PASOK's electoral victory, strengthened its presence among university students and, more specifically, among the young population of the Greek metropolitan centres. House occupations exploded immediately after the elections of 1981, provoking an unexpected violent repression (Souzas 2015). On various occasions, the centre-left governments of PASOK expressed a kind of moral shock and panic in front of an emerging massive social subject, which was perceiving itself politically under the terms of Toni Negri's conceptualisation of the "social proletariat". During the 1980s, networks of leftists, autonomists and anarchists engaged in significant battles against police brutalities and state repression. Due to the conditions of detention in prisons and living in the military camps, the prisoners' and soldiers' rights became critical focal points of collective action. Over the next decade, the radical Left led massive occupations in high schools and universities, expressing youth discontent provoked by educational reforms of both right-wing and centre-left governments (Sklavenitis 2016). Another important feature of the 1990s concerns the gradual formation of a solidarity movement in response to growing xenophobic and racist sentiments, caused by the massive influx of migrants after the collapse of the Balkan "socialist" regimes. Radical left and anarchist groups formed a dense nationwide network of social and migrants' centres, thus creating open social spaces for migrants to organise their collective action.

Finally, austerity economic policies of the second PASOK's government (1985–1989) also triggered a sustained strike wave, led by the big trade unions of the private and public sector. During 1986 and 1987, according to data published by the Ministry of Labour, 2,715,595 employees participated in different national or sectoral strikes, reacting against cuts in wage increases (Kouzis 2007, 237–238; Katsoridas and Lambousaki 2012, 84). PASOK's government, facing severe economic problems, introduced neo-liberal policies to limit rising inflation, to adjust the balance of payments and to decrease the public financial deficit. Aiming to achieve these goals, PASOK's "stabilisation programme" adopted neo-liberal monetarist formulas for the first time in Greece: "salary reductions, cuts in public expenditure, restrictions in money supply and increases of interest rates in addition to the devaluation of the Greek drachma, unexpectedly occurred in 1985" (Stathakis 2007, 45). Neo-liberal pension reforms and privatisations of public enterprises, implemented by the Right-wing government during 1990 to 1992, fuelled a new strike peak, although the latter was followed by a long period of relative peace in labour relations, primarily due to rising unemployment, but also as a consequence of the institutionalisation of collective bargaining norms and procedures between trade unions and employers' associations (Kouzis 2007, 240–242; Katsoridas and Lambousaki 2012, 85–86).

From Genoa 2001 to Athens riots 2008

After the collapse of the "socialist regimes" in USSR and the other countries of Eastern Europe, the Greek Left entered a period of profound crisis. Attempts to unify the conventional Left, which in 1989 concluded in the formation of the Left Coalition (LC), soon proved short-lived. The results of the general elections of 1993, 1996 and 2000 confined the fragmented parliamentary left in a marginal position in the Greek party system (Vernardakis 2011). Especially in the aftermath of the 1996 elections, economic and political elites successfully coined a new narrative around the goal of economic inclusion of Greece into the Euro-zone. *Modernisation* was proclaimed as the new national endeavour capable of securing prosperity for all citizens through the implementation of institutional reforms according to EU standards. Practically, the slogan of *modernisation* was selected as a "neutral term" to signal the ideological shift of PASOK's leadership towards neo-liberal principles and policies promoting the primacy of the markets (Stathakis 2007, 20).

Counter narratives opposing neo-liberalism and austerity policies in Greece can be traced back to the mid-1990s, originating from the influence of the Zapatistas revolution in Chiapas, Mexico; various anti-war initiatives on the occasion of the bombings in Yugoslavia; anti-austerity Euro-marches; and finally the Battle of Seattle in 1999 (Imig and Tarrow 2001; Kotronaki 2015; Iakovidou 2016). Furthermore, the anti-neo-liberal collective action frames systematically elaborated during the first three annual meetings of the World Social Forum (WSF) in Porto Alegre, under the slogan "another world is possible", created an international movement-centric space for the articulation of countless nation-wide (old and new) social movements and local resistances. Greek activists and intellectuals who had participated in previous anti-neo-liberal networks and movements exploited the opportunities given by the WSF to re-strengthen their common ideological references, political bonds and organisational resources. Additionally, Greek political and social movement organisations, in a status of dormancy during the 1990s, were reinvigorated in a series of European appointments to contest International Monetary Fund (IMF) and EU policies during international summits.

One of the first occasions in this direction was given by the S26 campaign proclaimed by the INPEG/PRAHA 2000. The 55th summit of the IMF and of the World Bank seemed to be an opportunity for the repetition of the Battle of Seattle in the territory of the "Old Continent". Greek activists calling for mass participation in the event stated:

We created the open Initiative Prague 2000 to participate in the campaign against the IMF conference. We seek Prague to become the Seattle of Europe. We want to make the voice of resistance heard by the expanding power of global capital.

(Ergatiki 2010)

The Greek Initiative Prague 2000, in its call, made clear that national struggles are tightly connected to transnational collective action; those national governmental policies and institutional reforms emerging out of the globalisation processes must be contested in a common global ground of resistance against neo-liberal barbarism. If Prague 2000 can be considered as the starting point in a long process of the movement's reactivation, Genoa 2001 clearly marked its course.

Contrary to the weak participation of the Greek delegation in Prague, 3,000 Greek activists embarked from Patras to Ancona port to take part in the anti-G8 international rally, organised by the Genoa Social Forum (Andretta *et al.* 2002; Kotronaki 2015). The Greek activists, surprised after the denial by the Italian police to permit entry to Italy to all 132 of them, were the first to encounter the police repression that escalated on 20 July 2001, leading to the murder of Carlo Giugliani. The "Greek Committee for the International Rally in Genoa" was soon replaced by a committee named "International Action" and finally by the Greek Social Forum (GSF), which was created immediately after the first meeting of the European Social Forum (ESF) in Florence, Italy (Kanellopoulos 2009; Kotronaki 2015). Previously, in October 2011, a network of radical-left activists and members of various parties was created and named "Dialogue Space for Left's Unity and Common Action" (DSLUCA), to promote the unity of the Greek Left parties to oppose neo-liberal policies in the realm of institutional politics.

It is interesting to underscore this dual path for the rise of the twenty-first century Greek radical Left, briefly depicted in the above paragraphs. Exploiting political opportunities created in the international arena of contention, radical Left political and movement organisations experimented with new forms of collaboration and identity-building. As the indigenous political elites were consolidating their ideological hegemony around the aim of *modernisation*, in practice implementing neo-liberal austerity policies and structural reforms, a counter frame began to take shape, uncovering the "collateral damages" of these processes. The demolition of the welfare state, the gradual privatisation of public goods and flexibility reforms in the labour market were viewed as parts of a coherent plan leading to the intensification of social inequalities, poverty and exploitation. The new collective action frame managed to articulate local and national issues to challenges and problems arising from the discourse concerning the implications of the ongoing globalisation processes, thus becoming a steady point of reference for all those willing to take part in the new transnational cycle of protest.

Although, a closer look at the initial and latter stages of anti-globalisation coalition formation in Greece reveals a complex mixture of differentiated and often divided collective actors, major divisions can be individuated between and inside diverse "movement families" (della Porta and Rucht 1995). Representatives of recognised labour unions participated together in various collective action events, with activists coming from new radical grass-roots unions, expressing especially the new workforce figure of precarious workers (Kretsos and Vogiatzoglou 2015; Zamponi and Vogiatzoglou 2015). NGOs coexisted with leftist political groups during ESF and GSF organising committees and public meetings. Anarchist groups marched in contentious demonstrations together with reformist party-youth organisations. But, aside from testing this new culture of coexistence, democratic dialogue and horizontal network relations, a sharp divide can be traced between those activists and organisations striving to invigorate grass-roots movement politics and those aiming to represent new cleavages into the central political national stage.

Anti-war mobilisations, opposition to the Athens 2004 Olympic Games, trade union strikes against the reform of the pension system and university students' occupations striving to block changes in the Greek Constitution (which typically still guarantees the public character of higher education), can be considered as the most visible collective action peaks during 2001 and 2006. In this same period, GSF effectively expanded its influence throughout the creation of grass-roots networks, bringing together activists operating in different movement, political and trade-union organisations. The 4th ESF meeting in Athens (2006) culminated in an unexpectedly massive demonstration, reflecting GSF's successful course, but also surprisingly marking its gradual demise. This paradox can be explained if we take into account that political organisations involved in GSF building were simultaneously active in the project for the unity of the Greek radical Left (DSLUCA) in the realm of electoral politics. A first step in this direction was made in the 2004 general elections when SYRIZA appeared as a radical-left party coalition. In the elections of 2007, almost all leftist party formations participating in GSF were incorporated in SYRIZA.

This shift from movement to party politics became highly visible during the 2008 riots that exploded after the cold-blooded assassination, by a police officer, of Alexis Grigoropoulos, a 15-year-old high school student (Papanikolopoulos 2016). Protest rallies and violent clashes erupted in all urban centres of the country, revealing the diffusion of deep feelings of grievance, especially among the Greek youth. Rising unemployment among young cohorts, unequal job opportunities and educational chances, visible social exclusion of the poor and of second-generation immigrants, in a context of flourishing consumerism and affluence of the privileged social strata, produced an unexpected violent reaction, lacking any tangible political content or demand (Serdedakis 2008). Radical Left activists participating in protest events proved unable to configure a viable communication channel to riotous crowds and develop a grounded political claim-making framework (Kouki 2011, 171).

December 2008 unveiled the Janus double, the inextricable and often contradictory faces of the radical Left: one representing grass-roots movement activity, the other rushing to become a recognised political force. Usually these two temporally coexisting tensions have a bitter end. The course from Genoa 2001 to December 2008 and the anti-austerity movement and party politics outcomes, during the years of recent crisis in Greece, can be portrayed as undeniable paradigms of this unwanted destiny.

Italy 1945–1973: the crisis of the traditional left, and the emergence of the "new grass-roots political militant"

In Italy, as in several other countries, social tensions increased in the aftermath of the First World War. The economic crisis of the late 1920s, the war's trauma, and the so-called "Russian example" – that is, the efforts to somehow follow the Russian Bolsheviks' successful rise to power and their country's transition into a socialist regime – were among the main social contention causes. The so-called "Red Biennium" (Biennio Rosso, 1919–1920), characterised by its massive strikes, armed factory occupations and self-management experiments, especially in the North of Italy (Bellamy and Schecter 1993), was part of a small constellation of similar insurrectional efforts that marked the period across Europe. It was followed by 20 years of fascist rule; the regime's repression; the long detention and death of Antonio Gramsci – perhaps the most important figure of the Italian Communist movement; the anti-fascist struggle with its strikes in the industrial cities of the North in 1943 and 1944; and the civil war of the same period, between the supporters of Mussolini's fascist regime and the loose coalition of Catholic Democrats and Communist partisans (Pavone 1991).

After a sensitive period of transition, the birth of the post-war Italian Republic was marked by the heavy shadow of the United States of America's influence on domestic politics, the strategic re-adjustment of the economy, the state's relentless efforts to marginalise the left-wing parties, and an increasing power of employers over workers.

The mobilisations that led to the fall of the extreme-Right government of PM Tambroni, in June 1960, proved to be the most concrete outcome of the official Left's institutional tactics; the argument raised was that one should struggle against a government suspected to have authoritarian tendencies. In June 1960, the communist-led union confederation CGIL organised a series of protests in Genoa and other cities of Italy, against what was perceived as an effort to re-legitimise the political representation of the fascists, through Tambroni's Christian-Democrats coalition with the extreme-right party MSI (*Movimento Sociale Italiano* – Italian Social Movement). The violent repression of the protests, which left several dead, contributed to the increase of tensions and disagreements inside Tambroni's own party, regarding its alliances and directions and, eventually, led to the government's fall.

A significant element of this early post-war period was the rapid expansion of the so-called *Case del Popolo* (*People's Houses*), that is, early social centres mostly founded and operated by members of the Communist Party and its trade union affiliates, the purpose of which was to provide to workers and their families a space for political involvement and debate, entertainment and socialisation. The

Case del Popolo emerged in Italy as early as 1893, following similar examples in France, Belgium and elsewhere (Maurizio Degl'Innocenti 1984), but were shut down during the fascist regime, and re-emerged in mass numbers after the war, as the Communist Party was looking for an efficient way to establish its presence in everyday life and counter the respective influence of the Catholic church and its de facto political representation, the Christian-Democratic party (Carloni 1991). The model proved very successful, and served as an inspiration in terms of practices and organisational procedures for what became, in later decades, the driving force of the Italian movements, that is, the social centres and their local and national networks.

Back in the 1960s, and more specifically in 1962, a significant event of the period was the protest organised in Turin by CGIL's metal-mechanics' union FIOM, which ended up in serious riots, hundreds of arrests and injuries. The Communist Party rushed to condemn the "provocations" conducted by "anarchists and internationalists". As the editors of the labour struggles' historical archive Chicago86 noted, "The rebellion of Piazza Statuto (Turin) signals, for the first time, the emergence of the mass worker in the class struggles" (Chicago86 2010). The Communist Party would soon realise that these young workers, who were often internal migrants originating from the Italian South, were unable and unwilling to follow the official party and trade union political lines. Their sudden entry in the Italian social and political scene would alter, once and for all, the social movement field of the country for years to come. Alongside the student movement, which also emerged during the tumultuous 1960s, criticising the division between manual and intellectual labour, those young proletarians contributed to the development of a mass subversive movement, the fruits of a common anti-capitalist understanding, which signalled its presence in hundreds and hundreds of strikes, protests and riots, and ultimately led to the "Italian 1968".

The most important characteristic of the 1968 mobilisations in Italy was the unprecedented alliance between the workers and the students. This alliance was founded on a mutual feeling of deep distrust, or perhaps even hatred, towards the post-war economic and political system of Italy; this sentiment was so widespread among youth that, for many of the activists, it represented an opportunity to engage the country in a revolutionary process.

Ultimately, though, the 1968 mobilisations failed, not only due to police repression, but first and foremost due to the movement's inability to bring forward new political institutions that would retain the anti-capitalist aspects of the movements themselves. Instead of new institutions, what emerged was political groups which, intentions aside, ended up pushing back to the mainstream political parties even those militant grass-roots activists who were criticising them.

The oil crisis of 1973 and its aftermath

The oil crisis of 1973 highlighted the weakness of the grass-roots political militants who held a key role in the 1960s mobilisations. The sharp increase in oil prices launched a financial crisis in Italy, which in turn provoked mass lay-offs in industries, as well as an overall worsening of working conditions in the factories.

In this context, the early theoretical contributions of 1960s' Workerism (Wright 2002), which assumed that young workers were driven by a strong tendency to *refuse* labour and the social configurations produced by employment relations, seemed, to say the least, paradoxical. It was actually the employers who would refuse the workers' labour, laying the latter off in mass numbers. Consequently, a new balance of power emerged in the industrial workplace and the employees' position significantly worsened, due to structural elements of the period's economy.

This led to the launching of a new period in practices, organisational formats and key frames of the Italian movement. As it became increasingly difficult for industrial action to bear concrete positive outcomes for the workers, the struggle expanded in what was termed "the social factory" (Gill and Pratt 2008), that is, the broader societal and economic configurations embracing the workers' everyday life, leisure and social rights.

Amongst the main issues emerging during this period were housing rights, the practices related to which included the "self-reduction" of the rent, bills and transport costs (Mullins 2013), as well as the occupations of public buildings and empty apartments (Marcelloni 1979). Through campaigns such as the above, popular mobilisation expanded beyond the narrow frame of class struggle, to include issues such as mutualism, community living and, more broadly, the act of *sharing* among workers.

A significant differentiation from the past was also related to the collective action means. Although mass political violence and clashes with the police forces were a frequent occurrence in Italy, at least since the late 1960s, in the post-1973 period the country witnessed the progressive enlargement of Left-wing armed struggle organisations founded in the Italian industrial North, such as the *Brigate Rosse* (Red Brigades) and *Prima Linea* (First Line). Armed organisations' activity culminated towards the late 1970s, perhaps arriving at its peak in 1978, with the kidnapping and consequent assassination of former Prime Minister Aldo Moro.

The reasons behind the phenomenon are complex and have been attributed to various factors, ranging from biographical and social psychological explanations of individual participants' behaviour (Weinberg and Eubank 1987), to the macro-analysis of the dynamics of state–society relations (della Porta 2006).

The response of the Italian State to the unprecedented armed organisations' challenge was to introduce progressively harsh repression at the legislative and protest policing level. Della Porta distinguished four periods of state response:

The first (1970–74) is characterized as "immobilist"; while left-wing terrorism was not recognized as a threat, right-wing terrorism, which was much more serious at that time, was protected by the Italian secret service. The second period (1974–76) is characterized by a decline in right-wing terrorism and a more serious attack on left-wing terrorism within a wider repression of organized and violent crime. The third period (1977–82), called the Emergency period, is characterized by a new wave of left-wing terrorism and increased repression that ultimately promoted terrorist recruitment. The fourth period (1982–89) represents the defeat of left-wing terrorism through new anti-terrorism policies, such as amnesty and repentance laws.

(della Porta 1992, 151)

The state response, alongside the progressive loss of popular support to the cause and methods of the armed struggle organisations, had a severe, long-term impact on the Italian social movements. Indeed, since the early 1980s, the level of political violence, both at the mass and the clandestine small-group level significantly decreased. This was not only due to the strong repressive arsenal offered to the police and judiciary forces, but also to the social de-legitimisation of political violence, in a society that would require years to recover from the trauma of the *Anni di piombo* (Years of Lead). Nevertheless, the repressive barrage of the late 1970s and early 1980s resulted in the imprisonment of tens of thousands of activists, resulting in a significant weakening of the Italian social movement as a whole.

In terms of organisational forms, the turbulent 1970s confirmed the Italian movement's break with the structures of the PCI. As Mullin stated,

the movement of 1977 had sought to extricate itself from a bankrupt political system that, in one crucial example, led to the PCI forming a government with the conservative Christian Democracy party (DC) beginning in 1973. For these young radicals, this "compromesso storico" (Historic Compromise) between the left and right begged the following question: what is the sense of a leftist orientation if it is not an alternative to the right? Above all, the movement was characterized by the overwhelming participation of young people, who decried the defunct, internecine squabbles between extra-parliamentary groups in the nine years following the revolt of 1968.

(Mullins 2013, 1)

Indeed, the two main extra-parliamentary Left political organisations of the period, *Potere Operaio* (Workers' Power) and *Lotta Continua* (Continuous Struggle) dissolved in 1973 and 1976, respectively, with their members rushing to populate the so-called autonomous groups that emerged during the same period. The autonomous groups could be divided into two broad categories: the "Autonomia Operaia" (workers' autonomy), that is, Marxist collectives which retained a rhetoric and agenda based on class struggle and workerism, and the counter-culture experiments, a constellation of smaller and larger projects ranging from pirate radio stations to political art groups, such as the *Indiani Metropolitani* (Metropolitan Indians) (Ginsborg 2003). The Autonomous collectives were particularly active in the universities, the launching place of the Movement of 1977, a massive mobilisation that included violent protests, faculty occupations and armed clashes with the police forces. The *Movimento di 77* was perhaps the most glorious moment of the post-war Italian movement, and has been commemorated ever since, albeit that the interpretations and analysis of the period by the activists who followed it vary significantly (della Porta *et al.* 2016).

The years after the lead: 1983–2001

During the 1980s, and despite the overall reduction of the activist population due to state repression and the demobilisation of thousands of participants, the Italian movement managed to re-organise around subjects that were also present in the struggles of the previous period: ecological issues, feminism, anti-nuclear mobilisation, and alternative lifestyles – in a sort of continuum with the counterculture initiatives of the previous decade – became fertile ground for the flourishing of dozens of collectives at the local and national level, that could be loosely categorised under the label of "new social movements". One may note the similarity of developments compared to other European countries during the same period.

These thematic struggles, but also broader efforts to intervene in the political scene, were organised in the *social centres*, spaces recuperated by the movement and organised over an assembly-based model of direct democratic participation (Moroni 1996).

The turn of the decade into the 1990s found Italy in great turmoil. On the one hand, the Soviet Union's collapse was followed, in 1991, by the demise of the PCI; its majority adopted a social-democratic platform, whilst a more radical minority split and formed *Partito Rifondazione Comunista* (Communist Refoundation Party – PRC). Furthermore, from 1992 onwards, the anti-corruption judicial operation *Mani Pulite* (Clean Hands), under which hundreds of politicians were prosecuted, contributed to the dissolution of Italy's post-war party system. By 1995, the Christian Democrat, Socialist and Communist parties had practically disappeared; the political vacuum was soon covered by ambitious figures such as Silvio Berlusconi, whilst at the movement level, the unprecedented political opportunity that had emerged, thanks to the disappearance of the constant post-war left-wing point of reference, the Communist Party, was sparking feverish debates among activists as to what path the main actors of the era, the social centres, should follow (Calia 2014).

From an organisational point of view, the most interesting development of the period was that of the loose social centre coalitions, formed at the national level in order to coordinate the struggles and increase the impact of the collective action. Towards the end of the 1990s, Fausto Bertinotti's PRC dissolved its youth branch and engaged in strong collaboration with a majoritarian social centre coalition, further strengthening their position.

The dominant frames at the time evolved around neo-liberalism, free trade, and globalisation, alongside ecological and sustainability issues. The Italian movement, which was always particularly open to international experiences, strongly supported the Zapatista revolution in Mexico; Subcommandante Marcos' calls for a genuinely global movement, firmly rooted in local struggles, resonated well with the everyday realities of the social centre activists: their horizontal networks of collaboration, their internationalist focus, and their strong engagement with neighbourhood- and city-level mobilisations (Sergi 2008). The Italian activists' contribution to the alter-globalisation movement, which sprang up all over the Western World during the same period, is of the utmost importance (Bennett *et al.* 2004).

The peak, and the breaking point, of this interesting mobilisation wave was the anti-G8 protest in Genoa, in 2001. Despite that, for the thousands of non-Italian activists who joined the local protesters, the Genova demonstrations were a unique transnational movement experience, unparalleled to anything that preceded or followed it, the incidents that followed the assassination of protester Carlo Giuliani and the violent clashes that accompanied it, left the Italian movement in disarray. Internal disputes, the collapse of the alliance between the PRC and the social centres, and the heavy physical and judiciary repression of the Genova protest participants are among the factors that contributed to this development.

Post-2001: precarious labour, housing rights and sustainable development movements

After Genova, social mobilisations in Italy developed in three distinct, yet often parallel, strands. First, the expansion of flexible labour, combined with the traditionally weak welfare state in most regions of the country, brought back to the public debate and movement focus issues related to workers' rights and well-being. Spearheaded by grass-roots trade unions, social centres and labour-related collectives, large protests were organised in metropolitan cities (Mattoni and Vogiatzoglou 2014). The anti-precarity activists launched innovative communication campaigns, aiming to construct and diffuse a collective identity for atypical workers (Mattoni and Doerr 2007). Some undertook social solidarity initiatives (e.g. legal and medical assistance to precarious workers, co-operatives and co-working spaces), in a way that reminisces workers' mutualist practices of previous periods.

Second, the housing rights' movement gained traction after the 2008 crisis and its accompanying austerity measures. In the cities of the North, the worsening rent/wage ratio rendered housing costs unsustainable for the most vulnerable population strata. The housing rights' activists adopted an aggressive strategy, building strong national alliance networks and occupying *en masse* abandoned buildings to house migrants and locals, as well as provide basic services (such as primary medical care and collective kitchens) to the tenants.

Third, several significant mobilisations emerged against "le grande opere" (big construction projects); the most important and long-lasting among them was the *No TAV*, against the construction of a high-speed train line in the Piedmont region of Northern Italy. It is important to note that these local movements differ significantly from traditional NIMBY (Not In My Back Yard) mobilisations that took place in other countries. The former placed emphasis on a refined and well-elaborated discourse on alternative development options, beyond the neo-liberal diktat, in a manner that allowed their scope to expand beyond local issues.

Finally, students were also present in two different mobilisation waves, the first duly named "The Wave" (*Onda*), in 2008, the second in 2010. An absence is also worth noting: Italy was missing from the list of Mediterranean countries that participated in the anti-austerity upsurge of 2010–2011. In October 2011, an attempt to launch occupy-style squares movement failed (Zamponi 2012), and ever since, the movement efforts to address austerity issues were scarce, although the country is far from having recovered.

Conclusion

The categorisation both of Italy and Greece as parts of the European South or alternatively as countries of the semi-periphery, runs the risk of obscuring the vast cultural, social, economic and political differences that separate them. Keeping in mind these differences, we tried to reconstruct their trajectory in the conjuncture of the post-war period, focusing on contentious politics and the role played by the radical Left in each country.

In Italy, under the electoral regime of the Christian Democracy and its various allies, the parliamentary socialist and communist left followed a reformist path finally leading to the acceptance of neo-liberal structural adjustments, introduced during the 1980s. The Italian radical Left, which emerged dynamically during the 1960s, expressed the grievances and demands of new social figures and social categories in the realm of labour and youth milieus, which remained unrepresented in the political centres of decision-making. The intensification of social and class struggles gave birth to a long cycle of protest which ended in the late 1970s, as a result of two congruent and escalating processes: social and political movements' radicalisation and harsh state repression. New social movements emerging in this period proved unable to transcend this fatal conflict, following the trajectory of institutionalisation observed in other western countries. In the late 1990s, under the influence of the Zapatistas and the Global Justice Movements' anti-neo-liberal campaigns and mobilisations, the Italian radical Left played a leading role in the Genoa anti-G8 summit and consequently in the formation of the European Social Forum. It is interesting, at this point, to underscore that besides the growing popular discontent against the EU anti-austerity policies, implemented by various governments in Italy after the explosion of the international economic crisis in 2008, and an attempt to give birth to an Italian *Idignados* campaign, Italy can be considered a missing link in the chain of anti-neo-liberal mobilisations in the South of Europe, a phenomenon which was mainly due to vivid contrasts between political and movement organisations.

In Greece, after the end of the civil war, the constitution of quasi-democratic political institutions reduced considerably any chances for the genuine expression of popular grievances, deriving from the harsh economic situation of the country and the restriction of political liberties and civil rights. Despite this unfavourable political environment, a movement for the democratic transformation of Greek society emerged during the late 1950s, exploiting diverse political opportunities that emerged after the sharp division in the camp of the winners of the civil war. The military coup d'état in April 1967 can be considered as a last desperate effort for the preservation of the post-civil war regime. The anti-dictatorial movement of "dynamic resistance" and the student revolt in Athens Polytechnic in 1973, both as a continuation of the pre-junta struggles and as the starting point of the coming post-junta period, marked the course of radical collective action after the collapse of the dictatorial regime. Factory and university occupations (1975–1979) represent the most crucial episodes under the influence of the new radical Left in Greece. The long cycle of protest for the democratic reconstitution of the Hellenic Republic finally led to the electoral victory of the socialist party (PASOK) in 1981, a party which proved capable of expressing popular expectations and demands which formed previews of social and political struggles.

During approximately the last two decades, a new protest wave rose against the implementation of austerity neo-liberal policies and reforms in Greece. Under the same influence observed in the case of Italy, internationally diffused sympathies on behalf of the Zapatista rebellion and the sensational events of the "Battle of Seattle" gave birth to radical-left movements and political initiatives. In contrast to the Italian case, two different paths were followed. An attempt to recompose activist networks and grass-roots initiatives, isolated in different thematic arenas, concluded successfully in the formation of the Greek Social Forum, and was by-passed by an effort for the unity of the radical Left in the realm of electoral politics, although producing poor results. The gradual shift from movement to electoral politics produced a gap – visibly manifested during the 2008 revolt in Greece – between the aggrieved population, especially the young, and the movement activists who were later absorbed by party politics. Maybe the same gap reappeared after the culmination of the Greek *Indignados* mobilisations and the electoral success of SYRIZA, who at the end of the day frustrated any expectation for an alternative Left policy, capable of leading Greek society out from the suffocating crisis spiral.

References

Alexandropoulos, Stelios, Nikos Serdedakis, and Iosif Botezagias. 2007. "The Geek Environmental Movement. From its Genesis to its Integration". *Greek Review of Political Science* 30: 5–31.

Andretta, Massimiliano, Donatella della Porta, Lorenzo Mosca, and Herbert Reiter. 2002. *Global, Noglobal, New Global. Le Proteste Contro il G8 a Genova*. Roma-Bari: Laterza.

Bellamy, Richard, and Darrow Schecter. 1993. *Gramsci and the Italian State*. Manchester and New York: Manchester University Press.

Bennett, W. Lance, Donatella della Porta, Mario Diani, and E. Johnson. 2004. *Transnational Protest and Global Activism*. London and New York: Rowman & Littlefield Publishers.

Botetzagias, Iosif. 2001. *The Environmental Movement in Greece, From 1973 to the Present: An Illusory Movement in a Semi-Peripheral Country.* Ph.D. thesis, Department of Politics, Keele University.

Calia, Claudio. 2014. *Piccolo Atlante Storico Geografico Dei Centri Sociali Italiani.* Padova: BeccoGiallo.

Carloni, Tita. 1991. "Case Del Popolo: Avanguardie Politiche E Tradizione Costruttiva". *Archi.* www.espazium.ch/case-del-popolo-avanguardie-politiche-e-tradizione-costruttiva (accessed 6 February 2017).

Chicago86. 2010. "La Rivolta Operaia Di Piazza Statuto Del 1962". *Chicago86.org.* www.chicago86.org/archivio-storico/lotte-operaie-anni-60-70-in-italia/scontri-di-piazza-statuto/103-la-rivolta-operaia-di-piazza-statuto-del-1962.html (accessed 5 February 2017).

della Porta, Donatella, and Dieter Rucht. 1995. "Left Libertarian Movements in Context: A Comparison of Italy and West Germany, 1965–1990". In *The Politics of Social Protest: Comparative Perspectives on States and Social Movements*, edited by Craig J. Jenkins and Bert Klandermans, 229–272. Minneapolis, MN: University of Minnesota Press.

della Porta, Donatella, Massimiliano Andretta, Tiago Fernandes, Eduardo Romanos, Francis O'Connor, and Markos Vogiatzoglou. 2016. *Late Neoliberalism and Its Discontents in the Economic Crisis: Comparing Social Movements in the European Periphery.* London and New York: Palgrave Macmillan.

della Porta, Donatella. 1992. "Institutional Responses to Terrorism: The Italian Case". *Terrorism and Political Violence* 4 (4): 151–170.

della Porta, Donatella. 2006. *Social Movements, Political Violence, and the State: A Comparative Analysis of Italy and Germany.* Cambridge: Cambridge University Press.

Ergatiki Allileggyi. 2010. "Prague 2000, Ten Years After. Anticapitalist Struggle Against IMF, Then …". *Ergatiki Allileggyi*: http://ergatiki.gr/article.php?issue=935&id=954 (accessed 20 September 2017).

Gill, Rosalind, and Andy Pratt. 2008. "In the Social Factory? Immaterial Labour, Precariousness and Cultural Work". *Theory, Culture & Society* 25 (7–8): 1–30.

Ginsborg, Paul. 2003. *A History of Contemporary Italy: Society and Politics, 1943–1988.* Basingstoke: Palgrave Macmillan.

Iakovidou, Iosifina. 2016. *Democracy Problems and Organizational Aspects in Open Movement Spaces. The Case of Social Forums.* Ph.D. thesis, Department of Political Sciences and History, Panteion University.

Imig, Doug, and Sidney Tarrow. 2001. "Mapping the Europeanization of Contention: Evidence from a Quantitative Data Analysis". Pp. 27–52 in *Contentious Europeans: Protest and Politics in an Emerging Polity*, edited by Doug Imig and Sidney Tarrow. Lanham, MD-Boulder, CO-New York-London: Rowman & Littlefield Publishers.

Kanellopoulos, Kostas. 2009. Constitution Processes and Social Movement's Theoretical Issues. The Movement Against Neoliberal Globalization. Ph.D. thesis, Department of Political Sciences and History, Panteion University.

Katsoridas, Dimitris, and Sofia Lambousaki. 2012. "The Strike Phenomenon in Greece. Evolution and Recorded Strikes in 2011". In *INE Notebooks 37*, coordinated by Giannis Kouzis, 75–227. Athens: INE/GSEE.

Kazakos, Panos. 2001. *Between the State and the Market. Economy and Economic Policy in Post-War Greece 1944–2000.* Athens: Patakis.

Kornetis, Kostis. 2015. *Children of the Dictatorship. Student Resistance, Cultural Politics, and the "Long 1960s" in Greece.* Athens: Polis.

Kotronaki, Loukia. 2015. *The Theory of Contentious Politics in the Praxis of Social Movements: the Movement Against Neoliberal Globalization* (Greece, 2000–2006). Ph.D. thesis, Department of Political Sciences and History, Panteion University.

Kouki, Hara. 2011. "Short Voyage to the Land of Ourselves". In *Revolt and Crisis in Greece. Between a Present Yet to Pass and a Future Still to Come*, edited by Antonis Vradis and Dimitris Dalakoglou, 167–180. Oakland, CA, Baltimore, MD, Edinburgh, London and Athens: AK Press and Occupied London.

Kousis, Maria. 2003. "Greece". In *Environmental Protest in Western Europe*, edited by Christopher Rootes, 109–134. Oxford: Oxford University Press.

Kouzis, Giannis. 2007. *The Characteristics of the Greek Trade Union Movement*. Athens: Gutenberg.

Kretsos, Lefteris, and Markos Vogiatzoglou. 2015. "Lost in the Ocean of Deregulation? The Greek Labour Movement in a Time of Crisis". *Relations industrielles/Industrial Relations* 70 (2): 218–239.

Louloudis, Leonidas. 1987. "Social Protest: From Protection of the Environment to Political Ecology". In *The Ecological Movement in Greece*, edited by Cristophoros Orfanides, 8–21. Athens: Meta ti Vrochi.

Marcelloni, Maurizio. 1979. "Urban Movements and Political Struggles in Italy". *International Journal of Urban and Regional Research* 3 (1–4): 251–268.

Mattoni, Alice, and Markos Vogiatzoglou. 2014. "Italy and Greece, Before and After the Crisis: Between Mobilization and Resistance Against Precarity". *Quaderni* (84): 57–71.

Mattoni, Alice, and Nicole Doerr. 2007. "Images within the Precarity Movement in Italy". *Feminist Review* 87 (1): 130–135.

Maurizio Degl'Innocenti. 1984. *Le Case Del Popolo in Europa: Dalle Origini Alla Seconda Guerra Mondiale*. Firenze: Sansoni.

McAdam, Doug, and Sidney Tarrow. 2010. "Ballots and Barricades: On the Reciprocal Relations between Elections and Social Movements". *Perspectives on Politics* 8 (2): 529–542.

McAdam, Doug, and Sidney Tarrow. 2013. "Social Movements and Elections: Toward a Broader Understanding of the Political Context of Contention". In *The Future of Social Movement Research: Dynamics, Mechanisms, and Processes*, edited by Jacquelien van Stekelenburg, Conny Roggeband, and Bert Klandermans, 325–346. Mineapolis, MN and London: University of Minessota Press.

Moroni, Primo, ed. 1996. *Centri Sociali. Geografie Del Desiderio: Dati, Statistiche, Mappe, Progetti E Divenire*. Milano: Shake.

Mullins, Jonathan. 2013. "What Remains of the Italian Left of the 1970s?" *World Picture* 8, (http://worldpicturejournal.com/WP_8/Mullins.html (accessed 20 September 2017).

Papanikolopoulos, Dimitris. 2016. *December 2008. Analysis and Interpretation: The Causal Mechanisms Behind the Protest Events*. Athens: Colleagues Editions.

Pavone, Claudio. 1991. *Una Guerra Civile: Saggio Storico Sulla Moralità Nella Resistenza*. Torino: Bollati Boringhieri.

Repousis, Maria. 2014. "Feminist Movement. From the Dynamic Establishment to the Gradual Incorporation". In *Greece in the Decade of 1980*, edited by Vasilis Vamvakas, and Panagis Panagiotopoulos, 624–626. Athens: Epikentro.

Seferiadis, Serafeim. 2008. "Collective Actions, Movement Practices: The 'Short' Decade of the 60s as 'Contentious Cycle'". Edited by Alkis Rigos, Serafeim Seferiades and Eyanthis Xatzivasileiou, 57–77. Athens: Kastaniotis.

Serdedakis, Nikos. 2007. "Democratization and Collective Action in Post-Junta Greece (1974–1981)". 4th ECPR General Conference, Pisa.

Serdedakis, Nikos. 2008. "Accumulated Social Discontent as the Cause of Dynamic Mobilizations", in *Epohi*: 14 December.

Serdedakis, Nikos. 2015. "Collective Action Continuities and Discontinuities During the Transition from 'Cachectic Democracy' to Metapoliteysi". In *Metapoliteysi. Greece in the Verge of Two Centuries*, edited by Manos Afgeridis, Efi Gazis and Kostis Kornetis, 99–115. Athens: Themelio.

Sergi, Vittorio. 2008. "I Municipi Autonomi Zapatisti in Chiapas (Messico): Appropiazione Simbolica, Spazi Ibridi E Potere Politico". *XXX Convegno Internazionale di Americanistica 2008*: 117–130.

Sklavenitis, Dimitris. 2016. *"Be Cool Gerasime..." Student Movement and Occupations 1974–2000*. Athens: Asini.

Souzas, Nikos. 2015. *Stop Talking About Death Babe. Politics and Culture in the Antagonist Movement in Greece (1974–1998)*. Thessaloniki: Nautilos.

Spourdalakis, Michalis. 1988. *PASOK. Structure, Infra-Party Crisis and Power Concentration*. Athens: Exantas.

Stathakis, George. 2007. "Neoliberalism in Greece and the Venture of Modernization". Pp. 33–56 in George Stathakis, *Fruitless Modernization*, Athens: Bibliorama.

Varika, Eleni. 1992. "Confronted with the Modernization of Institutions. A Difficult Feminism". In *Women's Greece*, edited by Eytixia Leontidou and Siggrid Ammer, 67–80. Athens: Enallaktikes Ekdoseis.

Vernardakis, Christophoros. 2011. *Political Parties, Elections and Party System. The Transformations of Political Representation*. Athens: Sakkoulas.

Voulgaris, Ioannis. 2001. *Post-Junta Greece 1974–1990*. Athens: Themelio.

Weinberg, Leonard, and William Lee Eubank. 1987. *The Rise and Fall of Italian Terrorism*. Boulder, CO: Westview Press.

Wright, Steve. 2002. *Storming Heaven: Class Composition and Struggle in Italian Autonomist Marxism*. London: Pluto Press.

Zamponi, Lorenzo, and Markos Vogiatzoglou. 2015. "Organising workers' counter power in Italy and Greece". *State of Power 2015. An Annual Anthology on Global Power and Resistance* (www.tni.org/en/stateofpower2015).

Zamponi, Lorenzo. 2012. "'Why Don't Italians Occupy?' Hypotheses on a Failed Mobilisation". *Social Movement Studies* 11 (3–4): 416–426.

3 Indignados, municipalism and Podemos

Mobilisation and political cycle in Spain after the Great Recession

Ibán Díaz-Parra, Beltrán Roca and Emma Martín-Díaz

The burst of the financial crisis evidenced the weaknesses of the Spanish economic model and its semi-peripheral position within the EU and the World-system. The implementation of austerity policies and cutbacks entailed a set of socio-economic, symbolic and political effects that substantially changed the Spanish political milieu. Although the economic crisis mostly became an excuse to deepen the neo-liberalisation processes that started several decades before (mainly consisting of deregulation of labour and privatisation of public services), its effect on the Spanish population facilitated a new opportunity structure where new political actors could enter the scene: in 2011 the 15M or *indignados* social movement, and after 2014 the new party *Podemos* and other municipal grassroots political groups and coalitions. It was possible because the economic crisis led to a crisis of representation as well as a crisis of expectations of well-being and social progress. The incompetence of public institutions to attend to the needs of the population in the context of austerity (together with corruption scandals and its connivance with financial and economic elites), drove a significant part of Spanish society to participate in massive social protests between 2011 and 2013. Later, the closeness of political institutions together with the lack of efficiency of street protests to address the popular demands, served as a catalyst for the transfer of militancy from social movements to new political groups. The electoral arena ended up reflecting both the divisions within Spanish society and the impact of the crisis on the popular classes.

This chapter describes such social processes. First, it will analyse the context of the political economy of the crises in Spain. It will also pay attention to social discourse on the crisis among the Spanish population. Second, it will examine the first responses to the crisis by the classic labour movement as well as by protest movements emerging in the context, characterised mainly by a frontal opposition to political representation and state institutions and a post-materialist nature. Third, this chapter investigates what we call the "materialist" turn of social movements (from 2012 to 2014). This turn was expressed in the focus on labour, housing and ethno-nationalist demands by new generations of activists. Fourth, it will describe the electoral turn of social protest with the rise of

Podemos and the municipalist initiatives. The in-depth study of these dynamics, especially focusing on the interplay between activism and political economy throughout the different stages of social protest, will shed light on the general discussion of anti-austerity movements and political parties in Southern Europe.

From the Spain of consumption to the Spain of austerity

The process known as globalisation, or the current stage of World capitalism, is characterised, as several authors have pointed out (Harvey 1990; Sassen 1991; Castells 1997), by the pre-eminence of financial and speculative activities, implying a constant growth of social and spatial inequalities. In this context, Nation-states are no longer the main holders of power of our age (Appadurai 1990), on behalf of international financial institutions such as the IMF and the WB at a global scale, or the ECB at a European scale. After the crisis of the stock market and the explosion of the bubble of the new economy of 2001, the role of these institutions, and of others such as the USA Federal Bank, focused on fostering the creation of money on all levels: cash money, bank money and financial money (Naredo 2006), on the basis of an unprecedented extension of debt, especially mortgage debt, in a process that had the characteristics of a pyramidal scheme fraud, since the debts were sustained one to another. The dynamic of expansion of money generated, among other factors, a significant growth in the construction sector and an unprecedented extension of consumption. Nonetheless, this process did not similarly affect all countries, either in the globe or in Europe. Although the financialisation of the economy is a hegemonic tendency at a global scale, Nation-states are still essential in the specific form that this tendency adopts in the different countries. This is basically due to two central reasons: (1) their ability to legitimise the dynamics imposed by international financial institutions, and to impose them on the population; and (2) their capacity to define the precise form that the process is going have within its national territory, generating "ad hoc" policies. This is the reason why the real estate boom did not similarly affect all the territories of the EU, and why Spain led Europe in a process that Fernández Durán (2006) named an "urbanising tsunami", promoting an increase in construction activity that was detached from the internal demand, and became the pillar of a highly speculative activity with both foreign and national agents participating. Without a set of state policies directed to support this speculation, one cannot understand the fact that in 2005 Spain began the construction of 800,000 buildings, bypassing the rates in France, Germany and the UK altogether – countries, not only with larger populations than Spain, but also with significantly higher income (Rodriguez 2005). The irrationality of this process was evident, but it was difficult to put into question before the Spanish population, which was aware that its purchasing power was linked to real estate activity, and that put their hope in the maintenance of this industry to the extent that its crisis meant the decline of the whole economic model promoted by the State. The sentence: "This cannot fall down because everything would collapse", was a constant phrase among bankers, urban developers, and in general among the population when it was becoming evident that the housing pool was not coherent with the existing demand, and "ghost towns" appeared far away from any kind of infrastructure of services and communications.

The support of the successive governments for construction as the engine of the Spanish economy was a constant since the last term of president Felipe González (1993–1996), but it intensified during the term of Aznar and continued during the government of Rodriguez Zapatero. Critical economists (Delgado 2011; Sampedro 2009) have stated that the construction boom, the increase of consumption and the growth of the GNP Spanish economy was accompanied by a constant decline of productivity, losing competitiveness within the EU, and an increase of family debt due to the rise of housing. The outbreak of the real estate bubble entailed a sharp retrenchment of economic growth, which decisively affected consumption capacity, implied a crisis for financial entities who were debt owners, and led 600,000 families (3.5 per cent of Spanish households) to lose their houses between 2008 and 2012 (Colectivo Ioé 2012).

At the beginning of the crisis, Zapatero's government refused to use the term "crisis", systematically using the term "economic retrenchment" instead despite all the objective indicators of the collapse. This refusal was repeated as a mantra by all of the members of the Government in their speeches before the mass media from April 2007 to April 2009. After that date, the executive began to recognise that a recession took place, but only in order to affirm that the country had begun the path to recovery ("green sprouts", according to the Ministry of Economy, Elena Salgado, in a statement one month before the elections for the European Parliament in June 2009). This attitude of refusal, and the optimistic discourse of the Government in a context of negative economic growth (–3 per cent), was strongly contested by both the media and public opinion. The manifest evidence of the crisis and the dramatic size of its effects, led the authorities of the European Council to press the government of Zapatero, who, with the support of the main party of the opposition, the conservative Popular Party, and making use of the fact that both had 90 per cent of the seats in the legislative chambers, agreed to modify article 135 of the Spanish Constitution, skipping the call for a referendum that would have been highly unpopular. The principle of budget stability consecrated as a priority before any other need or interest by the Constitution reform, entailed an immediate wage cut for public employees, represented as a privileged sector in a context of growing unemployment, and, consequently, incapable of generating the wealth needed for overcoming the crisis. With this discourse, the elites looked for, and achieved, the acquiescence of wide sectors of the population, generating a certain sense of "privilege" among the public employees themselves before a wave of evictions and a dramatic fall in employment. More serious, due to its greater social impact, was the radical drop of the budget in regional governments, in charge of public services such as health care and education, and public institutions with social goals. The unrest in the economic situation spread job insecurity and social exclusion among more and more sectors of population. The awkward attempts by the Government to reject the gravity of the situation drove to an anticipated call for general elections in which the Popular Party got an absolute majority. From the very moment of its constitution, the new Government was obliged to adopt drastic measures to avoid the collapse of the financial system, in a standoff due to the lack of payment of debt and, above all, the irresponsible practices of the banks. This situation skyrocketed the risk premium and drove the Government to ask the EU for a bank rescue of €100,000 million, that the State employed to restructure the bank system by means of the FROB (Fund for Organised Bank Restructuring). Thus, private debt turned into public debt. The fact that the money invested in, in the words of the social movements and critical sectors of the Spanish society, "saving the banks and not the people", was justified by the Government using three discursive pillars: (1) The rejection that it was a case of a rescue, but instead a "loan under very favourable conditions" (in the words of the Ministry Luis de Guindos in a statement of 9 June 2012); (2) the "received heritage" from the disastrous economic management of the Socialist government, that forced them to claim enormous sacrifices from the population; and (3) blaming of the Spanish society, "which had lived beyond their means".

At the same time as when the government passed these "austerity" measures that increased the social and regional breach to unprecedented rates since the 1970s (Cáritas 2013; Informe FOESSA 2014), a set of corruption scandals arose involving members of the Popular Party. As a result, in the general elections of 2015, although it received the most votes, it was not enough to form a government. This situation was repeated in the following elections in June 2016, despite the growth experienced by this political group, to a great extent motivated by a campaign of fear launched extensively by the mass media, which connected the fear of the economic crisis with the fear of political instability.

It is worth analysing the practices and discourses of the different sectors of Spanish society in two ambits inherently linked to the current economic crisis: consumption and austerity policies. Alonso *et al.* (2011) published research on consumption and crisis, drawn on the analysis of the discourses of several focus groups. Among other findings, the authors pointed out that a mimetic process was undertaken by all social groups, influenced by the mass media, that led to an inversion of consumption patterns, from the massive consumption of the years prior to the crisis to new patterns of saving and frugality. In addition, the authors stated that blaming the crisis on the irresponsible behaviour of the population had deeply influenced them, to the extent that it was regarded as the main cause of the crisis. Nonetheless, the authors identified meaningful differences, though not in the ambit of consumption, where the majority still opted for saving and frugality. The authors highlighted that there was no convergence in the sense of a structural or temporal transformation of consumption patterns. While some interviewees thought the crisis was a mistake to learn from and not repeat, others understood the retraction of consumption as something temporary, which would reverse as the economic situation changed. In contrast, in the ambit of the blame for the crisis, the authors observed an important change from the perception of the majority of the citizens as mainly responsible, given their irrational consumption, to a more concrete attribution of responsibilities to the bank and the political class, given the serious cases of corruption revealed by the mass media. This study points out a tendency that is easily verified in analysing the electoral behaviour of the Spaniards in the last two general elections: as the critical consciousness among the population scales up, the fear before "an absolute crisis of the model of labour citizenship" also grows, even at a higher rate (Alonso 2007).

> What seems to be happening is that, before the in-depth and scope of the recession, for the first time in decades the Spanish political and socio-economic models seems to have entered into a profound crisis of social legitimacy, what anticipates a scenario of change and uncertainty in the following years.
>
> (Alonso *et al.* 2016, 35)

The *indignados* and the first responses to the crisis

The general strike of 2010 and first trade union response

The burst of the economic crisis did not automatically result in high levels of mobilisation. During the first stage of the crisis, the socialist government of José Luis Rodríguez Zapatero was so clearly backed by UGT and CCOO that authors such as Redondo (2015) noted that major unions lost the autonomy they had gained in the 1990s. Nevertheless, the situation changed by May 2010, when the socialist government, following the demands of the European Council and the International Monetary Fund (IMF), launched an "austerity" plan allegedly in order to reduce the financial deficit. Major trade unions reacted by breaking off negotiations on labour market reforms taking place at the time, and the government passed the Labour Bill unilaterally on 6 June. The trade unions CCOO and UGT called for a general strike on 29 September.

The general strike of 2010 marked the beginning of a period defined by a "boxing and dancing" trade union strategy (Luque and González Begega 2014). Campos Lima and Martín Artiles (2011) referred to it as an "ambiguous relationship between general strikes and social pacts". As in other southern European countries, the Spanish trade unions resorted to collective action and, particularly, to the general strike to show discontent about austerity measures and cutbacks (Köhler *et al.* 2013); but at the same time the major unions demanded the restoration of a social agreement, what Hyman (2001) called a model of trade unionism oriented towards social pacts.

On February 2011 – only four months after the general strike – CCOO and UGT signed a tripartite agreement on pensions, accepting the increase of statutory retirement age from 65 to 67 years. The fact that in 2009 and 2010 trade unions opposed this agreement, and changed their position in 2011, reflects the tensions between different identities in the major trade unions. On the one hand, some scholars argued that trade unions acted as responsible social partners moderating their demands in order to avoid the intervention of the IMF over the country and lessening supra-national pressure (Campos Lima and

Martín Artiles 2011). Others, in turn, argued that the resort to tripartite agreements was a response to the weaknesses revealed during the general strike and an attempt to prevent being excluded from social dialogue (Antón 2012). It was, thus, a movement that sought to preserve their political influence (González Begega *et al.* 2013).

The "boxing and dancing" strategy will be present throughout the crisis, as a result of the tension between unions defending the interest of the working class by means of collective action, and operating as "responsible" social partners in order to maintain their political influence.

The rise of the 15M as a New Social Movement

By mid-2011, trade unions lost their leading role in social protest as a new actor turned up: the 15M or *indignados* (outraged). This new social movement demanded deep reforms in the political system and had a very critical attitude towards the institutions, including trade unions (Castells 2013; Fernández *et al.* 2014, 119). Although the relationship between trade unions and the *indignados* changed as the crisis went on, the initial disaffection with the unions of the 15M reflected the perception of a large part of the Spanish population.

Several authors have described the set of protests in which the 15M was forged, demonstrations running from May to October 2011 and tents in the squares of the main cities of Spain (Pastor 2012; Castells 2013; Moreno Pestaña 2013; Romanos and Sádaba 2015). The movement was born from a protest on Facebook on 15 May 2011 under the slogan "Real democracy now! Take the streets. We are not a commodity in the hands of politicians and bankers", and promoted by a small network of activists. It ended in a massive and horizontal mobilisation against the consequences of the economic crisis, manifesting the extended disenchantment with the political system. Without the initial support of any political party, trade union or civil society organisation, a growing number of activists organised protests in hundreds of cities with large attendance and impact. Protest camps, square occupations, networks, assemblies, work commissions and protests expanded rapidly throughout the country, building a new movement characterised by self-management and the use of new information and communication technologies (Castells 2013).

The specific and unprecedented character of the 15M is clear; however, the relationship to earlier mobilisations can also be traced, and initially it fits in the model of the "new social movement". Although in general terms protests caught the most experienced activists off guard in most cities, the background of the activists of the organiser entity Real Democracy Now (*Democracia Real Ya-DRY*) is well known. Many of them were linked to the most significant struggles, which took place in the first decade of the twenty-first century, such as the global justice movement, which had special relevance in Spain around 2003, the demonstrations under the slogan "May Day" between 2005 and 2007, or the protests due to housing problems in 2006. These actions coincided with what could be called an advanced stage of new social movements, including environmentalism, feminism, squatter movement and others. These movements share many ideo-logical positions characteristic of: post-workerism, self-management and a certain rejection of institutions. With a great use of new communication technol-ogies (including virtual), horizontal forms of organisation, spontaneous and other tendencies would be imitated by the 15M (Díaz-Parra and Candón 2014).

These previous movements are clearly connected to the 15M: from the campaigns developed in the previous period to the first protests, such as the tents of *Juventud Sin Futuro* (Youth Without Future) or *No les Votes* (Do Not Vote for Them), born in protest to the well-known "Sinde Law" which attempted to control the Internet and intellectual property (Candón 2013), amongst other measures. These influences are evident in the manifestos adopted once the initial moments of greater vagueness had passed. Thus, the call for demonstrations for 15 October of Real Democracy Now clearly made reference, together with the Tahir Square demonstrations, the Zapatistas or the lack of democracy of supra-national institutions such as the IMF, WTO or G8, to the discourse of the global justice movement. Similarly, the interac-tions with these movements were very recognisable during the first year of the movement. For example, the housing movement ended up launching the Platform of People Affected by Mortgage (*Plataforma de Afectados por la Hipoteca-PAH*), with which the 15M developed a noticeable synergy after the summer of 2011 paralysing evictions and, later on, carrying out re-housings (Díaz-Parra 2014).

Two elements of the continuity of the social movements of the previous two decades are especially relevant for our analysis. First, in relation to the inter-class or post-workerist character of the movement, the social composition of the foundational mobilisations was, without a doubt, heterogeneous. Young people, from diverse class backgrounds (albeit mainly from the middle class), were over-represented both in the occupations of the squares and the occupation of social centres during the first year. The core of experienced activists, who were gradu-ally joining the movement, came from this group. In addition, the incorporation of senior citizens, including militants from the mobilisation cycle of the political transition: neighbourhood associations, trade unions, radical-left parties, etc. was perceivable. However, the demonstrations managed to attract an extremely heterogeneous crowd in terms of demographic, ideological and social back-grounds (Díaz-Parra and Candón 2014). The vagueness and pursuit of consensus of the initial call for mobilisation was such that it was not, in fact, very appeal-ing to the already mobilised activists but, on the contrary, it managed to appeal to an enormously diverse sector of the population which disagreed with the social and political crisis experienced by the state. Some of the slogans that people used to call out and write on the placards in the first demonstrations were very significant: "We are neither from the left nor from the right". The founda-tional statement of the mobilisation of 15 May 2011, written by DRY, describes well this non-partisan – and under certain perspectives apolitical – discourse, demanding an ethical revolution and appealing in a considerably ambiguous manner to a very general audience:

We are normal and ordinary people. We are like you: people who wake up in the morning to study, to work and to job-hunt, people who have family and friends. People who work hard every day to earn a living and to provide a better future for those surrounding us. Some are more progressive, others more conservative. Some are believers, others not so.

Second, the 15M had a very critical discourse against institutions, including trade unions, just as they rejected political parties. Although this coincides to a great extent with earlier demonstrations and campaigns of social movements, it is also an element that contributed to the massive support that generated the movement.

The rejection of unions – particularly the major ones, CCOO and UGT – was, however, compatible with the awareness of the need to somehow approach these organisations, as they contributed experience, continuity and organisational support. This was evident in the August and September 2011 protests against the reform of the Spanish Constitution. The socialist government had yielded to pressures from Angela Merkel to include budget deficit controls in the Constitution under the guise of "calming the markets". This issue was voted for in parliament with the support of the Popular Party, then in the opposition, in the month of August and with little or no public debate. On 5 September, the day before the vote in the Senate, both the *indignados* and the trade unions organised parallel demonstrations in Madrid with different slogans calling for a referendum on constitutional reform. Both demonstrations converged in the *Puerta del Sol* and, as Manuel Castells recounted, one of the protesters carried a placard with an ironic message: "unions, thanks for coming" (Castells 2013, 119), which reflected the ambivalent relationship between *indignados* and labour organisations: reproaching their previous indifference and lack of support in former demonstrations on the one hand, while on the other, celebrating unions' backing of that particular protest.

The materialist turn of social protest: 2012–2014

The turn on labour issues

The attitude of 15M towards labour notoriously changed during its first two years. In the first period of mobilisation commencing in May 2011, there was an explicit rejection of any kind of conventional organisation, including trade unions. The 15M movement can be characterised in this first version as a postmaterialistic and anti-conventional politics movement of protest. From the end of 2011 and during 2012 and 2013, which were years of intense mobilisation and protest against austerity policies, a notorious collaboration with social and political organisations took place. This change involved, among other things, a progressive move towards labour issues.

From the beginning of the movement, there was also a particular attitude regarding the labour issue. The foundational statement made very general references to unemployment and precarity, similar to anti-globalisation movement discourses, which were repeated in further statements and meetings. It was when the 15M began to create some structures, albeit very basic and unstable ones, and mainly commissions, that some structures focused on labour issues appeared. This was very evident in the office against labour precarity launched by the 15M of Madrid in the social centre Patio Maravillas, a building that was squatted before 2011 and linked to certain factions of the local autonomous movement. Another example is the commission on labour of the Barcelona 15M which made a great effort to coordinate grass-roots struggles. Other commissions with less scope, such as the one in Seville, also carried out specific struggles, such as supporting local strikes or protests against high unemployment rates, with the occupation of an employment office in March 2012. The demands were very similar to those of radical unions: to forbid collective dismissals, and ensure public employment, the distribution of work and a minimum wage for the unemployed. The statement of the labour commission of Barcelona also denounced the "co-optation of the trade union elite" and simultaneously highlighted the past achievements of the labour movement and the need to defend them from labour reforms.

On the other hand, the participation of the *indignados* in the general strikes of 2012 was remarkable. The 15M assemblies, by this time decentralised by city areas and generally connected by local coordination, promoted the creation of "critical fronts" within the demonstrations in which they tended to converge with radical trade unions. The Madrid call criticised the uselessness of major unions and their leaders whereas they introduced discursive elements of both autonomous movement and radical unions such as to "visibilise aspects which the unions are not able to visibilise" (such as social problems affecting other sectors of the population) or carry out an "inclusive strike" – that is, including not only the workers, but also the retired, the young and the unemployed. Apart from active participation in the demonstrations, the different neighbourhood assemblies got involved in the picket lines, and in many cases called for a consumption strike or action more oriented towards the territory than the industry (in contrast to traditional union action).

The *indignados* movement developed a greater affinity with radical unionism – represented in Spain by organisations such as CGT, SAT or CNT – than to the major trade unions. CCOO and UGT, despite having deployed different strategies to converge with 15M and having launched several protests and general strikes (Köhler *et al.* 2013), attempted unsuccessfully to call on social dialogue, possibly due to its structural weaknesses and tensions (Köhler and Calleja Jiménez 2013). The convergence, after all, has been neither constant nor homogeneous in each city and among activists. In the first assemblies of the 15M, negative and conservative discourses on trade unions predominated (Fernández Rodríguez *et al.* 2014). The attitude of the radical unions towards the 15M on the other hand, was also diverse and changeable: from an initial mistrust, due to the undefined origin of the initiative and to not sharing some of the objectives, to an enthusiastic attitude because of its mobilisation capacity and horizontal organisation (Roca and Díaz-Parra 2017).

As time passed, the movement evolved and the initial mistrust towards trade unionism in general, and towards radical unions in particular, was diluted. This is related to factors which point in different directions – on the one hand, to the loss of massive participation in the assemblies and protests (only the most convinced activists remained) and on the other hand, to the politicisation of part of the new militancy. The initial militant profile, as inexperienced and not politicised, was changing, especially after the ending of the city square occupations and the creation of multiple neighbourhood assemblies. In those, the previously marginal long-term militant profile, usually linked to left-wing organisations, became increasingly important. The affinity between the *indignados* and the radical unions crystallised, amongst other ways, in the great attendance and participation in initiatives promoted by organisations such as CGT, SAT and CNT, which found in the economic crisis a convergence with the 15M, a loss in legitimacy of the major unions and greater opportunities to grow. This new context also favoured a climate of convergence among radical unions. Thus, under different names, such as the "unitary front" or "critical front", coalitions of radical unions, civil society organisations and 15M assemblies have played a key role in the collective action against austerity policies. Numerous mobilisations from 2012 reflect this convergence between radical unionism and the *indignados*. During the general strikes of 2012, for example, the coalitions of 15M and the smaller unions had a massive attendance. CGT's statement before the general strike of 14 November 2012, for instance, illustrates how radical unionism counted on the support of many 15M assemblies in its mobilisations, which were separate from those called by the main unions (Roca and Díaz-Parra 2017).

The turn on housing issues

In a similar way to labour, from the beginning of the movement there was also a particular attitude regarding the housing issues. First, 15M has one of its more obvious precedents in the 2006 decent housing movement, born from a series of spontaneous mass mobilisations, self-convocated by SMS messages, to protest the prohibitive price of housing which excluded large sectors of the population from the market, especially young people. The movement was able to create housing assemblies in many Spanish cities, which soon collapsed as a result of its uncoordinated and inefficient nature (in the opinion of Aguilar and Fernández 2010) and its most durable product was the creation of the PAH some time after, which would have a main role in Spanish politics after 2011. Second, there are strong links between 15M and the squatting movement. Successively, with the dismantling of the first camps, there was a wave of occupation of abandoned spaces. In many cases, squatted social centres sought to carry out a similar function to that achieved in plazas during the preceding period: the Madrid Hotel in the capital (Abellán *et al.* 2012), Valcárcel in Cadiz and the Encarnación abandoned market hall in Seville. Some others were adapted to house evicted families and crisis victims. Martínez and Domingo (2014) talked of a convergence process between 15M and the squatter movement, which would have a decisive effect on the movement's libertarian tendencies.

However, the transition between mobilisation first erupting and the later decentralisation to neighbourhoods was accompanied by the social consequences of the crisis being placed at the forefront. Both long-term and youth unemployment proliferated, as did forced evictions, so the individual mobilised by 15M began to take part in the housing movement (Díaz-Parra and Jover 2016). From the time of decentralisation to neighbourhood assemblies (the second half of 2011) the movement fed off the new recruits attracted by the mobilisation cycle. Within the context of the proliferation of resistance as disobedience in the face of evictions, usually coordinating 15M assemblies and PAH local groups, the assemblies saw themselves popularised to a certain degree. The organisation of resistance in defiance of evictions was a major qualitative leap which enabled forced and accumulated legitimacy to be used to fight what came to be perceived as injustices, with practical outcomes. Here, in some cases, there was direct continuity from 15M; this was evident in Andalusia. The housing movement in 2012 and 2013 was led in Seville by the 15M housing commission, and by anti-eviction platforms, strongly related to 15M, in Córdoba and Granada. Alternatively, at the State level and in other regions of the country, especially Catalonia but also in Madrid, PAH (Platform for those Affected by Mortgages) experienced significant increases in militant activism, activity and media presence. After 2013, with the decline of 15M local assemblies, most of the housing movement was carried on by PAH, also in Andalusia where it had no relevance before.

Along with the resistance against evictions, the other main topic in the housing movement in 2012 and 2013 was the squatting. As said before, some of the building squattings organised by 15M in 2011 were used for housing crisis victims. This tactic was broadly used after 2012. In Seville, a network of housing advice offices underpinned by neighbourhood assemblies was set up. These sparked collective squatting in buildings belonging to banking organisations called *Corralas*, linked to the assemblies. About a dozen empty buildings were squatted in Seville metropolitan area for housing evicted families in 2012. The spread of the Andalusian *Corrala* movement, mainly to other Andalusian cities, was complemented by a similar campaign initiated by the PAH in Catalonia (Díaz-Parra and Solanas 2015).

However, few results were achieved by the housing movement. As with the resistances to the evictions, collective squatting achieved a level of social support as was never seen before. Nevertheless, this did not prevent them from ending, with only a few exceptions, in police evictions. At the same time, the benefit to evicted persons or in situations of social exclusion passed by regional governments, such as the one of Andalusian government that included the temporary expropriation of empty bank-owned houses for social rents, were appealed by the central government at the Constitutional Court, which suspended them in a precautionary manner.

The rise of nationalism disconnected from the nationalism of identity

The defining feature of the so-called Spanish *Transition*, from a dictatorship to a parliamentary democracy in 1977, is related to the so-called "nationalism problem". The ethnic and territory diversity within the Spanish State was recognised during the first biennium of the Second Republic (1931–1933), although the process was suddenly interrupted with the Civil War and the ulterior dictatorship. Logically, in that context, the nationalist aspirations, long and fiercely repressed during the Francoist regime, broke out strongly in the debate about the model of the State, in which nationalist forces played a key role, imposing the so-called "State of Autonomies" by means of a complex process that cannot be described in this work. It can be sufficient to point out that, for the particular cases of the two territories where nationalism has been the hegemonic political force most of the time – Catalunya and Euskadi – the two political parties that have ruled, the coalition Convergencia I Unió, the first, and the Basque Nationalist Party (PNV in Spanish), the second, have played a central role in the political management of the parliamentary democracy, activating and deactivating the identity demands in a process of negotiation with the State. In this negotiation process, the convergence stood out in relation to the economic model to be implemented, only disagreeing about the distribution of State resources among the territories. This does not mean that all Basque and Catalonian nationalisms, or other nationalisms with minor social projection, such as the Galician, Andalusian, and Valencian, can be identified with conservative positions, but that these positions have been hegemonic in those territories where nationalism seized political power. This situation has changed significantly as nationalisms that join ethnic issues with class issues, such as the Catalonian CUP or the Basque Bildu, have increased their social influence, challenging their territorial representation spaces to the conservative forces, especially as the economic crisis and the subsequent cuts have scaled-up to more and more sectors of the population.

Classical theories on nationalism, proposed by Gellner (1983) and Smith (1977), have used, although with different nuances, the dichotomy between cultural nationalisms and civic nationalisms. According to this perspective, cultural nationalisms are based on emotional arguments containing a strong affective component. With important exceptions, this has been the predominant approach in the analysis of peripheral nationalisms within the established Nation-states. This is the origin of the distinction between ethnonationalisms, a concept which implies ethnicity as the determinant factor, and State nationalisms, a definition which emphasises the citizen's social pact as the union bond. The works of Ignatieff (1998) on the Balkan nationalisms and the book of the Syrian-French writer, Amin Maalouf (1998) on murderous identities, also followed this line. This tradition has been hegemonic in social sciences, but was far from being unanimous. Tom Nairn (1977), in *The Break up of Britain*, gives more weight to the class factor than ethnicity and citizenship, breaking with the dichotomy between cultural nations and civic nations. From his point of view, unequal development is the driving force of nationalisms and those territories located in the periphery of the states were the most interested in raising the flag of nationalism. A few years later, and following this same materialist approach, Hechter and Levi (1979) revisited the theory of internal colonialism in order to highlight that it is precisely the peripheral situation within a given state that determines the adscription to a nationalist project.

Nevertheless, this state-of-the-art conceptualisation began to change as financial globalisation processes destabilised the balance between the state and the market. In 1997, Castells published his trilogy *The Information Age*, focusing his second volume on the "power of identity" and identifying nationalisms such as the Quebecer and Catalonian ones as project identities (Castells 1997). Kaldor, in her article "Nationalism and Globalisation", argued that "the current wave of nationalism has to be understood as a response to globalization and not as evidence for the enduring nature of the national idea" (Kaldor 2004, 161).

Following the premises suggested by Castells and Kaldor, we think that the rise of the self-determination movements in Spain, particularly in Catalonia, and to a lesser degree Euskadi, are manifestations of a reflexivity process understood within the framework of the transformations of the Nation-states, resulting from globalisation and leading to a triple crisis: of competences, of legitimacy and of representation. In this context, the self-determination movements fit into the model of project identity suggested by Castells, and must be seen as a response to a situation of structural crisis for the model of the Nation-state, which characterised the first modernity (Beck 1997), and worsened due to the economic crisis that affected particularly the EU. These new nationalist movements make it impossible for researchers to maintain the dichotomy between ethnic and civic nationalisms considering the crisis of the citizenship model of modernity (Brown 1999). In this sense, these new nationalist movements in Catalonia and Euskadi coincided with the model of project identity proposed by Manuel Castells, which responded not only to a political crisis of the State, but also to the economic and financial crisis of 2008. And this is so for various reasons: First, the nationalist feelings and movements have intensified due to the current economic crisis and the general social unrest generated by austerity public policies. Second, identity references lose weight in these movements in relation to the aspiration of constructing, from self-determination, a new economic model which overcomes the contradictions sharpened by the neo-liberal policies of the Nation-state. This explains why numerous persons from the ambit of new social movements, initially not sensible to the independentist project, have ended up joining the self-determination project.

In conclusion, self-determination movements reflect a significant discursive and programme shift in ethno-nationalism. The new nationalist projects appear as a solution to the social problems generated by a Nation-state that has lost competence in the framework of the EU and the globalisation processes, and also due to the antisocial cutback measures.

The electoral turn: from 2014 to today

The lack of impact of collective action on State institutions and public policies during the first years of the crisis, led a group of militants of the organisation *Izquierda Anticapitalista* (Anticapitalist Left), which was a small Trotskyist party that played an active role in the 15M and was formerly integrated in *Izquierda Unida* (United Left), together with several university researchers and professors, to launch a new political party. This new party aimed at translating the electoral arena to the demands of anti-austerity forces, and, in particular, of the 15M movement (Iglesias 2015). The electoral turn of part of the 15M was also a result of the limits of the autonomous perspective that prevailed amongst its members. During 2013, these reflections were also part of the debates of the leftist Internet-based TV show, *La Tuerka* (The Screw), hosted by Pablo Iglesias, who was a lecturer in Political Science at the Universidad Complutense de Madrid. By this time, many activists felt that the movement needed to leap at the chance and create an electoral force. One informant, a member of the Local Board of *Podemos* in Seville explained it in this manner:

> I come from the social movements and, within them, from what has been called political autonomy. For some time now, I have been thinking that we need a new paradigm that fosters a movement with the capacity to change the institutions. I have also had a feeling of tiredness about certain voluntarism that has put social action ahead of political action which has shown to be useless beyond particular and isolated victories, such that it is unable to go further. I had a sense of anguish before the silences between concrete struggles.
>
> (LS, April 2014)

In January 2014, some 30 intellectuals and activists signed a public manifesto titled "Moving ahead" stating that

> popular mobilisation, civil insubordination and confidence in our own forces are essential, but it is also forging the keys in order to open the doors that they want to close to us: bring to the institutions the voice and the demands of the social majority.

The document ends by calling for a "unitary and ground-breaking candidacy, headed by people who put into practice new forms of relations with politics, and who constitute a real challenge to the bipartisan regime of PP and PSOE, which have kidnapped our democracy" (Público 2014). In March 2014, they founded the new party under the name of *Podemos* (We can), inspired by Obama's successful campaign, in order to participate in the elections for the European Parliament.

The communication strategy of the party and its leader, Iglesias, succeeded in attracting the attention of the mass media, and *Podemos* gained five seats in the European Parliament and 1.2 million votes (Errejón 2015). After this event, the presence in the international and national mass media of the political formation skyrocketed rapidly. Its discourse soon filled the political space that the PSOE had left empty after several decades of neo-liberal reforms: that of social democracy. In this landscape, a growing number of former 15M activists and the forms of other social movements, non-mobilised citizens and former members of other political groups who were disappointed with their organisations, joined the numerous *Círculos* (local branches) of the new party throughout the state and even in dozens of foreign cities. The new party set up its organisational structure to a great extent following the model of the networks formed by the 15M assemblies (Romanos and Sádaba 2015); however, institutional participation demanded a greater level of centralisation.

The identification between the circles and the neighbourhood assemblies of the 15M was noticeable. JC, an activist who took part in the 15M and now is a member of *Podemos* (Seville), recognised this fact:

> The main difference is that we do not debate now about how to organise protests, but about government programs. Due to the characteristics of a party, we had to create a formal organization and the organizational debate is, hence, mandatory. At last we speak about efficiency too, but we have to find an intermediate point between efficiency and democracy, to create a citizen-party and not an ordinary structure. It strikes me, for example, that the proposals are voted, something that did not used to be done in the assemblies of the social movements, but it is also about consensus building. However, finally it is the same neighbourhood assembly of the 15M with new members and new tasks, but it's the same spirit. May the 15th, 2011 was really the most important political event for our generation. I thought that because of the cultural change that it meant, but *Podemos* has materialised it, and nobody says now that the 15M was useless.
>
> (JC, October 2014)

Interviews and direct observation have shown a radical change in the behaviour towards State institutions and conventional politics by a significant number of activists. On the other hand, this change has been perceived sympathetically by most of the activists not directly involved in the creation of new electoral coalitions. The public and private rejection of institutional participation by activists who remained in autonomous movements was surprisingly very small, at least in the first instance.

It can be said that the circles of *Podemos* reproduced the spatial project of the 15M, this time articulated around the expectations for the political representation of a party. Nonetheless, it broke with some of the main characteristics of 15M, leading to a contradictory and unavoidable conflictive process. Whereas the circles bear the aspirations of radical democracy based on the micro-local scale of the neighbourhood and direct representation, the institutional participation implies some degree of centralisation. The harmonisation between both demands and the conception of the electoral turn as a tactic issue, became detached from the general strategy of bottom-up building. However, this was in contradiction to the fact that the project was essentially introduced from the top, from a small group of intellectuals, from the capital city of the State and with a great prominence of the traditional mass media (centralised by its own nature).

Consequently, the turning towards the institutions came together with an effective centralisation, which crystallised in the foundational congress of *Podemos* – also called the "Citizen Assembly: Yes we can" in November 2014. In it, the list of candidates endorsed by Pablo Iglesias won with more than 80 per cent of the votes of militants and sympathisers. The winning organisational structure was based on a general secretary and a coordination board elected by the general secretary. The line marked by this candidature focused on winning the general elections, dismissing the participation with the brand *Podemos* to the impending municipal elections in order to avoid risks. The political document of the team of Iglesias, titled "Of course we can", pointed out the limits of the cycle of mobilisations that started in 2011: "While in the street the voices of protests grew in what has been a whole cycle of social mobilization within the institutions, the right accumulated an unprecedented power" (page 3); the document also proposed the goal of replacing the "regime" of the Transition and the need for a turn towards political pragmatism (page 7).

Comparing Iglesias' proposal with that of his competitors can be enlightening. The proposals of his competitors were endorsed by some of the most traditional activists and explicit members of the Anti-Capitalist Left. This last proposal advocated for municipal elections, defended the extension of more power to the circles, and aimed at diluting the power of the cadres of the party to a greater extent. The general secretary would have been an office of three spokespersons with a citizen assembly with plenty of responsibilities. In the following internal elections, the direction positions were taken by the group around the central leader, Pablo Iglesias, while the opposition, with profiles closer to the traditional grass-roots activism, tended to be marginalised.

The political orientation that emerged from the foundational congress of *Podemos*, at the same time as vindicating the 15M movement and recruiting a large part of its activists, assumes the hegemonic spatial project around the state institutions. The chosen format of a centralised party is a main component of the State project, assuming organisation around instituted State scales (nation-state, state-regions and local state) and a temporality determined by instituted state elections. Moreover, the political line shows a clear spatial selectivity oriented to the nation-state primacy in political strategies.

The tension of the centralisation-decentralisation was translated as the creation of the local branches of the party and its spatial organisation. For example, in the case of Seville, a list of candidates who were formally backed by the followers of Pablo Iglesias won with a small margin (60 votes) to another one created from the circles and which included numerous well-known activists of the city, many of whom were very active in the 15M and in former struggles. This type of polarisation took place all over the country, and in most cases resulted in favour of the candidates endorsed by the central direction.

With the municipal elections on 24 May 2015 on the horizon, activists launched hundreds of municipal candidatures throughout the Spanish territory, most of them supported by *Podemos* and, in some cases, by other leftist political forces. Ada Colau, a spokesperson of the Mortgage Affected Platform, together with activists and representatives of several left parties, led a platform with the objective of participating in municipal elections in Barcelona in May 2015. The experience of Barcelona soon became a reference for other parts of the country. First in Madrid and then in hundreds of cities, activists from diverse movements began to create citizen platforms to participate in local elections and to articulate channels for political action at the community level. The transfer of militancy from the 15M assemblies to the new electoral initiatives had an effect on the decline of social protest.

Before the sudden avalanche of militants who had the aim of avoiding the recruitment of people who could spoil the image of *Podemos*, the direction of the party promoted a set of political, organisational, and ethical documents that included different mechanisms aimed at preventing the direct participation of the *Podemos*-brand circles in the municipal elections. This decision favoured the multiplication of municipalist candidatures who had the support of *Podemos* or who were directly launched by members of the party.

The candidatures fostered by *Podemos* finally seized power in the two most important cities, Madrid and Barcelona, but also in many other relevant cities such as A Coruña, Cádiz or Zaragoza. In other cities, they gained hundreds of seats on city councils. Notoriously, some of the first measures adopted by the new governments of these cities were related to demands of the housing movement.

As time went on, the media campaign against *Podemos* intensified, eroding the public image of its leaders and its social support. Nevertheless, in the general elections of December 2015 and June 2016, the coalition of *Podemos* with other leftist forces (*En Comú Podem*, *Compromis* and *En Marea*) received the third most votes. In particular, the coalition *Unidos Podemos* (with *Podemos*, United Left, *Compromis*, *En Marea* and *En Comú Podem*) received in 2016, 71 seats out of 350 (5,049,734 votes: 21.1 per cent). The conservative PP gained 137 seats (33.03 per cent: 7,906,185 votes); and the Socialist Party gained only a slight victory over *Podemos*: 85 seats, and 5,424,709 votes. These were historical results. Never in the recent history of Spain had a radical-leftist force achieved such electoral support. The results unleashed a profound crisis within the Socialist Party. The PP could only govern with the support (or abstention) of PSOE. PSOE also had the option to take office with the support of *Podemos*, but this would imply giving some ministries to representatives of the new party, and signing a political agreement that would be uncomfortable to pro-austerity powers. Both options are negative for the future of PSOE. Throughout 2016, negotiations among political parties took place without success. The PP government had been in office temporarily during that time. The divisions within PSOE and the difficulties in forming a new government reflect how the burst of *Podemos* substantially altered the Spanish political landscape, and, how the opportunity window opened by the 15M will probably have unexpected and long-lasting effects on Spanish society.

Acknowledgements

This work has been supported by the Ministry of Economy and Competitiveness of Spain, project "Sindicalismo y nuevos movimientos sociales en la construcción de la democracia: España, 1976–2012" (code HAR2012-38837).

References

Abellán, Jacobo, Jorge Sequera, and Michael Janoschka. 2012. "Occupying the #Hotel-madrid: A Laboratory for Urban Resistance". *Social Movements Studies: Journal of Social, Cultural and Political Protest* 3–4 (11): 320–326.

Aguilar, Susana, and Alberto Fernández. 2010. "El movimiento por la vivienda digna en España o el porqué de un fracaso de una protesta con una amplia base social". *Revista Internacional de Sociología* 68 (3): 679–704.

Alonso, Luis E. 2007. *La crisis de la ciudadanía laboral*. Barcelona: Anthropos.

Alonso, Luis E., Carlos J. Fernández, and Rafael Ibáñez. 2011. "Del consumismo a la culpabilidad: en torno a los efectos disciplinarios de la crisis económica". *Política y Sociedad* 48 (2): 353–379.

Alonso, Luis E., Carlos J. Fernández, and Rafael Ibáñez. 2016. "Entre la austeridad y el malestar: discursos sobre consumo y crisis económica en España". *Revista Española de Investigaciones Sociológicas* 155: 21–36.

Antón, Antonio. 2012. "Dificultades y perspectivas para el sindicalismo". *Inguruak* 51: 81–93.

Appadurai, Arjun. 1990. "Disjuncture and Difference in the Global Cultural Economy". *Theory, Culture and Society* 7: 295–310.

Beck, Ulrich. 1997. *Was is Globaliserung? Irrtümer des Globalismus – Antworten auf Globalisierung*. Francfort del Meno: Shurkamp Verlag.

Brown, David. 1999. "Are there Good and Bad Nationalisms?" *Nations and Nationalism* 5 (2): 281-302.

Campos Lima, Maria da Paz, and Antonio Martín Artiles. 2011. "Crisis and Trade Union Challenges in Portugal and Spain: Between General Strikes and Social Pacts". *Transfer* 17 (3): 387–402.

Candón, José. 2013. *Toma la calle, toma las redes. El movimiento 15M en internet.* Sevilla: Atrapasueños.

Cáritas. 2013. *De la coyuntura a la estructura: los efectos permanentes de la crisis. Documentación Social* 166. Madrid: Cáritas.

Castells, Manuel. 1997. *The Information Age: Economy, Society and Culture. Volume II: The Power of Identity*. Cambridge, MA: Blackwell Publishers.

Castells, Manuel. 2013. *Redes de indignación y esperanza*. Madrid: Alianza.

Colectivo IOÉ. 2012. "Más de 600.00 hogares han perdido su vivienda desde 2008". Barómetro Social de España http://barometrosocial.es/archivos/320.

Delgado, Manuel. 2011. "La Economía Andaluza durante las Tres Últimas Décadas: 1981–2011". In *Andalucía: identidades culturales y dinámicas sociales*, edited by Celeste Jiménez and José Hurtado. Sevilla: Aconcagua, 85–122.

Díaz-Parra, Ibán. 2014. "Acción social en la postmodernidad? Okupación y movimiento por la vivienda en Sevilla". *Anduli: Revista Andaluza de Ciencias Sociales* 12: 13–35.

Díaz-Parra, Ibán, and José Candón. 2014. "Espacio geográfico y ciberespacio en el movimiento 15M". *Scripta Nova* 470 (18).

Díaz-Parra, Ibán, and Jaime Jover. 2016. "Social Movements in Crisis? From the 15-M Movement to the Electoral Shift in Spain". *International Journal of Sociology and Social Policy* 9–10 (36): 680–694.

Díaz-Parra, Ibán, and Marta Solanas. 2015. "De aquel cemento estos lodos. Vivienda, desahucios y okupación en la crisis española". *Servicios Sociales y política social* 108 (32): 101–120.

Errejón, Iñigo. 2015. "We the people. El 15M: Un populismo indignado?" *ACME: An International E-Journal for Critical Geographies* 14 (1): 124–156.

Fernández Durán, Ramón. 2006. El Tsunami urbanizador español y mundial (versión ampliada) www.nodo50.org/ramonfd/tsunami_urbanizador.pdf (accessed 20 September 2017).

Fernández, Carlos J., Rafael Ibáñez, and Miguel Martínez Lucio. 2014. "Radical Trade Unionism in Spain: The Re-Invention and Re-Imagination of Autonomy and Democracy Within and Around the Union Movement During the Past Century". In *Radical Unions in Europe and the Future of Collective Interest Representation*, edited by Heather Connolly, Lefteris Kretsos, and Craig Phelan. Bern: Peter Lang.

Fundación FOESSA. 2014. VII Informe sobre Exclusión y Desarrollo Social en España www.foessa2014.es/informe/.

Gellner, Ernest. 1983. *Nations and Nationalism.* Oxford: Blackwell.

González Begega, Sergio, David Luque, and Ana Guillén. 2013. "Las organizaciones sindicales ante las políticas de ajuste del Estado del Bienestar: los casos de España y Portugal". Paper presented at the XI AECPA Congress.

Harvey, David. 1990. *The Conditions of Postmodernity: An Enquiry into the Origins of Cultural Change.* Malden, MA: Blackwell Pulishers.

Hechter, Michael, and Margaret Levi. 1979. "The Comparative Analysis of Ethnoregional Movements". *Ethnic and Racial Studies* 2 (3): 249–280.

Hyman, Richard. 2001. *Understanding European Trade Unionism Between Market, Class, and Society.* London: Sage.

Iglesias, Pablo. 2015. "Understanding Podemos". *New Left Review* 93: 7–22.

Ignatieff, Michael. 1998. *The Warrior's Honor. Ethnic War and the Modern Conscience.* NewYork: Henry Holt & Co.

Kaldor, M. 2004. Nationalism and Globalization. *Nations and Nationalism* 10: 161–177.

Köhler, Holm-Detlev, and Juan Pablo Calleja Jiménez. 2013. *Trade Unions in Spain. Organisation, Environment, Challenges.* Berlin: Friedrich-Ebert-Foundation.

Köhler, Holm-Detlev, Sergio González, and David Luque. 2013. "Sindicatos, crisis económica y repertorios de protesta en el sur de Europa". *Anuari del Conflicte Social* 2012: 1013–1052.

Luque, David, and Sergio González Begega. 2014. "Sindicatos contra gobiernos? Parálisis del intercambio político en el sur de Europa". Paper presented at CABISE Congress, Oviedo.

Maalouf, Amin. 1998. *Les identités meurtrières.* Paris: Éditions Grasset & Fasquelle.

Martinez, Miguel A., and Elena Domingo. 2014. "Social and political impacts of the 15M movement in Spain". Paper presented at XIX Conference *Alternative Futures and Popular Protest*, 14–16 April 2014. Manchester: Manchester Metropolitan University.

Moreno Pestaña, José Luis. 2013. "Democracia, movimientos sociales y participación popular. Lógicas democráticas y lógicas de distinción en las asambleas del 15M". In *Movimientos sociales, participación y ciudadanía en Andalucía*, edited by Agustín Coca and Javier Escalera. Sevilla: Aconcagua.

Nairn, Tom. 1977. *The Break-Up of Britain: Crisis and Neo-nationalism.* London: Verso.

Naredo, José Manuel. 2006. "Economía, poder y megaproyectos". Jornadas de Economía Crítica, Barcelon. March 2006.

Pastor, Jaime. 2012. "La emergencia del 15M en Madrid: un nuevo actor sociopolítico en escena". *Anuari del Conflicte 2011*: 175–190.

Público. 2014. "Intelectuales y activistas llaman a 'recuperar la soberanía popular' con una candidatura para las europeas". *Público*, 14 January 2014.

Redondo, Nicolás. 2015. "Renovarse o morir: el sindicalismo ante el futuro". *Claves* 238: 17–23.

Roca, Beltrán, and Ibán Díaz-Parra. 2017. "Blurring the Borders Between Old and New Social Movements: The M15 Movement and the Radical Unions in Spain". *Mediterranean Politics* 22 (2): 218–237.

Rodríguez López, Julio. 2005. "La vivienda en España. Los ciclos largos y las estadísticas". *El País*, 2 November 2005.

Romanos, Eduardo, and Igor Sádaba. 2015. "La evolución de los marcos (tecno) discursivos del movimiento 15M y sus consecuencias". *Empiria 32*: 15–36. doi: empiria. 32.2015.15307.

Sampedro, José Luis. 2009. *Economía humanista. Algo más que cifras.* Madrid: Debate.

Sassen, Saskia. 1991. *The Global City: New York, London, Tokio.* Princeton, NJ: Princeton University Press.

Smith, Anthony D. 1977. *Theories of Nationalism.* London: Duckworth.

4 Political opportunities, threats and opportunism

Examining SYRIZA's rise in crisis-ridden Greek politics

Kostas Kanellopoulos[1]

Introduction

Since the financial crash of 2008, the world system has entered a phase of severe and multi-levelled crisis (Harvey 2010; Rodrik 2011). Unlike the recent capitalist crises of the last two decades, this time the epicentre of the crisis was the advanced Western democracies (Reinhart and Rogoff 2009). Almost all Western economies went into recession, public debt grew and countless jobs were lost. Western governments reacted to the crisis at first by bailing out their financial sectors and then by imposing upon their population austerity measures and structural adjustment programmes in order to restart the economy. The latter is especially true for European countries. The political consequences of these policies soon played out on the electoral stage: incumbents in almost all European countries were punished in the elections (Beissinger and Sasse 2014; Kriesi 2014; Kousis and Kanellopoulos 2014). However, these shifts did not occur by themselves; in between, a series of mass anti-austerity protests erupted that destabilised the political alignments across Europe illustrating the significance of the interactions between protests and elections (McAdam and Tarrow 2010, 2013).

Greece, a Eurozone member, was one of the European countries most severely hit by the financial crisis. Due to its large deficit, Greece could not borrow money from the international markets to recapitalise its huge public debt and came dangerously close to bankruptcy. By that time the EU intervened, jointly with the IMF, and offered a rescue package to the Greek government. The EU, the ECB (European Central Bank) and the IMF formed a Troika that provided financial aid to Greece and as an exchange, the centre-left government of PASOK (Greek socialists) signed a "Memorandum of Understanding" agreeing on the structural adjustment reforms and the austerity measures that had to be imposed upon the economy and the Greek population. Analogous "Memoranda" soon followed for other EU countries.

In Greece as elsewhere, the "Memorandum" received fierce opposition from the beginning (in the spring of 2010). The main trade unions declared consecutive general strikes and the political parties and organisations of the left mobilised in mass protests to overthrow the agreement. The high frequency of protests that were synchronised at the national level, the high number of participants, the broad cross-class coalitions that involved a large number of challenging groups and the general public, made many scholars argue for the emergence of a sustained anti-austerity campaign in Greece (Kousis 2013; Diani and Kousis 2014; Kanellopoulos *et al.* 2017).

The continuous mobilisation of a significant part of the Greek population has not managed to stop austerity but it had a clear impact on the reshaping of the Greek political system (Kouvelakis 2011; Mavris 2012; Spourdalakis 2013, 2014; Kousis and Kanellopoulos 2014). PASOK and ND, who used to obtain jointly over 80 per cent of the popular vote and form self-reliant governments, jointly received around 30 per cent of the votes in the May 2012 elections and 42 per cent in the June 2012 elections, while a tiny and marginal neo-Nazist group secured over 6 per cent of the votes in both elections and gained parliamentary representation (Teperoglou and Tsatsanis 2014).

But the most impressive changes occurred on the Left side of the political spectrum: the, until then dominant, political force of the Greek Left, the Communist Party of Greece (KKE), was overshadowed by the tremendous rise of SYRIZA (Coalition of the radical Left) from 4.5 per cent of the votes in 2009 to 16 per cent in May 2012 and 27 per cent in June 2012. Consequently, in the January 2015 elections, SYRIZA rose to 36 per cent and became the biggest party in the Greek parliament. SYRIZA, then, chose to form a coalition government with the chauvinist far-right party of Independent Greeks (ANEL) on the basis of their common anti-Memorandum rhetoric. Soon after, an unfortunate negotiation period with the Troika, the SYRIZA/ANEL government capitulated to Troika's demands, agreed on a new "Memorandum" in order to receive another financial rescue package, and started imposing harsh austerity measures and selling off the remaining public enterprises and infrastructures of the country.

Certainly, the anti-austerity movement in general and SYRIZA in particular took advantage of the favourable structure of political opportunities created by the actual bankruptcy of the Greek economy and the tactical mistakes of the Greek ruling parties but, as previous research has argued, opportunities do not precede protest but are revealed by it (Goodwin 2012).

The findings of my research show that a large segment of the population in Greece was so outraged and shocked by the economic situation that they felt "...morally obliged to protest immediately, regardless of the chances for success and at times despite the high risks associated with some forms of protest" (Goodwin 2012, 293). The fact that Greece is, still, an advanced capitalist democracy and thus, relatively conducive to disruptive forms of contention, also provides a variety of mobilisation resources. But the analytical approach of political and economic opportunities and threats only partially explains questions like: Why did SYRIZA profit most from the Greek anti-austerity campaign and not the bigger (until 2012) and by far most organisationally powerful, KKE? Why did ANTARSYA (a coalition of the anti-capitalist left) that followed the same coalitional logic of SYRIZA and was even more active in the streets, not manage to grow in the polls and remain marginalised at the same time when, at the opposite side of the political spectrum, the equally and even more marginal (until 2012) Golden Dawn (an overtly neo-Nazist organisation) managed to become the third most powerful political party in Greece? Why did SYRIZA, a party of Eurocommunist provenance that was traditionally inhabited by left-wing intellectuals and academics, twice form a governmental coalition with a far-right party? And last but most important, how did SYRIZA manage to transform itself so rapidly and so smoothly into a pro-austerity party that imposes privatisations and neo-liberal policies?

To examine the above questions, a more strategic-interaction approach, that takes into account the actions of all the main actors, is needed and even more so, an elaborate conceptualisation of political opportunism in the cases, at least, of mass social and political protests. Thus, in the following sections I will first try to distinguish between political opportunities as they are used in the social movement literature and political opportunism as it appears and operates in politics, then I will present the interactions between the main actors in the Greek anti-austerity protest field and, finally, I will offer some findings from two research projects that: a) testify to the importance of the perception of threat in social movements, and b) support the argument for SYRIZA's opportunism in contrast with KKE's and ANTARSYA's more ideologically coherent stance.

Political opportunities and opportunism

The concept of political opportunities is widely contested in contemporary social movement literature (Meyer 2003; Meyer and Minkoff 2004; Goodwin and Jasper 1999, 2012). Many scholars use the concept to describe the broader political context within which a social movement is developed (Eisinger 1973; Kitschelt 1986; Kriesi 1995; Kriesi et al. 1995), while for others it also points out the specific political conjuncture or circumstance the movement faces that influences and shapes its trajectory (McAdam 1996; Tarrow 1996, 1998). Thus, political opportunities could be distinguished among the more structural and static ones and the more circumstantial and dynamic ones (Kriesi 2004). The former consist of evaluation of polity elements like the degree of openness in the political system, the degree of its separation of power, the degree of state centralisation, and the existence of long-lasting political cleavages (Kitschelt 1986). The latter consist of evaluation of elements like the stability or instability of that broad set of elite alignments that typically undergird a polity and the presence or absence of elite allies during a mobilisation (McAdam 1996). In short, some elements comprise the structural side of the concept while others the opportunity side.

But beyond the above distinctions, the concept of political opportunities has been criticised for its weak explanatory value. There are numerous cases of social movement emergence without the existence of any significant political opportunities or even more so, when the opportunity structure was negative for collective action (Kurzman 1996; Rasler 1996; Francisco 1996). On the other hand, there are also cases where opportunities were favourable but social movement actors did not take advantage of them (Sawyers and Meyer 1999). Other scholars criticise the overstretching of the concept (Gamson and Meyer 1996), and others its structural bias (Goodwin and Jasper 1999).

Trying to overcome the biases and discrepancies of the concept, many scholars have suggested turning our attention to how social movement activists frame, create, or attribute political opportunities (Gamson and Meyer 1996; Tarrow 1996; McAdam *et al.* 2001). Novel and more elaborate attention has been paid to the evaluation of political threats (Goldstone and Tilly 2001), while the concept of discursive opportunities has been introduced to discuss how activists interpret and seize opportunities (Giugni *et al.* 2005).

Finally, a recent trend in the literature suggests a more strategic approach to collective action by taking into consideration the interactions among all the players of the arena in a given contest (Jasper 2004, 2012; Jasper and Duyvendak 2015). However, what seems to be neglected in the literature is a conceptualisation of social movement goals and their interplay with political opportunities that would, also, allow for a better conceptualisation of the latter.

Social movements, as Tilly suggested long ago, are not single actors (Tilly 1985). This means that many different actors usually form a social movement, a protest campaign or even a single demonstration. Consequently, these different actors have different goals and, even more so, they use different means to pursue their goals. But, besides this inherent diversity of goals, a social movement and/ or a protest campaign in order to be held together and to be sustained is in need of a common goal that all interested parts agree, even as a least common denominator, that it is important. For instance, those who participated in and comprised the civil rights movement in the USA, beyond their many differences, had in common and agreed on the pursuit of granting civil rights. In our case, the least common denominator of the actors that form the anti-austerity campaign is precisely the fight against austerity policies and neo-liberalism (see also Peterson *et al.* 2015). And as a matter of fact, whole social movements and specific protest campaigns are usually named after this least common denominator.

On their part, political opportunities may be favourable, or not, during the emergence of a social movement and facilitate, or not, its evolution but this does not necessarily mean that they are also favourable and they will facilitate the achievement of a social movement's primary goal. In our two previous examples: civil rights for the black population in the southern States of the US were eventually granted but ceasing austerity policies and neo-liberal reforms in southern Europe has not yet occurred. In other words, social movements and protest campaigns may emerge, grow, and decay without actually succeeding in achieving their primary aims.

Of course some outcomes are always produced out of collective action and some actors that are part of a movement or a campaign may achieve some of their goals. It is important, thus, to study the strategic interaction of various movement actors in order to understand which actors manage to achieve which, and what sort of, goals.

In practice, major actors within a social movement or a protest campaign differ from other major actors precisely on the grounds of their different goals.

Also, these different actors face and come across different political opportunities and threats. Not all the actors of a movement or a campaign enjoy the same degree of access to the political system, attract the same allies, or face the same repression from state authorities. And as actors are differentiated by their goals, these different goals, in a way, attract, and are shaped by, different opportunities.

When some actors choose to pay attention mainly to the available and/or perceived opportunities regardless of any specific strategic goal, either because this goal does not exist or is not so specific, then, I argue, we are in front of the phenomenon of opportunism. The term is taken from the classic authors of Marxism and describes the situation when an actor prioritises tactics over strategic goals, and takes advantage of all available opportunities and means in order to achieve direct outcomes (Lenin 1902, 1918). However, most of the time, these direct outcomes are not compatible with any strategic goal.

The concept of opportunism is largely neglected in contemporary social movement literature. Goodwin (2012) has recently published a chapter with the revealing title "Are protestors opportunists? Fifty tests" where he comes to very fruitful conclusions regarding the uses and misuses of the concept of political opportunities but he does not discuss opportunism in its classic and political usage. The differentiation between the seizure of political opportunities and opportunism may prove useful in our quest to better understand the interplay between political opportunities/threats and goals since it touches upon exactly the cases when certain social movement actors seize the opportunity and achieve their goals but these goals are actually in sharp contrast with the goals of the movement.

Data sources and research methods

In order to conduct an organisational study of the Greek anti-austerity campaign, we first selected the most active organisations/groups that appeared in a previous protest event analysis (Kousis 2013), and then carried out new research based on the Social Network Analysis (SNA) method (Kanellopoulos 2015).[2] Our sample included 34 organisations/groups: 15 of them are trade unions and trade union factions and fronts, 14 of them are political organisations/parties,[3] and five of them are social movement organisations (SMOs). We distributed an extended questionnaire to core members of our sample organisations/groups asking not only questions about the other groups they collaborate with and whether they share resources, information, and so on, but also questions about claims-making and the perception of opportunities and threats. These questionnaires were distributed to randomly selected core members of the 34 organisations/groups before or after important organisational meetings or assemblies. The response rate was 42 per cent (114 out of 242). Additionally we conducted in-depth interviews with one representative from each of these 34 organisations/groups asking questions concerning tactics and strategy, the evaluation of the conflict and the stance towards alliance building.

For the purposes of this chapter, I am using the semi-structured interviews with core members of SYRIZA, KKE and ANTARSYA to understand the strategic interactions between them (see the next section) and two questions from the questionnaire – one about the self-placement of the respondents on the 1–9 left-right axis combined with another question to evaluate specific answers related to the structure of political opportunities and threats as it is typically used in the relevant literature (McAdam 1996; Goldstone and Tilly 2001).

Trying, then, to develop a more refined analysis of the tactics of our main actors, I make use of the Discursive Actor Attribution Analysis (DAAA) method.[4] This method is actually an instrument for the standardised measurement of the backbone of a controversial discourse.[5] DAAA is primarily designed for coding newspaper reporting, but can also be adapted to coding other material like other media reporting (TV or radio), press releases, programmatic papers, websites etc. (Roose *et al.* 2014). The actor attribution is the unit of analysis. In its simplified form, the actor attribution is the answer to the question: "Who makes whom publicly responsible for what?" It is the combination of an attribution sender (AS) stating the attribution, an attribution addressee (AA) to whom the attribution is directed, and the attribution issue (AI). These three parts are linked in the guiding question: "Who (AS) makes whom (AA) publicly responsible for what (AI)?" This trio forms the core of an actor attribution.

The DAAA method describes and explains systematically which actors interpret the situation in which way. The claims-making approach brings to light the actors who appear in reporting and analyses their views. This allows for a causal explanation based on the strategic action in specified structural positions.

The data for this chapter were derived from the systematic coding of five quality newspapers and articles from Reuters press agency. The total period covered was from 28 September 2009 to 30 September 2013. The selection of newspaper issues was based on artificially rotating weeks (for the 1st week we picked Monday, the 2nd Tuesday, the 3rd Wednesday, etc.). Our complete dataset included 11,809 attributions of responsibility. The analysis, here, is based on the data of 401 attributions, which have as origin attributions of responsibility initiated by SYRIZA, KKE, and ANTARSYA.

The interactions between opportunists and ideologists

The anti-austerity campaign and the changes in the Greek political system are inextricably linked. On the one hand, mass and sustained social and political protests contributed to re-alignments in the Greek political system while on the other hand, these protests were largely shaped by the active involvement of the political parties of the Left (Kanellopoulos *et al.* 2017; Kanellopoulos and Kousis 2017). The Greek case resembles analogous cases in Latin America when the local governments started imposing IMF-style policies (Almeida 2007). In Greece as in Latin America countries, the established political parties of the Left acted as social movement organisations – called for or actively supported strikes and demonstrations – and along with the trade unions of the public sector that

everywhere oppose privatisations, and counting on the anti-neo-liberal sentiments of the general public, managed to significantly alter the respective political systems (Almeida 2010).

In the Greek anti-austerity protest movement, two sets of actors were especially crucial: (a) the central trade unions GSEE (Confederation of Greek
workers) and ADEDY (Central union of civil servants) and (b) the political
parties/organisations of the Left either those with parliamentary representation
(KKE and SYRIZA) or those without (ANTARSYA and some smaller groups).

GSEE and ADEDY called numerous general strikes against the consecutive
austerity and neo-liberal reform packages that were voted on in the parliament.
The big demonstrations around these strikes were actually the backbone of the
protest campaign throughout the 2010–2014 period. After SYRIZA/ANEL's
compromise in 2015, GSEE/ADEDY called for and organised again strike demonstrations but, except for some top trade union officials, very few people
marched under their banners.

The central trade unions as parts and pieces of the dominant system of political and social representation and mainly controlled by PASOK were not trusted
by the workers or the Left factions in the unions (Vogiazoglou 2014). GSEE and
ADEDY, out of structural necessity, had to protest against measures and reforms
that worsen labour relations and dramatically affect the well-being of most
workers but their tactic was mainly to press for softer measures, and wait until
the anticipated crisis ended, in order to negotiate for better wages and working
conditions out of the much-expected economic growth.

In contrast to GSEE/ADEDY moderation, the tactics adopted by the political
parties/organisations of the Left and by many rank and file trade unionists were
more confrontational and far more challenging for the established political system.

SYRIZA was formed before the elections of 2004 as a coalition of the rather
moderate-Left parliamentary party of SYNASPISMOS (a pre-existing coalition
of the remnants of the Euro-Communist party with a faction stemming from
KKE and some ecologists) and some tiny extra-parliamentary groups with Trotskyite and Maoist tendencies. The new coalition had low mobilisation capacity
and very limited influence on trade unionism but its rank and file were very
active in almost all the social and political protests after 2004. In the anti-
austerity campaign, SYRIZA participated in GSEE/ADEDY demonstrations
while criticising the leadership of the trade unions. Also, the leadership of
SYRIZA and the party members enthusiastically embraced the short-lived but
massive *Indignados* protests that erupted all over Greece in June 2011. The
declared tactic of SYRIZA since the beginning of the crisis was that of "unity in
action" and open calls for cooperation with all "anti-Memorandum" forces with
the goal of forming a government of "national and social salvation".[6] In using
the conceptualisation of *modes of coordination* proposed by Diani (2015), we
could argue that SYRIZA was mainly acting on the grounds of the *coalitional
mode of coordination*, which is promoted by units where alliance-building is
instrumental to them and which assign limited importance to longer-term goals
and broader values (see Kanellopoulos *et al.* 2017).

KKE traditionally enjoyed a broader membership than SYNASPISMOS and later, SYRIZA, as well as much broader mobilisation capacity. It also controlled many trade unions and its influence in the organised labour movement was significant (Bithymitris 2010). KKE participated in all the anti-austerity protests except for those initiated by the *Indignados* since the party considered them apolitical and quasi-nationalist. And most importantly, KKE members and trade unions marched in most demonstrations separately and at a safe distance from the rest of the participants. The party adopted a clearly demonstrated tactic of "class unity" that serves the strategic goal of overthrowing capitalism and transforming the relations of production. In doing so, KKE usually operated under the organisational mode of coordination, which assigns limited importance to cooperation and alliances and more attention to the preservation of the party's autonomous decision-making capacity (Kanellopoulos *et al.* 2017). The communist ideology is central in KKE, while many see the party's tactics as sectarian and vanguardist (e.g. Spourdalakis 2014, 355).

ANTARSYA is itself a coalition of ten different extra-parliamentary political organisations that was formed in 2009. Its members and supporters actively participated in all anti-austerity protests, including those initiated by the *indignados*. ANTARSYA employs an anti-capitalist ideology, is more prone to alliance-building and accuses KKE of sectarianism. During the anti-austerity campaign of 2010–2014 ANTARSYA was, in practice, "united in action" with SYRIZA but never agreed to form a political alliance together.

Throughout the anti-austerity campaign, SYRIZA's tactics were in close interaction with those of KKE and ANTARSYA. On the one hand, SYRIZA was continually asking the other political forces of the Greek Left to form a united front in order to confront PASOK and ND in the polls. According to SYRIZA's analysis, PASOK and ND were corrupt and responsible for Greece's bankruptcy. Furthermore, the "Memoranda" with the Troika were not the results of the economic crisis but the causes of the crisis. The "Memoranda" were the results of PASOK's and ND's inability and unwillingness to negotiate properly with the Troika that destroyed the Greek economy. SYRIZA wanted to form a government of the left to overthrow the "Memoranda" regime, cancel Greece's debt and impose Keynesian policies to restart the economy without, at the same time, putting at risk the participation of Greece in the EU and the Eurozone.

On the other hand, KKE and ANTARSYA were rejecting SYRIZA's calls and offers as unreliable and illusionary. According to them, Greece's exit from the Eurozone, the EU and NATO are preconditions for the country's social transformation towards socialism and thus, preconditions for any viable political and social alliance. Also, for KKE and ANTARSYA the Greek crisis and the subsequent "Memoranda" were the results of the global capitalist crisis of 2008 and the only possible way to overcome the crisis is to have a clear anti-capitalist strategy.

SYRIZA's proposals offered the protest movement a political dynamic and a shortcut to favourable outcomes – namely the seizure of political power. The anti-austerity movement would achieve its goals when SYRIZA would take office and fulfil its promise to tear up the Memoranda of Understanding with the Troika and, as a government of the Left, alter the austerity policies. This tactic proved very effective indeed for SYRIZA since the electoral power of the party rose enormously in the elections of May 2012, June 2012 and January 2015 and SYRIZA almost quadrupled its membership. SYRIZA's success pressured KKE and ANTARSYA. As a matter of fact, in between the elections of May 2012 and June 2012, both parties lost nearly half their voters to SYRIZA (Mavris 2012; Tsakatika and Eleftheriou 2013).

However, electoral success in the elections for the parliament was never a primary goal for KKE and ANTARSYA. Thus, both parties rejected SYRIZA's calls for unity and continued to participate on the same side with SYRIZA at the same social and political protests. This situation, of course, changed after SYRIZA's capitulation to Troika in the summer of 2015. Since then, KKE, ANTARSYA, LAE (a major left split of SYRIZA in the summer of 2015), the trade unions and some new actors in the protest social field, like the farmers and the associations of self-employed, forcefully opposed SYRIZA-led austerity policies in the streets.

Perceptions of threats, opportunity availability, and attributions of responsibility in the Greek anti-austerity campaign

According to McAdam's classification, the key dimensions of political opportunity (McAdam 1996, 27) are (1) the relative openness or closure of the institutionalised political system, (2) the stability or instability of that broad set of elite alignments that typically undergird a polity, (3) the presence or absence of elite allies, and (4) the state's capacity and propensity for repression.

If we take into account the above classification, the Greek anti-austerity campaign represents a case where all opportunity features were favourable: (1) Greece has an open access democratic political system where social and political protests are not only frequent and allowed but also have managed to influence policymaking many times in the recent past (see Lountos 2012; Hamann *et al.* 2013); (2) since the eruption of the Greek debt crisis, major elite realignments occurred, business interests were fighting each other and the ruling political parties were divided about the decision to sign or not a Memorandum with the Troika;[7] (3) parliamentary parties like KKE and SYRIZA, and to a lesser extent ND, along with the powerful trade union confederation of GSEE and ADEDY, acted as powerful elite allies of the anti-austerity campaign; and (4) the Greek state's capacity for repression is high but given the democratic institutional design and the high volume of the mobilisations besides, the state's propensity for repression has remained at rather low standards.

But, the major actors inside the anti-austerity campaign seem to have not perceived as favourable the structure of political opportunity. In our research concerning the organisations/groups that called and coordinated the campaign, we asked core members to evaluate by answering yes or no to which of the following hypotheses they agreed: (H1) we can take advantage of the institutions of political representations in order for our claims to be heard; (H2) the division of Greek economic and political elites provides an opportunity for action; (H3) in the present circumstances we can take advantage of the presence of powerful elite allies; (H4) the Greek state's capacity/propensity for repression is not high; (H5) besides the repression, if we do not mobilise our life will become worse; (H6) none of the above.

The results are striking. Experienced activists seem to pay very little attention to both structural and circumstanced opportunities. In contrast, they take into serious consideration the existing political threats. They acknowledge the state's high capacity/propensity for repression but they decide to mobilise because the cost for their lives if they do not will be larger. In other words the exogenous shock of the financial collapse and the subsequent harsh austerity measures imposed on Greek society appear to be the sole sufficient conditions for mobilising (see Table 4.1).

The above assumption is especially true for those who position themselves to the Left side of the political spectrum. As we can see in Table 4.2, the Greek anti-austerity campaign was mainly formed and shaped by leftists who perceived austerity as a major threat.

Table 4.1 Perception of opportunities and threats

Type of opportunity/threat	Frequency (N = 114)	Valid per cent
H1: Access to the system	18	15.8
H2: Elite division	15	13.2
H3: Existence of allies	4	3.5
H4: Declining repression	9	7.9
H5: Cost of inaction bigger than cost of repression	100	87.7
H6: None of the above	5	4.4

Source: Independent project "Social movement networks in Greece".

Table 4.2 Left–right positioning and perception of the cost of inaction

		Left–right axis 1–9						Total
		0	*1*	*2*	*3*	*4*	*6*[1]	
H.5	0	4	5	2	2	0	1	14
	1	18	55	24	2	1	0	100
Total		22	60	26	4	1	1	114

Source: Independent project "Social movement networks in Greece".

Note
1 The 1–9 left-right axis goes only up to 6 because there were no responses for positions 7–9. Position 0 is for those who refused to place themselves to the 1–9 axis.

Another statistically significant finding is that for those few who see an opportunity in the open access to the political system, there is again a strong correlation with their leftist self-positioning (see Table 4.3).

Since most of the core activists of the anti-austerity campaign are members of political parties on the left, they are also participating in the political system. As party members they want to increase the power of their party within the political system and, thus, take advantage of the available political institutions and means. But the available opportunities are not the same for all the parties.

In the GGCRISI project, we found 401 attributions of responsibility were raised by SYRIZA, KKE and ANTARSYA. Of these, 76 per cent were raised from SYRIZA, 21 per cent from KKE and only 3 per cent from ANTARSYA (see Figure 4.1).

These findings testify to the differences in the available discursive opportunities for the different actors. Although SYRIZA, until 2012, was a smaller party than KKE, it enjoyed far more visibility and its public speech was widely reproduced in the press. SYRIZA, in contrast to KKE and ANTARSYA, was an

Table 4.3 Left–right positioning and perception of open access to the political system

		Left–right axis 1–9						Total
		0	*1*	*2*	*3*	*4*	*6*[1]	
H1	0	21	53	21	0	1	0	96
	1	1	7	5	4	0	1	18
Total		22	60	26	4	1	1	114

Source: Independent project "Social movement networks in Greece".

Note
1 The 1–9 left-right axis goes only up to 6 because there were no responses for positions 7–9. Position 0 is for those who refused to place themselves to the 1–9 axis.

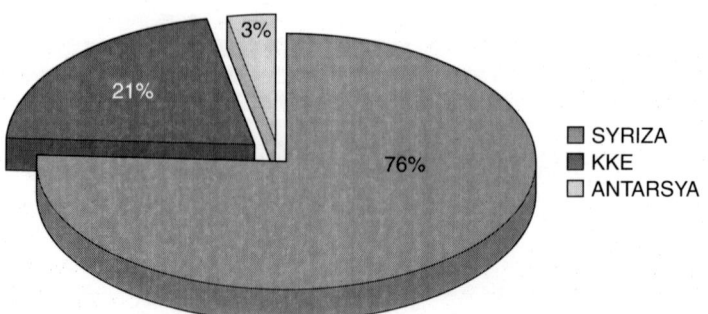

Figure 4.1 Attributions of responsibility per political party.

Source: "The Greeks, the Germans and the Crisis" project (www.ggcrisi.org).

accepted partner in the polity and the party's voice concerning the Eurozone crisis, which drew a lot of attention.

SYRIZA's more favourable position in the Greek political system is also exemplified by the choices of attribution addressees the party is making. In Figure 4.2, we depict the main actors SYRIZA chooses to address. First of all, SYRIZA is "talking" (either by blaming or by demanding) to the Greek government/the Greek ruling parties (69 per cent). Then, EU/Troika is addressed 15 per cent of the time followed by the attributions addressed to SYRIZA's interior (7 per cent). The Greek people/workers/protesters are addressed 6 per cent of the time while the corporations/rich only 2 per cent of the time.

This picture is different in KKE's preferences in attributing responsibility. There, the Greek government/ruling parties are addressed 60 per cent of the time but the second most important addressee is the Greek people/workers/protesters (22 per cent) where KKE calls them to action. Fifteen per cent of the time KKE is talking to EU/Troika and 2 per cent of the time to SYRIZA, answering the calls for cooperation.

Half of ANTARSYA's attributions are addressed to the Greek government/ruling parties, 36 per cent of the time ANTARSYA is addressing (mainly by blaming) the EU/Troika, and 14 per cent of the time it is addressing the corporations/rich.

The choice of addressees is important because it reveals with whom the attribution sender wants to interact. The engagement of all anti-austerity actors with the government is of course expected and normal. But it is SYRIZA that is clearly more oriented to the political system while KKE appears to be more prone to the Greek people/workers confirming its close relation with the trade unions and the Greek working class (see Figure 4.3). ANTARSYA, which certainly enjoys far less visibility than the others and its sample is very small, appears to pay particular attention to distanced pillars of the capitalist system like the EU/Troika and the corporation/rich (see Figure 4.4).

Equally important for our attempt to discern the tactics of each political party that has actively participated in the anti-austerity campaign are the attribution

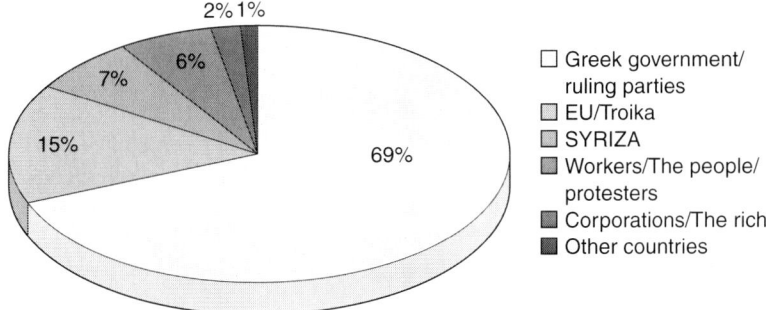

Figure 4.2 SYRIZA addressees.

Source: "The Greeks, the Germans and the Crisis" project (www.ggcrisi.org).

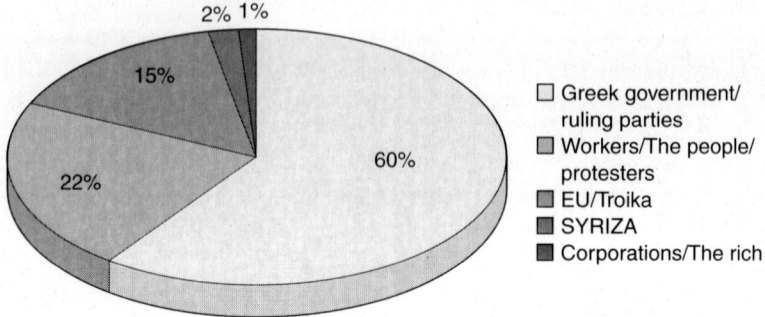

Figure 4.3 KKE addressees.

Source: "The Greeks, the Germans and the Crisis" project (www.ggcrisi.org).

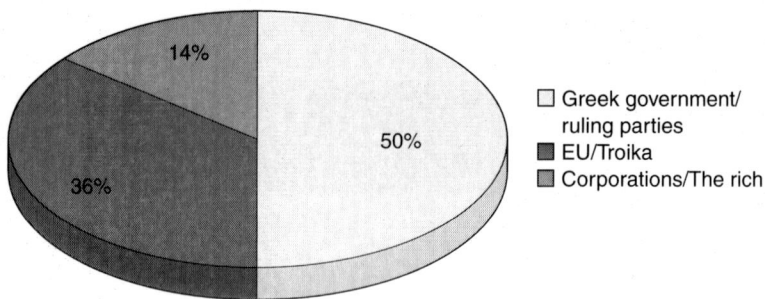

Figure 4.4 ANTARSYA addressees.

Source: "The Greeks, the Germans and the Crisis" project (www.ggcrisi.org).

issues. The attribution issue is at the core of the attribution of responsibility. The definition of the issue is largely dependent on the sender's perspective in the form in which it is reported. Moreover, the specific issues around which each actor decides to intervene in the public phere are characteristic for each actor's political priorities and concerns.

In our sample here, SYRIZA is primarily concerned with "political decisions/ negotiations" (18 per cent) and then deals with "economic policy"[8] (15 per cent) and "Eurozone crisis management/memoranda" (11 per cent). Labour market policy issues are also important in SYRIZA's discourse (10 per cent) followed by "socio-political behaviour"[9] (9 per cent). SYRIZA also discusses "debt refinancing" (5 per cent), calls upon other countries for solidarity (5 per cent), talks about "burden distribution" among classes (2 per cent), national sovereignty (2 per cent), "democracy" (2 per cent) and demands elections (2 per cent) (see Figure 4.5).

On the other hand, KKE (see Figure 4.6) is primarily dealing with the "Eurozone crisis management/memoranda" (23 per cent) and then deals with

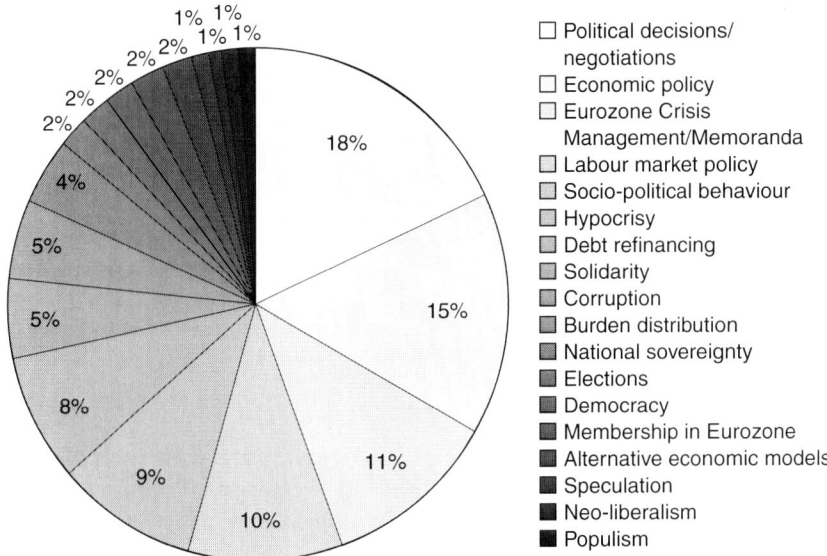

Figure 4.5 SYRIZA issues.

Source: "The Greeks, the Germans and the Crisis" project (www.ggcrisi.org).

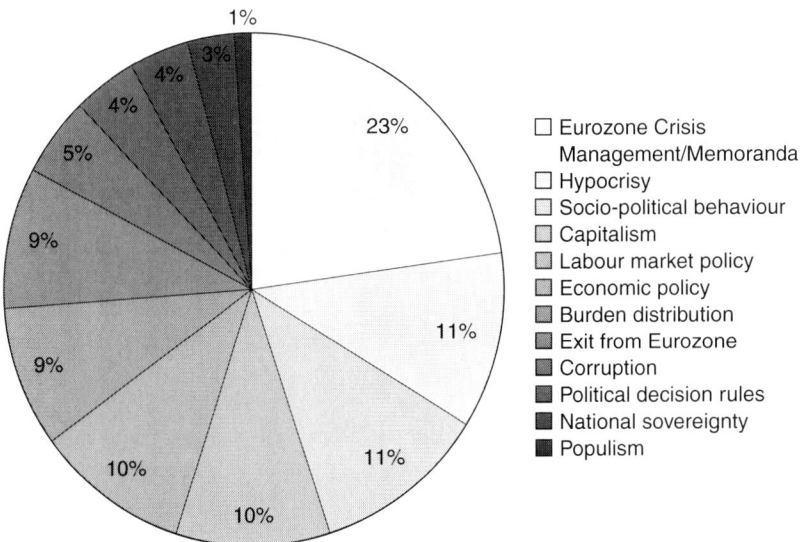

Figure 4.6 KKE issues.

Source: "The Greeks, the Germans and the Crisis" project (www.ggcrisi.org).

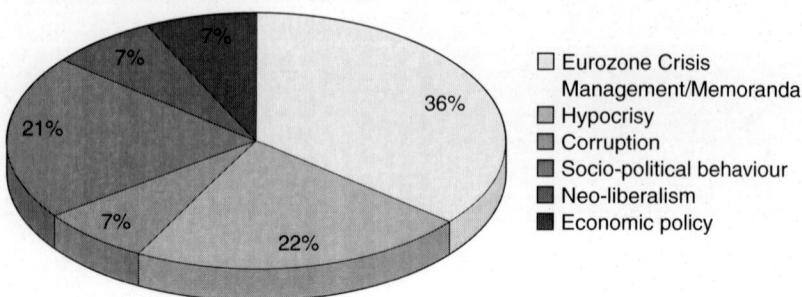

Figure 4.7 ANTARSYA issues.

Source: "The Greeks, the Germans and the Crisis" project (www.ggcrisi.org).

"socio-political behaviour" (11 per cent) and "labour market policy" issues (10 per cent). In KKE's discourse, "capitalism" (10 per cent) and "burden distribution" among classes (9 per cent) are important, while the party also discusses "economic policy" (9 per cent), political decisions/negotiations (4 per cent) and "national sovereignty" (3 per cent).

ANTARSYA (Figure 4.7), like KKE, appears to discuss more about "Eurozone crisis management/memoranda" (37 per cent) and "socio-political behaviour" (21 per cent). ANTARSYA is also very concerned with the issues of "hypocrisy" (21 per cent) and "corruption" (7 per cent).

Our data reveal a high concern among all Left parties in Greece for this last set of moral issues. SYRIZA and KKE also talk extensively about "hypocrisy" (8 per cent and 11 per cent respectively) and "corruption" (4 per cent for both parties). But the commonalities in their discourse stop there.

KKE is framing the crisis on more ideological terms, pointing to a systemic change while SYRIZA seems to seek solutions within the system by focusing on political decisions, rules and negotiations.

Concluding remarks

The collapse of the Greek economy in 2010 posed an exogenous shock to Greek society. Greece lost one-fifth of its GDP in less than five years, unemployment rose to an EU record of 27.5 per cent, poverty and social exclusion rates also hit record numbers. The old political system of the country also collapsed, since trust in national and EU political institutions had hit zero. Conditions were favourable for collective action to defend labour rights and fight against austerity measures. An impressive anti-austerity protest movement indeed emerged and accelerated the changes in the political system.

The structure of political opportunity was, in many aspects, favourable but, as our research reveals, it was the perception of threat posed by austerity for the well-being of numerous people that actually sparked and sustained the anti-austerity mobilisation. When, in January 2015, SYRIZA (one of the main initiators and champions of the anti-austerity protest movement) rose to power, many believed that austerity policies would stop and the era of "Memoranda" would end.

SYRIZA managed to gain the most out of the protest movement because on the one hand more and "better" political opportunities were available to SYRIZA compared with those for the other players in the arena and because on the other hand, SYRIZA's tactic was essentially oriented towards the seizure of available political opportunities, regardless of whether or not this tactic would lead to the achievement of the protest movement goals. SYRIZA as a coalition (until 2013) was inherently prone to political unity and not an ideological one. Tactics were prioritised over strategy and especially after the economic collapse of 2010 the occupation of political power (through the parliamentary route) became a self-evident goal, although without any serious reference to more strategic principles and aims. Therefore, SYRIZA's opportunism is, by and large, responsible for both its electoral success and its subsequent failure to fulfil its promises as a government.

In 2015, after a dramatic sequel of negotiations, tactical and communicative manoeuvres, for instance, the July 2015 referendum (Tsatsanis and Teperoglou 2016), SYRIZA finally capitulated to Troika's demands, signed a new Memorandum and started enforcing new harsh austerity measures and neo-liberal reforms upon an already devastated economy and an impoverished population (Kouvelakis 2016). The party split and the anti-austerity campaign started over again in late 2015 with SYRIZA's government this time the target of the protests (Kanellopoulos and Kousis 2017).

SYRIZA's rise sparked a heated and highly politicised debate among scholars of Greek politics. Scholars that oppose SYRIZA attribute both its rise and its pro-austerity transformation to populism (Pappas and Aslanidis 2015; Aslanidis and Rovira Kaltwasser 2016) and even characterise the whole anti-austerity protest campaign as a "populist social movement" (Andronikidou and Kovras 2012; Aslanidis 2016). On the other hand, scholars of left-wing populism reply by reminding of Laclau's (1977, 2005) usage of the term that in mass democracies all parties should try to address the "people" in order to be successful in the elections (Stavrakakis and Katsambekis 2014). According to this logic, SYRIZA's success was due to its ability to address the people and seize the available political opportunities.

As a matter of fact, and seen from a contentious political perspective, political opportunities, and especially political and economic threats, were crucial for the emergence and the evolution of the massive anti-austerity protests and eventually to the collapse of the old political system but as this chapter has tried to show, opportunism, or in other words the unconditional seizure of opportunities, does not necessarily lead to the achievement of the anti-austerity campaign's goals.

Notes

1 Dr. Kostas Kanellopoulos is a Researcher at the University of Crete. Please address all correspondence to konkanel8@gmail.com.
2 The organisational study of the Greek anti-austerity campaign was conducted as independent research by Kostas Kanellopoulos, Konstantinos Kostopoulos, Dimitris Papanikolopoulos and Vasilis Rongas in 2013. However, the analysis and the arguments in this chapter here reflect only the author's view.
3 Out of these 14 political organisations/groups, five are part of SYRIZA (SYNASPIS-MOS, its youth organisation and three more groups), five are part of ANTARSYA, two are part of KKE (the main party and its youth organisation) and two more groups do not belong to any of the previous political formations. We have studied all these organisations/groups independently because: (a) typically they are autonomous organisations, and (b) we wanted to examine their differences towards alliance-building.
4 Data for this part of the chapter stems from the research project "The Greeks, the Germans and the Crisis", a joint Greek German project, funded by the General Secretariat for Research and Technology (GSRT) of the Ministry of Education and Religious Affairs, Culture and Sports of Greece and the German Federal Ministry for Education and Research (BMBF). The project mainly analyses the contentious debate in the Eurozone crisis with a special focus in Greece and Germany that one might plausibly expect to represent the two extremes in the debate. The project was co-coordinated by Jochen Roose (for Germany) and Maria Kousis (for Greece) and conducted by two groups of researchers, one at Freie Universität Berlin and one at the University of Crete. We gratefully acknowledge Martin Wettstein's (University Zürich) very helpful coding tool "angrist" which has facilitated the coding process.
5 In the project, we follow Koopmans and Statham in defining an instance of political claims making as

> a unit of strategic action in the public sphere that consists of the purposive and public articulation of political demands, calls to action, proposals, criticism, or physical attack, which actually or potentially affect the interests or integrity of the claimants and/or other collective actors.
> (Koopmans and Statham 1999, 206; Koopmans *et al.* 2005, 24)

6 The goal of "national and social salvation" was set by the leader of SYRIZA in his inaugural speech as Prime Minister on 26 January 2015.
7 The main oppositional party in 2010, the conservative New Democracy (ND), opposed the "Memorandum" and asked for a structural adjustment programme without austerity measures. When ND made a spectacular policy turn in early 2012 by forming a coalition government with PASOK and voting in parliament for a second Memorandum, the party split and as a result, in the elections of May 2012, ND achieved the lowest result of its history. ANEL was the party that emerged out of ND's split in 2012.
8 "Economic policy" in the GGCRISI codebook refers to some more specific issues like taxation, trade regulation, competition policy, privatisations etc., while "Eurozone crisis management/memoranda" refers to the specific interventions and Troika mechanisms like the EMS/EFSF and direct reference to Memorandum content.
9 "Socio-political behaviour" issues mainly refer to protests/contention/resistance or to attitudes like frustration/passivity and political awareness.

References

Almeida, Paul. 2007. "Defensive Mobilization: Popular Movements against Economic Adjustment Policies in Latin America". *Latin American Perspectives* 34 (3): 123–139.

Almeida, Paul. 2010. "Social Movement Partyism: Collective Action and Oppositional Political Parties". In *Strategic Alliances: Coalition Building and Social Movements*, edited by N. Van Dyke and H. McCammon, 170–196. Minneapolis, MN: University of Minnesota Press.

Andronikidou, Aikaterini, and Iosif Kovras. 2012. "Cultures of Rioting and Anti-Systemic Politics in Southern Europe". *West European Politics* 35 (4): 707–725.

Aslanidis, Paris. 2016. "Populist Social Movements of the Great Recession". *Mobilization* 21 (3): 301–322.

Aslanidis, Paris, and Cristóbal Rovira Kaltwasser. 2016. "Dealing with Populists in Government: The SYRIZA-ANEL Coalition in Greece". *Democratization*, DOI: 10.1080/13510347.2016.1154842.

Beissinger, Mark, and Gwendolyn Sasse. 2014. "An End to 'Patience'? The Great Recession and Economic Protest in Eastern Europe". In *Mass Politics in Tough Times: Opinions, Votes, and Protest in the Great Recession*, edited by N. Bermeo and L. Bartels, 334–370. Oxford: Oxford University Press.

Bithymitris, Giorgos. 2010. "Greek Trade Union Movement Strategies in the Context of European Integration: The Case of Metal Sector". Unpublished doctoral dissertation, Social Policy Department, Panteion University of Social and Political Sciences, Athens.

Diani, Mario. 2015. *The Cement of Civil Society*. New York: Cambridge University Press.

Diani, Mario, and Maria Kousis. 2014. "The Duality of Claims and Events: The Greek Campaign Against Troikas's Memoranda and Austerity, 2010–2012". *Mobilization* 19 (4): 387–404.

Eisinger, Peter. 1973. "The Conditions of Protest Behavior in American Cities". *American Political Science Review* 67 (1): 11–28.

Francisco, Ronald. 1996. "Coercion and Protest: An Empirical Test in Two Democratic States". *American Journal of Political Science* 40 (4): 1179–204.

Gamson, William, and David Meyer. 1996. "Framing Political Opportunity". In *Comparative Perspectives on Social Movements: Political Opportunities, Mobilizing Structures and Cultural Framings*, edited by D. McAdam, J. McCarthy and M. Zald. Cambridge: Cambridge University Press.

Giugni, Marco, Ruud Koopmans, Florence Passy, and Paul Statham 2005. "Institutional and Discursive Opportunities for Extreme-Right Mobilization in Five Countries". *Mobilization* 10 (1): 145–162.

Goldstone, Jack, and Charles Tilly. 2001. "Threat (and Opportunity): Popular Action and State Response in the Dynamics of Contentious Action". In *Silence and Voice in the Study of Contentious Politics*, edited by R. Aminzade, J. Goldstone, D. McAdam, E. Perry, W. Sewell, S. Tarrow and C. Tilly, 179–194. Cambridge: Cambridge University Press.

Goodwin, Jeff. 2012. "Conclusion: Are Protestors Opportunists? Fifty Tests". In *Contention in Context: Political Opportunities and the Emergence of Protest*, edited by Jeff Goodwin and James Jasper, 277–300. Stanford, CA: Stanford University Press.

Goodwin, Jeff, and James Jasper. 1999. "Caught in a Winding, Snarling Vine: The Structural Bias of Political Process Theory". *Sociological Forum* 14 (1): 27–54.

Hamann, Kerstin, Alison Johnston, and John Kelly. 2013. "Unions Against Governments: Explaining General Strikes in Western Europe 1980–2006". *Comparative Political Studies* 46 (9): 1030–1057.

Harvey, David. 2010. *The Enigma of Capital*. Oxford and New York: Oxford University Press.

Jasper, James. 2004. "A Strategic Approach to Collective Action". *Mobilization* 9 (1): 1–16.

Jasper, James. 2012. "Introduction: From Political Opportunity Structures to Strategic Interaction". In *Contention in Context: Political Opportunities and the Emergence of Protest*, edited by J. Goodwin and J. Jasper, 1–33. Stanford, CA: Stanford University Press.

Jasper, James, and Jan Willem Duyvendak, eds. 2015. *Players and Arenas: The Interactive Dynamics of Protest*. Amsterdam: Amsterdam University Press.

Kanellopoulos, Kostas. 2015. "Social Movement Networks and Contentious Politics in Greece During the Economic Crisis: Theoretical Issues and Research Practices". *Greek Sociological Review* 2–3: 97–118.

Kanellopoulos, Kostas, and Maria Kousis. 2017. "Protest, Elections and Austerity Politics in Greece". In *Living under Austerity: Greek Society in Crisis*, edited by A. Placas and E. Doxiadis. New York and Oxford: Berghahn.

Kanellopoulos, Kostas, Konstantinos Kostopoulos, Dimitris Papanikolopoulos and Vasileios Rongas. 2017. "Competing Modes of Coordination in the Greek Anti-Austerity Campaign 2010–2012". *Social Movement Studies* 16 (1): 101–118.

Kitschelt, Herbert. 1986. "Political Opportunity Structures and Political Protest: Anti-Nuclear Movements in Four Democracies". *British Journal of Political Science* 16 (1): 57–85.

Koopmans, Ruud, and Paul Statham. 1999. "Political Claims Analysis: Integrating Protest Event and Political Discourse Approaches". *Mobilization* 4 (2): 203–222.

Koopmans, Ruud, Paul Statham, Marco Giugni, and Florence Passy. 2005. *Contested Citizenship: Immigration and Cultural Diversity in Europe*. Minneapolis, MN: University of Minnesota Press.

Kousis, Maria. 2013. "The Nationwide (all-Greek) Campaign Against Memoranda and Austerity Policies". *Greek Sociological Review* 1: 33–41.

Kousis, Maria, and Kostas Kanellopoulos. 2014. "Impacts of the Greek Crisis on the Contentious and Conventional Politics, 2012–2012". In *The Social Impacts of the Eurozone Debt Crisis*, edited by G. Tsobanoglou and N. Petropoulos, 443–462. Athens: Gordios Books.

Kouvelakis, Stathis. 2011. "The Greek Cauldron". *New Left Review* 72: 17–32.

Kouvelakis, Stathis. 2016. "SYRIZA's Rise and Fall". *New Left Review* 97: 45–70.

Kriesi, Hanspeter. 1995. "The Political Opportunity Structure of New Social Movements: Its Impact on Their Mobilization". In *The Politics of Social Protest. Comparative Perspectives on States and Social Movements*, edited by J. Craig Jenkins and Bert Klandermans. Minneapolis, MN: University of Minnesota Press.

Kriesi, Hanspeter. 2004. "Political Context and Opportunity". In *The Blackwell Companion to Social Movements*, edited by D. Snow, S. Soule and H. Kriesi. Oxford: Blackwell.

Kriesi, Hanspeter. 2014. "The Political Consequences of the Economic Crisis in Europe: Electoral Punishment and Popular Protest". In *Mass Politics in Tough Times: Opinions, Votes, and Protest in the Great Recession*, edited by N. Bermeo and L. Bartels, 297–333. Oxford: Oxford University Press.

Kriesi, Hanspeter, Ruud Koopmans, Jan Willem Duyvenda, and Marco Giugni. 1995. *New Social Movements in Western Europe: A Comparative Analysis*. Minneapolis, MN: University of Minnesota Press.

Kurzman, Charles. 1996. "Structural Opportunity and Perceived Opportunity in Social-Movement Theory: The Iranian Revolution of 1979". *American Sociological Review* 61 (1): 153–170.

Laclau, Ernesto. 1977. *Politics and Ideology in Marxist Theory: Capitalism, Fascism, Populism*. London: New Left Books.

Laclau, Ernesto. 2005. *The Populist Reason*. London: Verso.

Lenin, Vladimir I. (1902) 2008. *What is to be Done?* Athens: Sychroni Epohi.

Lenin, Vladimir I. (1918) 1996. *State and Revolution*. Athens: Sychroni Epohi.

Lountos, Nikos. 2012. "Radical Minorities, a Decade of Contention and the Greek December 2008". In *Violent Protest, Contentious Politics, and the Neoliberal State*, edited by S. Seferiades and H. Johnston, 183–191. Surrey: Ashgate.

Mavris, Yiannis. 2012. "Greece's Austerity Election". *New Left Review* 76: 95–107.

McAdam, Doug. 1996. "Conceptual Origins, Current Problems, Future Directions". In *Comparative Perspectives on Social Movements: Political Opportunities, Mobilizing Structures and Cultural Framings*, edited by D. McAdam, J. McCarthy and M. Zald. Cambridge: Cambridge University Press.

McAdam, Doug, and Sidney Tarrow. 2010. "Ballots and Barricades: On the Reciprocal Relations Between Elections and Social Movements". *Perspectives on Politics* 8 (2): 529–542.

McAdam, Doug, and Sidney Tarrow. 2013. "Social Movements and Elections: Toward a Broader Understanding of the Political Context of Contention". In *The Future of Social Movement Research*, edited by J. Stekelenburg, C. Roggerband and B. Klandermans, 325–346. Minneapolis, MN: University of Minnesota Press.

McAdam, Doug, Sidney Tarrow, and Charles Tilly. 2001. *Dynamics of Contention*. Cambridge: Cambridge University Press.

Meyer, David. 2003. "Political Opportunity and Nested Institutions". *Social Movement Studies* 2 (1): 17–35.

Meyer, David, and Debra Minkoff. 2004. "Conceptualizing Political Opportunity". *Social Forces* 82 (4): 1457–1492.

Pappas, Takis, and Paris Aslanidis. 2015. "Greek Populism: A Political Drama in Five Acts". In *European Populism in the Shadow of the Great Recession*, edited by Hanspeter Kriesi and Takis S. Pappas, 181–196. Colchester: ECPR Press.

Peterson, Abby, Mattias Wahlström, and Magnus Wennerhag. 2015. "European Anti-Austerity Protests – Beyond 'old' and 'new' social movements?" *Acta Sociologica* 58 (4): 293–310.

Rasler, Karen. 1996. "Concessions, Repression, and Political Protest in the Iranian Revolution". *American Sociological Review* 61 (1): 132–152.

Reinhart, Carmen, and Kenneth Rogoff. 2009. *This Time is Different: Eight Centuries of Financial Folly*. Princeton, NJ: Princeton University Press.

Rodrik, Dani. 2011. *The Globalization Paradox: Democracy and the Future of the World Economy*. New York and London: W.W. Norton and Company.

Roose, Jochen, Maria Kousis, and Moritz Sommer. 2014. "Discursive Actor Attribution Analysis: A Tool to Analyze How People Make Sense of the Eurozone Crisis". Paper presented at the 8th ECPR General Conference, Glasgow, UK.

Sawyers, Traci, and David Meyer. 1999. "Missed Opportunities: Social Movement Abeyance and Public Policy". *Social Problems* 46 (2): 187–206.

Spourdalakis, Michalis. 2013. "Left Strategy in the Greek Cauldron: Explaining SYRIZA's Success". *Socialist Register* 49: 98–119.

Spourdalakis, Michalis. 2014. "The Miraculous Rise of the 'Phenomenon SYRIZA'". *International Critical Thought* 4 (3): 354–366.

Stavrakakis, Yiannis, and George Katsambekis. 2014. "Left-wing Populism in the European Periphery: The Case of SYRIZA". *Journal of Political Ideologies* 19 (2): 119–142.

Tarrow, Sidney. 1996. "States and Opportunities: The Political Structuring of Social Movements". In *Comparative Perspectives on Social Movements: Political Opportunities, Mobilizing Structures and Cultural Framings*, edited by D. McAdam, J. McCarthy and M. Zald. Cambridge: Cambridge University Press.

Tarrow, Sidney. 1998. *Power in Movement: Social Movements and Contentious Politics*. Cambridge: Cambridge University Press.

Teperoglou, Eftichia, and Emmanouil Tsatsanis. 2014. "Dealignment, De-legitimation and the Implosion of the Two-Party System in Greece: The Earthquake Election of 6 May 2012". *Journal of Elections, Public Opinion and Parties* 24 (2): 222–242.

Tilly, Charles. 1985. "Models and Realities of Popular Collective Action". *Social Research* 52 (4): 717–748.

Tsakatika, Myrto, and Costas Eleftheriou. 2013. "The Radical Left's Turn Towards Civil Society in Greece: One Strategy, Two Paths". *South European Society and Politics* 18 (1): 81–99.

Tsatsanis, Emmanouil, and Eftichia Teperoglou. 2016. "Realignment under Stress: The July 2015 Referendum and the September Parliamentary Election in Greece". *South European Society and Politics* 21 (4): 427–450.

Vogiatzoglou, Marcos. 2014. "Trade Unions in Greece: Protest and Social Movements in the Context of Austerity Politics". *WSI-Mitteilungen* 5: 361–368.

5 Building the "contraption"

Anti-austerity movements and political alternative in Portugal[1]

Elísio Estanque, Hermes Augusto Costa* and Dora Fonseca**

Introduction

Austerity became a dominant word in Portuguese society at least from the end of 2010. In fact, by 29 September 2010, the former socialist Prime Minister, José Sócrates, announced that pay cuts of between 3.5 per cent and 10 per cent would affect civil servants earning more than €1,500 a month. This decision (applied since January 2011) was part of the "Stability and Growth Programme 3" (PEC 3) and followed other previous measures taken by the Portuguese Government, namely: "PEC 1" (March, 2010), mainly supported by measures to contain expenditure and increase revenue; and "PEC 2" (May, 2010) aimed at additional measures for budget consolidation. Meanwhile, in the same vein of PEC 3, on 11 March 2011 an additional austerity package (PEC 4) was announced. However, it was rejected days later in the Parliament by all the parties in opposition. Consequently, the Socialist Prime Minister resigned and a right-wing coalition (Social Democratic Party, PSD, and Christian Democratic, CDS) came to power and ruled the country from June 2011 to October 2015. In short, this coalition was primarily responsible for implementing the austerity measures.

The year of 2011 unveiled a protest cycle that unfolded until 2013. The context was one of acute crisis in various domains and fostered harsh opposition against austerity supporters, prompting divisions among political elites regarding solutions. Social movements were organised in response to the oppressive dynamics of austerity measures of *Troika* (comprising the International Monetary Fund, the European Central Bank and the European Commission) in the overall context of neo-liberalism (Costa and Estanque 2017). The austerity measures resulting from the *Memorandum of Understanding* (MoU) signed with the *Troika* in May 2011, and the subsequent amendments to the employment law, raised controversial issues, such as greater flexibility in the labour market, the devaluation of wages, an increase in working hours (Costa 2012) and a general process of income transfer from labour to capital (Leite *et al.* 2014).

The cycle of anti-austerity contention between 2010 and 2013 in Portugal reveals a complex picture, where traditional actors, including trade unions and left-wing political parties, emerged as key actors. This gave rise to a period of intense polemics in the political arena, since the former right-wing majority refused to accept a new Prime Minister (António Costa, the leader of the Social-ist Party) who "lost" elections in late 2015. However, a "defeated" leader achieved power and was able to draw the "squared of the circle", negotiating and forging agreements among the divided forces of the Left. This government solu-tion, because of its supposed fragility and lack of consistency, became known as the "Contraption"[2] (*"Geringonça"*, in Portuguese). But more than a year later it still resisted and could even avoid some difficult obstacles.

Austerity, crisis and social protests

According to Dagnino (1998), it can be said that those collective actors fought for the right to participate in the definition of the very system they acted upon. In that context, social movement protests tried to keep their distance from partisan logics in order to maintain neutrality that would grant them a broader character. In that light, one can ask if they have succeeded in keeping the distance just mentioned. How did anti-austerity social movement organisations (SMOs) interact with those traditional political actors? Were they immune to any influ-ence whatsoever? Were they safe from co-optation and instrumentalisation?

If austerity struggles have become the unifying "big issue" that created greater synergies between the trade union movement and other groups or socio-occupational movements (Costa and Estanque 2017), they also set the ground-work for interaction dynamics between those protests and political parties. Having as an empirical background the 2011–2013 protest cycle in Portugal, our goal is to elaborate on this contentious matter. We will begin by clarifying the existing connection between austerity, crisis and political participation, followed by a more incisive approach of the relationship between social movements and democracy in times of austerity. In the fourth and following sections, we embrace a contentious debate within which political parties, trade unions and social movements enter into dialogue and bring about a new political alternative.

Especially in southern Europe, the driving factor for participation in demon-strations was dissatisfaction with the functioning of democracy (Campos Lima and Martín Artiles 2013). Such dissatisfaction was associated with changes observed in Portugal after 2011. The labour market has been the area most affected by extremely violent austerity policies, evident in high unemployment rates (mainly among young people), salary and pension cuts, blockage of profes-sional carriers, proliferation of precarious forms of work, dismissals, and the reduction of trade union and collective bargaining power, among other things (Estanque and Costa 2012, 2014). The origins of these new trends can be traced back to the end of Fordism and of the *thirty glorious years*. The *precarious con-dition* that marks the twenty-first century was fostered by a profound reconfigu-ration of working conditions. The fallacy of the promise of "meritocracy"-based, working-class "upward mobility", with considerable impacts in the socio-political arena has become evident. Besides the "traditional" working class, social struggles of the 20th and 21st centuries encompass the "beneficiaries" of the welfare state, including new socio-professional categories (teachers, doctors, civil service officials, etc.). A scenario of that kind amplified the probability of protests in general.

Since the end of 2010, with the onset of austerity, there has been a new intensification of forms of social protest and strike activity (Costa *et al.* 2014; Costa and Estanque 2017). Trade unions were extremely active and resorted to various forms of action. Between 2010 and 2012, there were 384 strikes in Portugal involving about 224,500 workers.[3] General strikes gained relevance as a type of strike that mobilises the whole of society. There were five general strikes in Portugal in the period 2010–2013. Three of them were combined actions, uniting the two main trade union confederations – General Confederation of Portuguese Workers or *Confederação Geral dos Trabalhadores Portugueses* (CGTP) and General Workers' Union or *União Geral de Trabalhadores* (UGT) – against austerity policies (24 November 2010, 24 November 2011 and 27 June 2013). On the other hand, the other two general strikes were called by only CGTP (one was held on 22 March 2012 and the other on 14 November 2012), also against the austerity of the government and the *Troika*. In general, public discontent peaked during the rescue programme, signed by the three traditional ruling political parties – PS (Socialist Party), PSD (Social Democratic Party) and CDS (Christian Democrats/right-wing), which imposed an "austerity society" model on the Portuguese (Ferreira 2012).

Thus, austerity's significance is not only economical. When we speak of austerity and crisis, it is legitimate to think that we are facing something that, more than defined by economic and financial criteria, results from an "imminently political" act (Santos 2012, 11) that produces impacts on different areas: inequalities, middle-class impoverishment, unemployment, indebtedness of the families or providence society (Santos 2012, 59; Estanque 2012). Moreover, in this sense, austerity constitutes "a form of political economy of a regressive nature" (Observatory on Crises and Alternatives 2014, 313), which incorporates changes in social relations and redefines the central place of work in the economy as well as the traditional role of the welfare state (Estanque 2013; Hespanha *et al.* 2014).

Consequently, austerity is intricately connected with democracy and, it can be said, its erosion. Portuguese anti-austerity movements were part of a transnational protest cycle in which democracy was a contentious issue in the sense that efforts were made to re-signify notions like citizenship, political representation and participation, or to counteract the refusal of economic democracy by impositions of financial markets under the form of technocratic governance. Through their renewed conceptions of direct and participatory democracy, those collective actors forged a potential resistance against the corrosion of democracy in the last couple of decades. Those trends aroused indignation in a general way, especially since the turn of the century. Austerity and the idea of inevitability were fostered not only by national political actors but also, and with great intensity, by international institutions, making space for an intense debate about the (non)democratic nature of the Portuguese bailout process. Constraints imposed by the MoU were regarded as non-democratic, namely by the CGTP and UGT (by the way, traditional actors of labour market were directly targeted by the MoU) despite the difference in tone between CGTP and UGT.[4] In that context, the efficiency of parliamentary representative democracy was widely questioned. Claims focused on opening the political decision-making process but also the "rehabilitation" of the "political class" through the contribution and action of left-wing parties and social movements.

A context like this is not the most favourable for political parties in terms of public opinion. In fact, public image of political parties was "damaged" overall as there was the perception that they were either powerless or compliant with regard to the imposition of austerity. In that sense, reasons to protest sprung from dissatisfaction with the functioning of democracy (in connection to wealth, welfare and increasing employment) associated with disaffection towards political parties as well as democratic institutions in a general sense. Although economic and social grievances played an important role, mobilisation and social protest were also an expression of meta-political motivation (Campos Lima and Martín Artiles 2013). Citizens were not at all satisfied with the responses of the political system to the economic and social problems.

According to the European Social Survey's (ESS) data for 2012,[5] Portugal registered one of the largest increases regarding the percentage of people who reported participating in at least one demonstration between 2008 and 2012. Conversely, it is also one with low levels of participation and associative affiliation and where confidence in the party and parliamentary system and in democracy in general also tends to be lower. Findings point to discontent with the performance of the economy and the working of democracy as a contributory factor accounting for mobilisation in Europe; this discontent was highest among young people and those with university education (Campos Lima and Martín Artiles 2013). A correlation seems to exist between people's position on the Right/Left political spectrum and their participation in mobilisations. Youths' claims tend to be channelled through social movements and not through parties or trade unions. A strong sense of "democratic disaffection" has been reported, representative of the distance of Portuguese citizens from political institutions, expressed in low levels of political participation and engagement, conventional (as participation in elections) and otherwise (alternative forms of civic activism) (Magalhães 2005). This gradual erosion of the weight and role of traditional forms of political participation has been punctuated by periods of intense mobilisation (Accornero and Pinto 2015). Especially from 2011 onwards, democratic disaffection played an important role in the unfolding of the protest cycle, increasing political activism and engagement amongst the Portuguese citizenry.

Social movements and democracy in times of austerity

The period at stake was a phase of heightened conflict and contention across the social system, marked by a rapid diffusion of collective action from a more mobilised to a less mobilised sector, amongst other things. This description corresponds to the definition of *protest cycle* (Tarrow 1995, 1998). Other characteristics, also present in the Portuguese case, are the geographical spread of conflict, emergence of non-organisational actions and of new groups/organisations, innovation in the repertoires of action, and the elaboration of new cognitive, cultural and ideological frames. It is worth saying that, despite levels of participation attained throughout the protest cycle, in the second half of 2013 and beyond there has been a cooling down of the frequency and intensity of protests. SMOs and "cyber platforms" expressed an acute discontent focused, in part, on the perception that traditional politics (typically represented by organisations like political parties and trade unions) were excessively bureaucratised (Estanque *et al.* 2015), and this, in association with other factors, precluded a true expression of citizens' claims and will. That being so, and as pinpointed by Campos Lima and Martín Artiles (2013), most of the recent social movements operate very much in the periphery of political and trade union organisations.

On a global scale, the various events and waves of protest in recent years share some common characteristics in that they are inspired by sections of educated youth, communicated through cyberspace, organised flexibly over networks, without identifiable leaders or centres, and spontaneous in nature. Such decentralisation increases participation and reduces vulnerability to repression, without calling into question coordination and deliberative functions. Media exposure – especially the role of cyberspace – means that the images and the drama of crowds in revolt, or the collective celebration of a victorious outcome, might trigger a copycat effect that could rapidly spread whenever the specificities of the local context prove favourable. Social movements and their organisations here at stake are considered to be network social movements that express, as proposed by Manuel Castells (2013), revolts and personal projects anchored in multi-dimensional experiences. They respond to an emotional mobilisation unchained by indignation before injustice, which can also be seen as a heterogeneous rebellion under the influence of a *middle-class drive* (Estanque 2015).

Manuel Castells also highlighted network social movements' capacity to generate new spaces of autonomy through their action. They are viral, reflexive in nature, non-violent by principle, embrace many different claims, and seek value change. Other features worth emphasising are the transnational nature of many of the established networks and the combination of material, political and identity-based demands. They seem to materialise autonomous organisation strategies from civil society regarding the State – a sign of civil society re-emergence (Cohen and Arato 2000).

The democratic issue attained great relevance during this protest cycle. Institutional democracy and democratic values tend to come under attack in periods of conflict and crisis. In the recent social context in Southern Europe, it should be noted that the formation of the wave of protests was intimately connected with a "return to materialism", especially concerning work and employment rights (Estanque *et al.* 2013; Costa and Estanque 2017; Quaranta 2016).[6] Such a return would be in line with Boltanski and Chiapello's *social critique*, the same critique identified in "old" social movements (Boltanski and Chiapello 2001). However, following the authors just mentioned, an *artistic* (or *cultural*) critique linked to the "new" social movements is also present, especially considering the presence of identity issues, the trans-class composition as well as the large presence of youth in these mass demonstrations. Thus, we need to focus our attention on the old tension between labour struggles issued from the sphere of production, on the one side, and most of the "new" social movements, connecting struggles of identity, culture or "post-materialism", on the other (Costa and Estanque 2017).

In any case, it is important to highlight that the (old) theories of the so-called New Social Movements (NSMs) are probably insufficient[7] for an accurate account of recent movements of protest and social rebellion. Network social movements are less exposed to co-optation by political parties, even though the latter can capitalise on the public opinion changes produced by them (Castells 2013). Despite their engagement in political debate, they neither create new political parties nor support governments, albeit, as discussed later on, in light of the Portuguese context, such reasoning does not hold.

Even if the issue of autonomy is a central one, social movement strategy and politics are always constrained by their internal dynamics and interaction with formal politics (Kriesi *et al.* 1995). Zald and Ash have defined social movements as "a purposive and collective attempt of a number of people to change individuals or societal institutions and structures" (Zald and Ash 1966, 329). For them, the organisations through which social movements can manifest themselves differ from bureaucratic organisations in two ways: they are aimed at changing society and its members; and wish to restructure society or individuals, not to provide it or them with regular service. Goals aimed at change subject movement organisations to vicissitudes which many other types of organisation avoid.[8] In spite of the fact that contemporary social movements act on and compose new organisational contexts, social movement organisations are by no means insulated from the outside world. They exist within political, economic and social contexts, and deal themselves with a dynamic internal context.

The Left, radicalism and the search for "alternative"

The life cycle, strategies and organisational forms of social movements are influenced by internal and external contexts (Zald and Ash 1966). The consolidation of a precarious society and the austerity regime (Soeiro 2015) made up the external context in which social movements were shaped, and influenced the options for certain strategies. Those options were also influenced by institutional attitudes towards the new collective actors. Formal political actors' reactions to movement actors' claims were a key factor. Social movement success is thought to go hand in hand with a decrease in autonomy (Zald and Ash 1966), and that, alongside the incorporation of some of their claims by political parties, can mean a greater interest for more conventional forms of doing politics.

The search for an alternative has been at the core of protests and, in recent decades, the question of an alternative has acquired a new meaning given that the future is not what is at stake (Estanque 2015). Conversely, as suggested by Arcary (2013), those who protest focus on the rejection of a humiliating past or a degrading present.

The rejection of past and present entails possibilities of change. The notion that "it can't possibly get any worse" may turn out to have a mobilising effect. Constructing an alternative requires a profound transformation (Eagleton 2003). In that sense, one should be aware of the difference between a reformist and a revolutionary period: whereas in the first case global revolution remains a dream and attempts are limited to change things locally; in a revolutionary period, radical global change is necessary for something to change at all (Žižek 2013). The social uprisings under analysis here are not revolutions in the sense described by Žižek, although in some cases, as in the so-called "Arab Spring", radical changes did occur.[9] Their characteristics do not point to the presence of a "revolutionary" potential, beside the fact that they put pressure on governments and institutions (Estanque 2015).

The concerns of the left and those of NSMs are, according to Kriesi *et al.* (1995), closely related. In particular, "new" left political parties normally appeal to the same constituency as NSMs, pursue the same goals to a large extent, and resort to forms of political action close to those of NSM. On the other hand, according to the authors just mentioned, both NSMs mobilisation capacity and political success are expected to depend closely on the support they receive from the organisations of the left.[10] Two aspects in particular should be taken into account: the configuration of power on the left and the presence or absence of the left in government.

Considering these theoretical lines, we shall look at the current trends of growing precariousness as well as the large fragmentation and metamorphosis of work. Given these transformations we think it could a logical statement to believe in a progressive process of proximity between traditional labour struggles and the new battles of the "brand new social movements" who are, to a large extent, related to economic and employment problems. In fact, this is one of the ambivalent dynamics in the recent cycle of demonstrations in the Portuguese case. Therefore, we will try to show some lines of that relationship composed by a complex mixture of tensions, complicities and contradictions.

Similarly to other parts of the world, Portugal came face to face with a wave of protests marked by the sense of indignation in 2011. According to Ortiz *et al.* (2013), the global protests of recent years[11] seem to unveil a lack of strategic direction, leadership and ideological reinvention, focusing on an alternative, (un) wittingly vague and distant. Protest agendas as well as modes of organisation and action stand out for being quite divorced from traditional political participation in most cases. In fact, protests between 2011 and 2013 entailed a political critique of the social and political order, challenged it, calling for new and radical forms of democracy.

Anti-austerity movements and political parties

The support of the old Left for NSMs can happen in situations where the latter bring forth issues that also mobilise their traditional social bases. A militant old Left is willing to support NSMs only on its own terms.[12] In other words, an alliance with NSMs could be interesting as long as those movements' concerns were reformulating the "old" working class struggles but still focussed on employment rights and rejecting precariousness. When the "old" left faced competition from "new" left parties, the chances of the former becoming closer to the NSMs, and inorganic protests, increase. In general, the presence of New Left parties is thought to play an important facilitating role concerning NSMs' campaigns.

New alliances between political parties and NSMs increase when the Left is in the opposition because the former will benefit from their challenges to the government, especially when those challenges are moderate and considered legitimate by a large part of the electorate. When becoming part of the government, the left is limited by institutional politics and pressures from dominant social forces, and will make compromises regarding their electoral promises.[13] In such cases, in spite of being possible, cooperation is a remote possibility because there is always the risk of NSMs' action getting out of control. It is worth mentioning that the relationship between the left and NSMs can vary according to the type of social movement. Also, the degree to which changes in the composition of government will affect the opportunities for NSMs will vary according to the strength of the state, the exclusiveness of elite strategies, and the details of the composition of the government.

In the case of Portugal, the claim for autonomy was a core value of anti-austerity movements, namely in relation to political parties and other (vested) interests. It was envisaged as a cornerstone in the construction of an alternative project, with citizens as the prime actors of that construction. They were to gain an active voice in political decisions, which were no longer only left to political parties and governments. That meant that social movements attempted to exclude parties from the battles they were leading. Adopting a partisan stance was a contentious issue inside "social movement organisations" throughout the entire protest cycle. It was contentious in a number of ways and constrained further developments until a certain point. Moreover, such a principle was difficult to sustain given the nature of claims at stake. In spite of the autonomy mentioned, left-wing political parties, as well as trade unions, turned out to be key actors in that context, facilitating and sustaining the discontinuous mobilisation of new forms of activism, while seeking to gain access to new constituencies through them. On the other hand, it can be argued that a nonpartisan stance was a sort of asset that allowed bringing new supporters to the "anti-austerity cause". At the same time that the new actors displayed major weaknesses, they also faced important challenges, due to the strained relationship they retained with the older social movements (trade unions and political parties), with that difficulty attributed to the absence of new ideological reference points around which to mobilise (Costa and Estanque 2017). In that sense, the initial general picture can be somewhat paradoxical. Nevertheless, in the context of austerity, connections between social movements and political parties became altogether clearer.

The first protest of this cycle, the Desperate Generation (*Geração À Rasca*),[14] was presented as ostensibly non-partisan, even anti-political in the sense of a rejection of established political parties. It took place on 12 March 2011, shortly after the presentation of the Stability and Growth Pact IV (the already quoted "PEC 4") by the Socialist government, setting the emergence of the anti-austerity movement in Portugal. Harsh new measures were being prepared, such as revising the labour law and new taxes. Discontent was displayed in the streets based on concrete deprivation experiences and degradation of life conditions and expectations. It was a "protest of a generation against the imposition of labour precariousness" that evidenced the prevalence of "carousel trajectories" (Diogo 2012), characterised by disqualifying integration experiences (Paugam 2000) and permeated by risk and insecurity among youths. Demands were articulated with issues related to representative democracy, its quality and of the political class altogether. The call for protest expressed dissatisfaction with three specific domains: political class, government politics and absence of future perspectives.

It has been said that chances of alliances between political parties and NSMs increase when the Left is in the opposition, as it can benefit from NSMs' challenges to the government (especially when moderate and considered legitimate by a large part of the electorate). Albeit being in opposition, the Socialist Party (PS) and the Communist Party (PCP) tried to keep their distance from the new collective actors. Taken as representatives of the "old" Left, both were utterly puzzled by the enormous mobilisation produced without political parties' or trade unions' support. They praised collective action, acknowledged the claims and were sympathetic as they were in line with their own. Despite all that, their reactions were of distrust given the belief that discontent had to be channelled through institutions in order to produce effects. Desperate generation activists, supporters and participants thought otherwise.

In the PCP's case, reluctance displayed can also be derived from its appointed close relationship with the General Confederation of Portuguese Workers (CGTP), the most representative trade union confederation (Cerdeira 1997; Estanque 2009; Estanque and Costa 2013; Stoleroff 1988). When it was founded, CGTP established itself as a "class-based, unitary, independent, democratic and mass trade union organisation, which has its roots and its principles in the glorious traditions of organisation and struggle of the working class and of Portuguese workers" (CGTP 2012, 2014). Action by the anti-austerity movements threatened to overshadow that of CGTP. Leaning on Hyman's typology (2001), it can be said that the confederation is a case of *class-based* trade unionism. If one bears in mind network social movements' characteristics mentioned beforehand – horizontal network pattern sustained by the Internet, absence of identifiable centres and formal leaderships, viral, reflexive in nature, and so on – it is not at all surprising that those political parties' attitudes were suspicious. Our argument is that such attitudes influenced those of PCP and vice-versa, giving the close relationship just mentioned.

A similar kind of argument holds for the Socialist Party's (PS) case. As highlighted by several authors, the confederation created in 1978 – the UGT – was aimed at counteracting the hegemony that CGTP (close to the PCP) enjoyed in Portuguese society. At its founding, the UGT was supported by the Socialist and

Social Democratic parties (Costa 1994). Assuming the role of the political and ideological rival of the CGTP, the UGT can be envisaged, again according to Hyman (2001), as an example of *society-based* trade unionism, given that it advocates for social integration and the promotion of social dialogue. In the CGTP case, the communist influence, coming from a party tied to a counter-power strategy, was inductive of a trade unionism of contestation (Estanque *et al.* 2015). In contrast, the socialist and social-democratic influence over UGT favoured a trade unionism of negotiation (Costa 1994; UGT 2013).

Following the argument partially formulated above and bearing in mind anti-austerity movements' general stance of clear opposition and less than mild affinity with negotiation, those movements would always be closer to the CGTP than to the UGT. It must be stressed, however, that "tensions" and "distrust" have always been a structural trait between the two fields. Therefore, CGTP's dominant position concerning the task of defending and promoting labour rights was in some sense threatened (at least in terms of prominence) by new collective actors' emergence. That being so, a more distant attitude by a PCP closely connected to the confederation was not at all surprising, since it would be in PCP's interest to preserve the prominence just mentioned. The same reasoning can be applied to UGT's case, even though the clear choice of negotiation over contestation drove the confederation and anti-austerity movements apart, with the expected effects in what concerns the attitudes of political parties supporting the first.

The case of the Left Bloc (BE) contrasts clearly with the previous. That party was more than simply sympathetic towards the emergent collective actors. It supported the protest in what could be called a "moral" sense. As previously mentioned, New Left political parties appeal to the same constituency as the NSMs, pursue the same goals to a large extent, and resort to forms of political action close to those of NSMs (Kriesi *et al.* 1995). In that sense, the support granted was not at all surprising given that the BE can be identified with a "new" left in some sense. That party has always claimed for itself the status of "the movements' party". Moreover, it strongly opposed the cuts introduced by the socialist government in office and embraced the struggle against labour precariousness, presenting a history of unofficial involvement with a social movement organisation called "Inflexible Precarious".[15] It can be argued that by supporting the emergent collective actors, the BE was trying to expand its sphere of influence. In what can be an excessively straightforward formulation, if the PCP "had" CGTP, the BE would "have" anti-austerity movements.

Moments of a protest cycle

On 12 March, 2011, such dissatisfaction was clearly evident in the most popular slogans heard in Lisbon and Porto:

> *"If they want precarious workers, they'll get rebels!"; "We want our lives back!"; "Salary theft!"; "The country is going to the dogs!"; "Enough of*

the trash economy!" "Precarious workers are not suckers!"; "The people united don't need a party!"; "Precarious work sucks"; "Don't make me emigrate"; "I want to be happy"; "Who elected the markets?"

(Costa and Estanque 2017)

This huge demonstration brought 300,000 people into the streets of the two main Portuguese cities (about 200,000 in Lisbon and 100,000 in Porto), and was the largest social protest in Portugal since the "Carnation Revolution" of 25 April 1974 (Campos Lima and Martín Artiles 2013, 357). It can be envisaged as a turning point in that trade unions ceased to have the monopoly on social and industrial action, which is perhaps why it briefly became the subject of public debate. This first protest is thought to have had both direct and indirect impacts. Soon afterwards, in May, the *Indignados* and the *Acampadas* of *Democracia Real Já*, in Madrid, Spain, transmitted a similar message and invoked the Portuguese example (Velasco 2011, cited in Costa and Estanque 2017), followed by the global wave of protest around the *Occupy Wall Street* movement, centred on New York, but with global repercussions (Vradis and Dalakoglou 2011; Harvey 2012; Baumgarten 2013).

In a similar way to most demonstrations and socio-political protest networks, the Desperate Generation protest was defensive in nature. The truth is that those who rebelled might be aware of what they did not want, but they did not know exactly what they did want. Despite the large mobilisation produced, both the protest call and organisation process were not mediated by any organisation. In that sense, it was spontaneous, which raised particular reactions from political actors. In a general way, it was considered a "healthy demonstration from civil society", in the sense that democracy allows expressions of discontent, with those expressions being valuable elements in terms of political agenda configuration. Nevertheless, those "healthy expressions" were further framed in two distinct ways. The coalition in government (centre-right) stuck to the "healthy" character while devaluating those same expressions; Left-wing parties' reactions were paradoxical.

The 15O protest (on 15 October 2011) – "United for global change" – was the second protest of the cycle and the first after signing the MoU. It was a global protest motivated by generalised indignation, which took place in hundreds of cities around the world. The slogan "Direct Democracy, Now!" was the most emblematic, together with "They don't represent us" or "We are the 99%". In a general sense, those slogans expressed indignation towards political leaders and denounced the shortcomings of democracy. The claims voiced radical perspectives that advocated a total rupture with the status quo, in line with the critique of representative democracy and of political actors previously conveyed by the "Desperate Generation". However, in contrast, the 15O was summoned by organisations linked to the extra-parliamentary radical Left. Together with the claims' radical nature, that fact aroused the suspicion of both socialists and communists. For those political parties, especially for the PCP, the very conception of political action, organised and driven by political parties, was at stake, or, better said, was being endangered.

The protests "Screw the Troika!" were at the protest cycle's height. The expression "Screw the Troika" ("Que se lixe a Troika", Portuguese acronym QSLT) condensed a set of meanings relative to the imposition of societies of austerity (Ferreira 2012) and incorporated several struggles aimed at counteracting that imposition. We had two big mass demonstrations under this slogan.

The first QSLT protest – called *"Screw the Troika, we want our lives back!"* – took place on 15 September 2012, in a context of economic and political crisis and social unrest. On that date, the announcement of the proposal of the right-wing coalition government to reduce employers' social security contributions from 23.75 per cent to 18 per cent and, in turn, increase employees' contributions from 11 per cent to 18 per cent (in what became known as the draft "Single Social Tax"/TSU) triggered harsh reactions. A group of citizens, in its majority linked to activism and previous mobilisations, summoned a new protest via Facebook. About one million people demonstrated angrily in most Portuguese cities, prompting the government to back down and withdraw the proposal. Demystifying the idea of inevitability and its absolute necessity allowed for rejecting the intervention and exigencies of the Troika and a proactive and combative attitude towards austerity. Austerity politics were after all political and ideological options. Therefore, the appeal to participation was broader and more inclusive than in previous protests. This event, similar to "12 March 2011", involved socio-occupational actors and also relied on a strong cyber-activist culture, in contrast to what had been standard trade union practice.

The second QSLT protest, mobilised with the motto *"Screw the Troika, It is the People who rule the most!"*, took place on 2 March 2013, after the approval of the State Budget for 2013, which foresaw salary cuts and a drastic reduction of public expenditure. The context was therefore one of austerity reinforcement. The call for protest was broad and inclusive and conveyed a harsh critique. It was openly against the state reforms and the announcement of €4 billion in cuts to state welfare spending. The tone of indignation, the claims for government dismissal and the rejection of the Troika rose in intensity and were more clearly formulated in comparison with previous protests. The mobilisation was considered a success because it brought to the streets hundreds of thousands of people who demanded a left-wing government.

The idea of unity between all sectors of the population, organised and non-organised and of different struggles, was present in both of the "Screw the Troika" protests. The nonpartisan character was not evoked as a guiding principle. Critical speech towards political parties and trade unions was softened, allowing it to attract other social sectors that had been maintained apart until that moment. As expressed in the second protest manifesto, the goal was to provide a "meeting point for various democratic anti-Troika currents". So, that was a precarious "unity" based on being "against" but not on prospective grounds. Differently from the previous ones, the second protest was around quite concrete claims: government's dismissal, expulsion of the Troika and anticipated elections. Participation was massive, up to hundreds of thousands overall, and, together with the enlargement of the social base, confirmed the disintegration of the consensus around inevitability. However, the government depreciated the dissatisfaction expressed in the streets.

The "Screw the Troika" protests presented a new character to the protest cycle. On the one hand, they reversed the fall into despondency after the first round of protests (the last one had been almost a year before); on the other, claims acquired demand a character not only more specific but also "more political" in conventional terms because they relied clearly on the distinction between the political Left and Right. Another new element was related to the amplification and diversification of support. In the case of the second "Screw the Troika" protest, the main trade union confederation and some left-wing parties openly supported the protest. The magnitude reached by the second QSLT protest can in part be explained by the presence of influential allies (Tarrow 1998). Political parties represented one of those influential allies (especially the Left Bloc).

If left-wing political parties were the influential allies of anti-austerity movements, those movements were, in turn, important allies in crucial moments, as in the general strikes mentioned (Fonseca 2016). Between 2011 and 2013, general strikes benefited from the context provided by anti-austerity protests, which was quite intense in terms of mobilisation and challenges. The chronological sequence suggests it: the 24 November 2011 general strike took place after "Desperate Generation" and 15O protests; the 14 November 2012 general strike was preceded by the first "Screw the Troika" protest; and the 27 June 2013 strike happened a few months after the second "Screw the Troika" protest, which was massive. In general, those protests produced sensitising impacts,[16] that is, they influenced public opinion in what concerns the inevitability of austerity and the potential of collective action. On the other hand, anti-austerity movements played an important part in the unfolding of general strikes registered in that period, reinforcing and expanding both strategies and the scope of the general strikes (Fonseca 2016). Anti-austerity movements provided, in that sense, opportunities for trade unionism renewal as new strategies and alliances were put forward, and, by doing so, produced a new political climate that favoured political change.

Beyond the movements: building the *"contraption"*

About a year after the last protest, the political landscape changed in Portugal. The elections on 4 October 2015 ushered in a changed parliamentary scenario that was indicating a major political shift (Estanque and Costa 2015). After four years of austerity, the election outcome was contradictory right from the start. The victory of the right-wing alliance between the Social Democratic Party (PSD), and the Christian Democratic Centre (CDS), opened up the possibility for an alliance of the Left, despite the high rate of abstention (44.14 per cent). The PSD-CDS coalition (in government since 2011) received the highest percentage of votes (36.86 per cent), followed by the Socialist Party/PS (32.31 per cent), the Left Bloc/BE (10.19 per cent) and the Portuguese Communist Party/PCP (8.25 per cent). Such an electoral outcome, in spite of protest activity mentioned above, was the result of a number of factors.

The Government (right-wing) discourse of inevitability fostered by the coalition prevented (or made more difficult) the construction of alternatives. The impression was that the adjustment programme prescribed by Troika was absolutely necessary. Alongside it, there was the "SYRIZA effect": in Greece, a leftist party came to power but continued with austerity policies. As a third factor, a combination of three defining issues is presented as a third factor: a divided left, the fact that it was the previous Socialist Party government that asked for Troika's help, and the judicial proceedings involving ex-Prime Minister and former socialist leader José Sócrates.[17] The three issues damaged the image of the PS. A fourth factor was the timid upturn in some economic and employment indicators over the last two years of government.

The right-wing alliance's victory proved to be a fragile one, undermined by prevailing discontent due to growing impoverishment, high unemployment, cuts and threats to the welfare state, and so forth. With no surprise, it was put at stake by the (more surprising) willingness of the left to converge. The BE doubled its votes (from 5.2 per cent to 10.2 per cent) and increased the number of seats in Parliament from eight to 19, in part as a result of the adoption of more moderate positions. On the other hand, the PCP maintained its share of the votes, but was overtaken by the BE, which also meant a symbolic defeat. Given this general background, the results of the elections were perceived by PS's secretary-general as an opportunity to put forward an alternative government. The fact is that the coalition government would not last long with all the parliamentary left against it. Political parties shown willingness to (or were forced to) dialogue. The rejection of a (more probable) centre-left government solution opened the way for what could be called a "political breakthrough".

Even though large sectors of the population welcomed the new political solution, some felt threatened and grew agitated by the possibility that a government of the left would become viable with support from Blockists and Communists, including the President of the Republic at the time. The fact that both the PCP and the BE were known for their Euroscepticism and/or radicalism played an important role in the construction of a sort of fear regarding a possible "left solution". Conversely, any kind of commitment from those two parties seemed to be, at the very least, surprising given their well-known positions. Despite all this, on 10 November 2015, a motion to reject the new coalition government was won by the parties of the left with 123 votes in favour and 107 against. A new government, led by PS, emerged from a Parliamentary agreement signed between PS, BE, PCP and the Greens. From the beginning, harmony between them was regarded by many as not long-lasting. Doubts about the guarantees to ensure the government's stability throughout the legislative period were abundant. The new government, in functions at that time, is one of PS's initiatives. The PCP and BE were left out, on their own wishes, owing to programmatic differences between them and the PS, especially regarding the European Union in general and the Budgetary Treaty and the renegotiation of the debt in particular (amongst others things). There are some "red lines", the crossing of which can endanger the prevalence of this peculiar (in the sense of "brand new" and "unexpected") political solution. Given that, the Portuguese political scene is chronically strained in some sense, as disagreement between parts involved is always a possibility.

Under a PS-led government committed to a number of reforms pushed by a more "radical" attitude from the PCP and the BE, a different spirit and a more ambitious course towards a more social, more cohesive Europe, can be sensed. Nevertheless, agreements reached remain somewhat fragile. One year of left-wing government has gone by and agreements signed have held so far. Some attempts have been made to reverse a considerable number of austerity effects, most of them are related to aspirations of the two other partners of the government solution (PCP and BE). We can mention aspects like these: (i) reversal of the privatisation of strategic corporations (like the Portuguese airways – TAP); (ii) restitution of wages, pensions, holiday and Christmas subsidies; (iii) minimum wage raise; (iv) reset of some national holidays; (v) enforcement of labour regulations' supervision; (vi) reinstatement of the 35 hours worked per week; (vii) creation of an unemployment benefit for independent workers (the so-called "green receipts") and the ending of other measures that have contributed to social dumping and the impoverishment of the Portuguese middle class. An important accomplishment has been the approval of regulations concerning the existence of precarious workers in the public sector (public administration and public enterprises). The new regulation foresees the integration of the state's "green receipts" (independent workers) as public servants, with all the rights it entails, and was pressed forward by the BE and PCP.

This left alternative has a number of impacts that are still to be fully assessed. However, the unfolding of the present legislature allows for making some considerations about its potentialities and/or limitations. From the very beginning, BE's and PCP's involvement in the government solution posed some questions, namely related with CGTP's behaviour. Since the confederation's allies are part of the political solution, will it change to a more "negotiation" style or will it honour a long contestation tradition? In a more general sense, are trade unions to be left out when explaining the success or failure of the political alternative? It can be said they have been important in the maintenance of social cohesion and thus in the government solution for continuity. In spite of its demands and combativeness, the CGTP has so far avoided more extreme or "last resort" measures, like general strikes – its main strategy in the previous period – allowing the government's programme to unfold (Estanque and Costa 2016).

The left solution is inherently ambiguous and unveils politics' tactical dimension. Accepting a left agreement required careful thought from the political parties involved. For the Socialist Party (PS), it meant making concessions to left-wing coalition partners, normally more radical, something that would most probably displease more conservative members and supporters and raise the opposition of both PSD and CDS. Even if such discontent will not affect PS's position in practical terms, it weakens its position overall. On the other hand, coalition partners (BE and PCP) stand in a kind of "ungrateful" position in the sense that it implies being in government and in opposition simultaneously. This in/out position is utterly ambiguous as it means cooperating/supporting and forming the opposition all at the same time. A "softer" opposition might displease their traditional social bases and mean a loss of support from those who protested against austerity. Conversely, both the BE and PCP are obliged to compromise, as any kind of refusal endangers the political alternative, leaving the country in a difficult position (as in Spain), and thus will be disadvantageous for them, at least in electoral terms. In sum, the political agreement between PS, BE, PCP and the Greens can both foster or be prejudicial for these political parties' current positions and their image in the political field. At the same time, it cannot be forgotten that the PCP faces strong competition from the BE and vice-versa (and the latter surpassed the former in electoral results recently). They compete for the same social support bases and try to advance their own perspectives in what concerns a viable Left alternative. Such a competitive attitude might be problematic in the near future.

Finally, when analysing the "success" or "survival" of the Left solution so far, one should not neglect the personal style of the actual Portuguese Prime-Minister. António Costa has displayed great adroitness in managing conflicting interests and positions. Contrasting with his predecessors both in office and in the PS's structure, Mr Costa inspires confidence. He is what can be called an "aggregating personality", that is, he stirs sympathy and has an appeasing influence, generating a collective consensus. During times of personalisation of politics, this has certainly been an asset for the Left solution so far.

Conclusion

The protest cycle from 2011 to 2013 acted as a catalyst for political change and was a paradigmatic milieu for relations between political parties and network social movements, at least in Portugal. Despite being frequently seen by the traditional actors (like trade unions) as having an inorganic and discontinuous character, social movements and their organisations are not isolated islands. Conversely, they emerge from and act within complex political landscapes. In that sense, political parties were part and parcel of the protest cycle, playing an important role even, if unintentionally sometimes. Left-wing political parties were social movements' important allies on many occasions. In embracing the claims of social movements, particularly those concerning labour relations and the defence of workers' basic rights, they rehabilitated their public image, which was very damaged in the last couple of years, especially in the period of Troika's bailout programme.

This unfolding relationship was, nevertheless, peculiar in the sense that attitudes from both parties responded to changes in the external and internal contexts of the organisations. Anti-austerity mobilisations have evolved from a straightforward rejection of political parties and "old" institutional actors – an anti-political stance and institutional distrust connected with radical perspectives of total rupture with the system – to a tacit acceptance of the new parliamentary solution. More precisely, left-wing political parties (BE and PCP) became possible allies in spite of their persistent differences (and tacit concurrence between them). A clearer and more realistic formulation of claims from social movements accompanied a phasing out of the harsh critique directed at political parties. Support granted by left-wing parties to the anti-austerity movement varied according to their "pretentions" to achieve power. Due to that support and their accomplishments, trade unions and political parties – especially PCP – changed their perceptions up to a point and started perceiving them as possible allies that could help bring down the government. Objectively, the protest cycle was used to put pressure not only on the former majority but also on those who did not offer any alternatives, allowing the continuity of "more of the same".

Being a chronic candidate to office, the Socialist Party was not as supportive as the Left Bloc (BE), instead displaying careful and ambivalent attitudes. As for the Communist Party (PCP), it also tried to keep a relative distance from the social movement, at least for a while. As an "old" Left representative, that political party "competes" with the "new" Left (the Left Bloc), which has called itself "The party of social movements". Though simple, such an explanation might clarify some positions assumed throughout the protest cycle.

As a matter of fact, austerity effects on the Portuguese population facilitated a new opportunity structure where new political actors could emerge – the "Desperate Generation" and "Screw the Troika" – and "old" actors intensified their action (the CGTP, for instance). On the other hand and different to Spain, where, as stated by Díaz-Parra *et al.* in Chapter 3 of this book, anti-austerity protests and social movements led to the emergence of a new political party (*Podemos*), in Portugal there was no consequence concerning the formation of a consolidated political actor. Portuguese mass protests were probably more intense in specific actions (12 March 2011, 15 September 2012 and 2 March 2013) but they disseminated and disappeared afterwards. So, the Portuguese movement dynamic did not foster organised networks and nuclei as in Spain. Here, the mentioned new political party sprung up from the closeness of conventional political institutions while their original force came from the bottom-up street protests and their network articulations. At the same time, the lack of efficiency of street protests in what concerns substantive impacts and "solutions" pushed some leaders to take action and *Podemos* came out. However, once again, contrary to what happened in its neighbour, the Portuguese movement dynamics paved the way for a new political solution in which "more radical" left-wing parties and class struggles played an important role.

Since the beginning (November 2015), the new parliament majority and the government led by A. Costa's leadership was under attack. First, the former Prime Minister, Passos Coelho, was particularly violent against this solution starting with criticisms like "the defeated party is going to rule" or "the new leader does everything to achieve power". After a while, the atmosphere evolved towards some other formulations like the one that remains to this day: "The Contraption"[18] Government. This notion, suggested by a right-wing opinion-maker, was initially directed to the Socialist Party, but public opinion picked it up and spread it out. Other observers, more sympathetic, have also named this political solution as "The flying cow", a metaphor to emphasise the "miracle" of watching a cow fly, similar to such surprising agreement among these different – and normally divergent – political parties. No matter how difficult it was, the political alternative in Portugal brought some important accomplishments regarding precarious work, social rights and working-class conquests, albeit not being considered a consistent solution. Until now (January 2017), it has worked and "the cow still flies"....

Notes

  * Elísio Estanque and Hermes A. Costa are senior researchers at the Centre for Social Studies (CES) and professors of sociology at the Faculty of Economics – University of Coimbra.

** Dora Fonseca is a junior researcher at CES and a team member of the above-mentioned REB-Unions project.

 1 This work benefited from the financial support of the Foundation for Science and Technology (FCT/MEC) through national funds and is co-financed by FEDER through the Operational Programme Competitiveness and Innovation COMPETE 2020 within the project REB-Unions – Rebuilding trade union power in the age of austerity: a review of three sectors (PTDC/IVC-SOC/3533/2014 – POCI-01-0145-FEDER-016808).

 2 "Contraption" ("*Geringonça*") refers to a strange looking device or apparatus, which seems to work or move in a very precarious and fragile manner.

 3 The data concern the private sector alone. Source: DGAEP – Directorate General for Administration and Public Employment, 2014.

 4 On the one hand, CGTP was clearly against the terms and targets of the MoU, pointing to the need for an immediate renegotiation of debt, interest and deadlines, in order to avoid further recession and increase the risk of unemployment and poverty. The UGT, on the other hand, was more cautious about the requirements of the MoU, stressing the need to respect the commitments made with the European Union and the IMF, in order to create conditions for renegotiation and the extension of time and interest (UGT 2011; CGTP 2014; Costa 2015).

 5 www.europeansocialsurvey.org.

 6 See also Chapter 3 of this book.

 7 The discussion about the meaning of "social movements" is the subject of different classification proposals. Salvador Aguilar (2001) proposed five types of social movements: (1) *primitive* (pre-industrial era): religious, forms of social banditry; (2) *classic* (eighteenth century to the first third of the nineteenth century): labour movement, nationalism movements, socialist movements; (3) *new social movements* (1960s to 1980s): ecologist movement, pacifist, feminist, sexual liberation; (4) *brand new social movements* (1990s): solidarity movements, NGOs, for a global civil society, movements of users of public services; (5) *peripheral and anti-systemic* movements (last third of the twentieth century and located in the periphery and semi-periphery of the world system), resistance movements to autocracies, Zapatista movement or landless movement/MST). More recently, Campos Lima and Martín Artiles (2013) have used the terminology "*brand new social movements*" ("*novíssimos movimentos sociais*") mainly to refer to movements with a capacity for attracting groups that the unions find difficult to organise: the unemployed, those in precarious work and young people in general.

 8 See Zald and Ash (1966).

 9 In the countries encompassed by the "Arab Spring" (Tunisia, Egypt and Libya), governments and regimes fell apart because of the magnitude and intensity of the street demonstrations.

10 The framework of analysis proposed by Kriesi *et al.* (1995) relies on the distinction between the "old" and "new" left. Such distinction may be criticisable given its blurred character.

11 Between January 2006 and July 2013, Ortiz *et al.* (2013) analysed global protests in 87 countries (covering more than 90 per cent of the world's population). The protests were promoted by four different groups: (1) *people's rights* (302 protests), which included protests of several types: ethnic, indigenous and racial, labour, freedom of association, religious issues, LGBT, immigrants, prisoners, etc.; (2) *global justice* (311 protests), especially against the IMF and other financial institutions, against imperialism, free trade and the G20, and on behalf of environmental justice and "global commons"; (3) *the failure of political representation and political systems* (376 protests), generally centred on denouncing the lack of real democracy, business influence, deregulation and privatisation, corruption, absence of justice emanating from the legal system, surveillance of citizens, against the war and the military industrial complex, etc. (4) *for economic justice and against austerity* (488 protests), especially focused on public services, tax justice, wage and working conditions, inequality, poverty and living standards, pension systems, fuel prices, food prices, etc. (Ortiz *et al.* 2013, 14).

12 When an "old" Left is non-pacified, divisions are usually between social-democrats and communists. The importance, the organisational and ideological makeup, as well as the strategies of the "two parts" of the Left, depend to a large extent on the institutional structures and prevailing strategies of a given country (Kriesi *et al.* 1995). The heritage of the prevailing strategies to deal with the challenges has a lasting impact on the strategies and the structure of the old Left. The heritage of exclusive strategies contributes to the radicalisation and split between Left currents. The split between Left currents may foster the further radicalisation of the labour movement. Such a tradition of extra-parliamentary action is likely to continue to affect the labour movement's strategies with regard to new social movements. Given that, parties of the old Left and the labour movement are seen as more likely to support the actions of new social movements in exclusive regimes. This tendency will be reinforced by the fact that exclusive strategies affect not only the relations between new social movements and polity members but also those among polity members themselves (which are more polarised in exclusive regimes, and, therefore, more likely to confront each other by way of extra-parliamentary mobilisation).

13 In general, a decrease of mobilisation levels is expected when the Left is in government for two reasons: on one side, reforms that can benefit social movements are foreseen and, on the other, social movements lose their most powerful ally (Kriesi *et al.* 1995).

14 The protest was launched via Facebook by four young people from Lisbon and announced as non-partisan, secular and pacifist. The adjectives used to define the protest had two effects. On the one hand, that definition was a source of attractiveness that allowed the expression of uneven interests – for instance, the non-partisan epithet allowed far-right participation, displeasing many people. On the other, it gave the protest a broader sense with the negative effect of making it more difficult to define a concrete direction as well as objectives. The name "Geração à Rasca" is, as pointed out by Accornero and Ramos Pinto (2015), a clear reference to a previous cycle of protest in the early 1990s, and especially to university and high-school student protests against the then PSD government's educational reforms. At the time, both media and political elites accused the mobilisation of students as serving only their particular interests: it was thus named Geração Rasca – the "Trashy Generation" (Seixas 2005 cited in Accornero and Ramos Pinto 2015). The 2011 protests recovered this title and gave it a new meaning.

15 The "Inflexible Precarious" (PI) was created in 2007, in Lisbon (Portugal's capital city), with the goal of giving continuity to the mobilisation accomplished with May Day (an action day against labour precariousness). The main objective was to fill the

void in relation to the struggle against labour precariousness. With May Day being a process limited in time, the constitution of an autonomous group, or social movement organisation, aimed at assuring the maintenance of social action targeting that problem seemed a logical step for those who had been involved. They took after FERVE (direct translation to English: fed up with these green receipts, but the acronym also means "spoil") a group that existed in Oporto, adopting however a more comprehensive focus that included all forms of labour precariousness. As a social movement organisation, the PI was informal, horizontal, with no hierarchies or formal leadership, and resistant to whatever form of bureaucracy.

16 See Kriesi *et al.* (1995).
17 José Socrates faced charges of corruption, tax fraud and illicit enrichment, in a judicial process still ongoing.
18 In Portuguese, the term is "*Geringonça*" (see note 2 above). The "flying cow" was also a result of the image of a toy (a flying cow), shown on TV, showing the Prime Minister offering it as a gift to his minister (in derisory fashion).

References

Accornero Guya, and Pedro Ramos Pinto. 2015. "'Mild Mannered'? Protest and Mobilisation in Portugal under Austerity, 2010–2013". *West European Politics*, 38 (3): 491–515.

Aguilar, Salvador. 2001. "Movimientos sociales y cambio social. Uma lógica o varias lógicas de acción colectiva?" *Revista Internacional de Sociologia* 30: 29–62.

Arcary, Valério. 2013. "Até onde vamos aguentar?" Available at http://raquelcardeira-varela.wordpress.com/2013/10/30/ate-onde-vamos-aguentar/.

Baumgarten, Britta. 2013. "Geração à Rasca and beyond: Mobilizations in Portugal after 12 March 2011". *Current Sociology*, 61 (4): 457–473.

Boltanski, Luc, and Eve Chiapello. 2001. *Le Nouvelle Esprit du Capitalisme.* Paris: Gallimard.

Campos Lima, Maria da Paz, and Antonio Martín Artiles. 2013. "Youth Voice(s) in EU Countries and Social Movements in Southern Europe". *Transfer* 19 (3): 345–363.

Castells, Manuel. 2013. *Redes de Indignação e Esperança. Movimentos sociais na era da internet.* Rio de Janeiro: Zahar.

Cerdeira, Maria da Conceição. 1997. "A sindicalização portuguesa de 1974 a 1995". *Revista Sociedade e Trabalho* 1: 46–53.

CGTP. 2012. Estatutos. *Boletim do Trabalho e Emprego*, Bulletin No. 17.

CGTP. 2014. Reforçar a luta dos trabalhadores contra a exploração e o empobrecimento (resolução 1.02.04). Lisboa: CGTP.

Cohen Jean, and Andrew Arato. 2000. *Sociedad Civil y Teoría Política.* México: Fondo de Cultura Económica.

Costa, Hermes A. 1994. "A construção do pacto social em Portugal". *Revista Crítica de Ciências Sociais* 39: 127–128.

Costa, Hermes A. 2012. "From Europe as a Model to Europe as Austerity: The Impact of the Crisis on Portuguese Trade Unions". *Transfer – European Review of Labour and Research* 18 (4): 397–410.

Costa, Hermes A. 2015. "Le syndicalisme portugais et l'austerité: entre la force des protestations et la fragilité des alliances". *Relations Industrielles/Industrial Relations* 70 (2): 262–284.

Costa, Hermes A., and Elísio Estanque. 2017. "Trade Unions and Social Movements at the Crossroads: A Portuguese View". In *Social Movements and Organized Labour.*

Passions and Interests, edited by Jürgen Grote and Claudius Wagemann. Farnham: Ashgate Publishers.

Costa, Hermes A., Hugo Dias, and José Soeiro. 2014. "As greves e a austeridade em Portugal: Olhares, expressões e recomposições". *Revista Crítica de Ciências Sociais* 103: 173–202.

Dagnino, Evelyn. 1998. "Culture, Citizenship, and Democracy: Changing Discourses and Practices of the Latin America Left". In *Cultures of Politics, Politics of Cultures. Revisioning Latin American Social Movements*, edited by Sonia E. Alvarez, Evelyn Dagnino, and Arturo Escobar, 33–63. Boulder, CO, Oxford: Westview Press.

Diogo, Fernando. 2012. "Precariedade no emprego em Portugal e desigualdades sociais: alguns contributos". *Observatório das Desigualdades*. Available at http://observatorio-das-desigualdades.cies.iscte.pt/index.jsp?page=projects&id=129.

Eagleton, Terry. 2003. *After Theory*. New York: Basic Books.

Estanque, Elísio. 2009. "Trabalho, desigualdades e sindicalismo em Portugal". In *Relaciones Laborales y Ación Syndicale. Relaciones Laborales Transfronterizas, Portugal-España*, edited by A. Buiza and E. Pérez, 127–150. Valladolid/Granada: Instituto de Estudios Europeos.

Estanque, Elísio. 2012. *A Classe Média: ascensão e declínio*. Lisboa: Fundação Francisco Manuel dos Santos.

Estanque, Elísio. 2013. "O Estado social em causa: instituições, políticas sociais e movimentos sócio-laborais no contexto europeu". In *Os Portugueses e o estado Providência. Uma perspectiva comparada*, edited by Felipe Carreira da Silva, 225–263. Lisboa: ICS, 225–263.

Estanque, Elísio. 2015. "Middle-class Rebellions? Precarious Employment and Social Movements in Portugal and Brazil (2011–2013)". *RCCS Annual Review* 7: 17–44.

Estanque, Elísio, and Hermes A. Costa. 2012. "Labour Relations and Social Movements". In *Sociological Landscapes: Theories, Realities and Trends*, edited by Dennis Erasga, 257–282. Rijeka/Croatia: INTECH, 257–282. Available at: www.intechopen.com/articles/show/title/labour-relations-and-social-movements.

Estanque, Elísio, and Hermes A. Costa. 2013. "O sindicalismo europeu no centro do vulcão: desafios e ameaças". *JANUS*. Available at: http://janusonline.pt/2013/2013.html.

Estanque, Elísio, and Hermes A. Costa. 2014. "Austerity Policies and Trade Unionism: A Glance at Portugal". *Global Labour Column* 190. Available at: http://column.global-labour-university.org/2014/12/austeritypolicies-and-trade-unionism.html.

Estanque, Elísio, and Hermes A. Costa. 2015. "Portugal's New Social and Political Context". *Global Labour Column* 219. Available at http://column.global-labour-university.org/.

Estanque, Elísio, and Hermes A. Costa. 2016. "Uma crítica construtiva ao sindicalismo". *Público*, 24 de fevereiro, 44.

Estanque, Elísio, Hermes A. Costa, and Manuel Carvalho da Silva. 2015. "O futuro do sindicalismo na representação sociopolítica". In *O Futuro da Representação Política Democrática*, edited by André Freire, 119–142 Lisboa: Nova Veja.

Estanque, Elísio, Hermes A. Costa, and José Soeiro. 2013. "The New Global Cycle of Protest and the Portuguese Case". *Journal of Social Science Education* 12 (1): 31–40.

Ferreira, António Casimiro. 2012. *Sociedade de Austeridade e direito do trabalho de exceção*. Porto: Vida Económica – Editorial SA.

Fonseca Dora. 2016. Movimentos sociais e sindicalismo em tempo de crise. O caso português: alianças ou tensões latentes? Unpublished doctoral dissertation, Faculdade de Economia da Universidade de Coimbra.

Harvey, David. 2012. *Rebel Cities. From the Right to the City to the Urban Revolution*. London: Verso.

Hespanha, P., Ferreira, S., and Pacheco, V. 2014. O Estado Social, crise e reformas. In: Reis J (org) *A Economia Política do Retrocesso. Crise, Causas e Objetivos.* Coimbra: Almedina, 189–281.

Hyman, Richard. 2001. *Understanding European Trade Unionism: Between Market, Class and Society.* London: Sage.

Kriesi Hanspeter, Ruud Koopmans, and Jan Willem Duyvendak. 1995. *New Social Movements in Western Europe: A Comparative Analysis.* London: UCL Press.

Leite, Jorge, Hermes A. Costa, Manuel Carvalho da Silva, and João Ramos de Almeida. 2014. "Austeridade, reformas laborais e desvalorização do trabalho". In *A economia política do retrocesso: crise, causas e objetivos*, edited by Observatório sobre Crises e Alternativas, 127–188. Coimbra: Almedina/CES.

Magalhães, Pedro. 2005. "Disaffected Democrats: Political Attitudes and Political Action in Portugal". *West European Politics* 28 (5): 973–991.

Observatório sobre Crises e Alternativas. 2014. Sete propostas alternativas para reconstituir a economia, a sociedade e a política. In *A economia política do retrocesso. Crise, causas e objetivos*, edited by J. Reis, 309–323. Coimbra: Almedina/CES.

Ortiz, Isabel, Sara Burke, Mohamed Berrada, and Hernan Cortez Saenz. 2013. *World Protests 2006–2013.* Initiative for Policy Dialogue, Columbia University, Friedrich-Ebert-Stiftung, Research Working Paper 274, New York.

Paugam, Serge. 2000. *Le Salarié de la Précarité. Les nouvelles formes de l'intégration professionnelle.* Paris: Presses Universitaires de France.

Quaranta, Mario. 2016. "Protesting in 'Hard Times': Evidence from a Comparative Analysis of Europe, 2000–2014". *Current Sociology* 64 (5): 736–754.

Santos, Boaventura de Sousa. 2012. *Portugal. Ensaio contra a autoflagelação.* Coimbra: Almedina.

Seixas, Ana Maria. 2005. "Aprender a democracia: jovens e protesto no ensino secundário em Portugal". *Revista Crítica das Ciências Sociais*, 72: 187–209.

Soeiro, José. 2015. A Formação do Precariado. Transformações no Trabalho e Mobilizações de Precários em Portugal. Unpublished doctoral dissertation, Faculdade de Economia da Universidade de Coimbra.

Stoleroff, A. 1988. Sindicalismo e relações industriais em Portugal. *Sociologia: Problemas e Práticas*, 4: 147–164.

Tarrow, Sidney. 1995. "Cycles of Collective Action: Between Moments of Madness and the Repertoire of Contention". In *Repertoires and Cycles of Collective Action*, edited by Mark Traugott, 89–116. Durham, NC: Duke University Press.

Tarrow, Sidney. 1998. *Power in Movement. Social Movements and Contentious Politics.* New York, Cambridge: Cambridge University Press.

UGT. 2011. *Memorando de Entendimento da Troika* (Resolução Secretariado Nacional, 12.05.01). Lisboa: UGT.

UGT. 2013. Estatutos. *Boletim do Trabalho e Emprego*, 29: 301–331.

Velasco, Pilar. 2011. *No nos Representan* (El Manifesto de los Indignados). Madrid: Bertrand.

Vradis, Antonis, and Dimitris Dalakoglou. 2011. *After December: Spatial Legacies of the 2008 Athens Uprising.* Oakland, CA and Edinburgh: AK Press.

Zald, Mayer N., and Roberta Ash. 1966. "Social Movement Organizations: Growth, Decay and Change". *Social Forces* 44 (3): 327–341.

Žižek, Slavoj. 2013. "Problemas no paraíso". In *Cidades Rebeldes: passe livre e as manifestações que tomaram as ruas do Brasil*, edited by Slavoj Žižek *et al.*, 101–108. São Paulo: Boitempo/Carta Maior.

6 When the Spring is not coming

Radical Left and social movements in Italy during the austerity era

Simone Castellani and Luca Queirolo Palmas

The economic crisis in Italy and the absence of an anti-austerity movement

From 2007 to 2013, the youth unemployment in the EU-28 grew from 15 per cent to 23 per cent (Eurostat 2017). The young and young adults were some of the hardest hit groups in EU during the recent economic recession, facing increasing expulsion or exclusion from the formal labour market.

Nevertheless, the crisis did not affect all EU countries in the same way. The unemployment data and GDP show a growing gap that separates North-Central Europe from South and East. In Italy, for instance, in the period 2013–2017, youth unemployment doubled from 21 per cent to 42 per cent (Eurostat 2017) and the GDP dropped from +2 per cent to –2 per cent (OECD 2017). The age cohort that suffered most from the recession in Italy was the one between 25 and 29 years, which had an unemployment rate of 33 per cent (Eurostat 2017). This means that many of these young people, mostly graduated, were never able to enter, except sporadically, the labour market.

These figures show the consequence of the crisis on the most unprotected part of the labour market, composed mainly of young workers and characterised by a high level of temporary jobs, which were the first ones to disappear (Migliavacca *et al.* 2015). The situation in Italy became increasingly worse after the EU commission and the ECB imposed "austerity measures" stated in the Fiscal Stability Treaty (2012), which was approved during the Mario Monti technocratic government, thanks to a right–leftwing consensus. The welfare system and public services, as well as the historical labour protections, were sacrificed on the altar of the GDP/deficit ratio and the control of public debt (Borghi 2013). Furthermore, if we take into consideration that this sacrifice overlapped with a structural lack of a welfare safety net, typical of the Southern EU countries (Ferrera 1996), we can understand why the Italian young generations faced increasing vulnerability and dependence on the older generations.

In spite of this disarming picture in Italy, a massive mobilisation did not rise against the anti-austerity measures imposed by the government, led by young people, as in the other Southern European countries (Roca Martínez *et al.* 2017). Following the theories of the Political Opportunity Structure (Kriesi 2007;

Kitschelt 1986; Giugni 1998), we can confirm in this case that social movements are born and develop not only in response to difficult contingent circumstances but within the opportunities that are given in a specific socio-historical context.

As highlighted by Bosi and Zamponi (2015), the contemporary economic crisis in Italy and its representation is no more dramatic than the crisis of the mid-1970s. Nevertheless, the outcomes in terms of mobilisation are just the opposite. The causes should not only be ascribed to the fact that they take place in different phases of the capitalist economy but also to the historical dialectic between social movements and parties, which mark the Italian context (della Porta 1996). As highlighted by Tarrow (1989) in his analysis of the mobilisation of the 1960s and 1970s, in Italy the participation in a social movement intensified when they were convinced of being able to find backing in, or put pressure on, leftist parties for increasing the possibility of success of the protest. In fact, the post-Second World War Italian context registered a continuous exchange between movements and left parties as well as the cases of double militancy, which ended in a reciprocal influence.

Nevertheless, to observe the evolution of the contemporary Italian social movement, the country's features have to be considered within a context of an information society where the nature of social movements change radically as well as those of the leftist parties, which after the Cold War do not represent an alternative to neo-liberalism, either in terms of ideologies or policies (Melucci 1996).

Starting from these premises, in this chapter we explore why the spring of the world occupy movements did not arrive in Italy. We will pay attention to the dialectic between movements and radical Left parties in recent Italian history, as well as to the transformation of the nature of the social movement in a globalised context. In this sense we will start our reflection on the largest anti-globalist and anti-war movement, which was born in the summer of 2001 in Genoa and marked the first decade of the new millennium. Next, we will pay attention to the rise of the localised single-issue protests which arose and spread all over Italy, focusing particularly on the cases of the *No Tav* and *No Dal Molin* movements. Then, we will analyse the emergence of the Five-Star Movement (M5S) on the political scene and its installation within a political space left empty by the radical Left, consolidating within the social movements. Finally, we will reflect on why, during the economic recession, the anti-austerity protests failed to take to the streets and embark on institutionalisation through the M5S.

The failed momentum: the marginalisation of the radical Left after the G8 protests

The G8 of Genoa in July 2001 can be assumed as a starting point in the analysis of the complex relationship between social movements and political actors. The protests against that meeting were organised by a huge coalition of different social subjects, thousands of organisations and associations mixing Catholics with communists, anarchists with scouts, trades unionists with vegans, gays and lesbians. This organisational density, converging on the platform of Genoa

Social Forum (GSF), shared the opposition to neo-liberal globalisation. The agenda of the movement was on global issues (debt, poverty, trade, migration, war); and it was opened by the protests against the WTO Conference in Seattle in 1999 using the window of visibility provided by this event. Although the actors in GSF presented different sensibilities and cultures, they started to elaborate a dialogue and to build a political space.

The multiplicity of organisations involved in GSF was unexpectedly exceeded by a multitude from all over Europe (300,000) responding to the call for mobilisation over several days: the movement began to be known as "the movement of movements" to reflect this heterogeneity as a richness. Moreover, this network, starting at a global level, worked also as a national political space. The right-wing government of Berlusconi had just won the election, and the previous centre-left government – a coalition called *L'Ulivo* (the Olive) – had prepared and imagined the G8 meeting. The movement of movements was almost completely isolated.

In 1998 *Rifondazione Comunista* – the main radical Left party (more than three million votes in the 1996 election, representing nearly 8.5 per cent of the voters) – withdrew its support of the government of *L'Ulivo* and of their soft neo-liberal policies, undergoing a split inside the party and the loss of half of MPs elected who formed an alternative pro-governmental communist party. In doing so, the radical Left became the only institutional political subject recognised as a possible ally and supporter of social movements. In 1999, the *L'Ulivo* Government participated in the NATO bombing of Serbia and was totally discredited amongst those in the peace movement, where Catholic tradition and networks play an important role.

During the Genoa demonstrations, the youth communist organisation of *Rifondazione* joined the *Tute bianche* (White Overalls), an umbrella organisation for hundreds of squat centres inspired by the experience of *Autonomia Operaia* (Worker Autonomy) and other autonomist extra-parliamentary radical groups of the seventies. Both comprised a new subject called *Disobbedienti* (Disobedients), which mixed direct action, mass organisation and self-management. According to the leaders of this project, the marriage aimed, somehow, to establish the end of the fracture between communists and autonomous groups, dating back to 1977.[1]

The movement in Genoa was militarily destroyed by a cruel repression (GSF 2002) – after decades had passed, once again police killed a young protester in the streets – but it opened a huge cycle of mobilisation for several years on different topics, at global and national levels. That experience of a harsh repression, which unveiled the fragility of democracy, acted also as a baptism for a new generation of thousands of activists in the new millennium. During those days of July 2001, the GSF was the basis for the formation of a new generation of radical-left leaders – such as Pablo Iglesias and Alexis Tsipras – of successful radical parties in contemporary Spain and Greece; nonetheless, none of the Italian leaders in the anti-G8 demonstration played a relevant role in national politics.

After 2001, Italy experienced an impressive cycle of demonstrations and strikes, whose dimension had few precedents in the political history of the country (Aa.Vv. 2002); the agenda also turned to national matters. The experience of the Social Forum, as a way to put together different cultural and political traditions, spread in almost every city. In March 2002, the main Trade Union – CGIL – gathered three million people in Rome to stop a labour counter-reform of the Berlusconi Government to ensure employers the right to freely dismiss. In November 2002, nearly one million people attended the Social Forum in Florence. Thousands mobilised against authoritarian acts of the right-wing Government and against the soft attitude of the political opposition. In February 2003, Rome had an overflowing gathering of millions of people against the announced invasion of Iraq. Several campaigns were joined by a multitude of demonstrators in the streets, calling for the free circulation of people and assaulting detention centres for migrants, or contesting temporary employment and flexibility policies in the labour market. Indeed, during the decade, precariousness became the norm for young people, a trend supported by governments of different political orientations. Job centres were boycotted and occupied, trains delivering weapons for war in Iraq were stopped by activists and railway workers; there were local actions, but the mobilisations operated as national campaigns, mixing direct actions and symbolic protests.

Briefly, in the three years following the G8, a massive movement of movements crossed Italy. It was a multitude acting on different topics: war, employment, democracy, migration, turning the global agenda national, and contesting both Right and traditional Left. No one in politics could represent it. Traditional unions had severe difficulties organising workers in precarious employment who comprised the main part of the youth workforce and they preferred to support the rights of older workers also because a huge part of those unionised are retired.[2]

Rifondazione was the only political actor who could enjoy some kind of trust in this landscape. But in 2006, when the new political elections were due to occur, leading people in the movement came back to their organisations, while *Rifondazione* opted once again to support the centre-left coalition – who went on to win the election by a very narrow margin – with the desire of bargaining with the Government for some results on a more radical agenda. It was a chimera that lasted only two years from 2006 to 2008. In 2008, Berlusconi won the election again.

What can we learn from this story? The movement was first strongly *captured* by the radical Left – many of their leaders were co-opted in the parliamentarian group of the party in the 2006 election – avoiding the birth of a new political space – but was subsequently abandoned. The space opened in that period by the movement of movements, for a larger political subjectivity and organisation was finally collapsing. Instead of challenging the Blairian attitude of centre-left parties by building a new and radical hegemonic project, able to transform and shift forward the legacy of communism in the twentieth century, *Rifondazione* finally chose to adapt a minority position inside a coalition implementing neo-liberal policies in a soft way. Social movements and the radical Left dramatically lost the momentum to transform the whole political system.

In the 2008 election, when Berlusconi won again, the radical Left disappeared as a parliamentary force and the structure of the party progressively collapsed under different divisions. The economic crisis began, and the EU management of the crisis used austerity as a device for destabilising class relations in favour of the capitalist class (Gallino 2011, 2012). "Austerity" became an overused word and the government started to implement massive social cuts on welfare and new policies of labour flexibility. Education was particularly affected and a new movement, called *L'onda* (The wave) – promoted by university students, professors and researchers – emerged the same year, occupying many universities all around the country. *L'onda* was the last national movement of some importance, the last mobilisation of universities, a space which always represented an indispensable social engine for any kind of mobilisation. However, *L'onda* was also the first movement to think of crises and austerity as original devices of control and social transformation; thus, any political representation stayed off the agenda (Caruso *et al.* 2010). From that moment, social movements started to become increasingly localised in specific community issues. Besides which, the political organisation of the M5S grew quickly, a new party mixing left and right-wing anti-system propositions in a post-ideological mood. This expressed, on a political level, a clear contestation of austerity as a European device in front of the other left and right coalitions, which were perceived as different sides of the same coin.

From the global to the local and return: the *No Tav* and *No Dal Molin* movements

One crucial dynamic in the articulation between the radical Left and social movements is the growth of single-issue mobilisations during the last decades. Apparently, these movements expressed a retrenchment to a narrower agenda, because they stood for a NO against some local project or infrastructural investment, mainly funded by public funds or driven by public actors (Caruso 2010).

Nonetheless, these NO movements opened the field to an in-depth discussion and a critique of a capitalistic way of life, a profit-driven society, and its impact on human and environmental well-being. In the social fabric of these movements, many radical Left activists were fully involved, trying to shift the contingent protest to a more critical stance on society. During the last decade, the phenomenon spread everywhere in Italy. From North to South, several groups with huge support from the local population engaged in battles on different topics: the opening of a high speed railway in Val Susa, the new US military base in Vicenza, the electromagnetic pollution in Sicily and the incineration plants in Parma, the mobile dikes in Venice, the new highway links in Liguria, the oil drilling in the Adriatic Sea or in Basilicata, the bridge planned to join Calabria and Sicily. Curiously, in an epoch of austerity and monetary constraints, these struggles challenged the meaning and the direction of public investments and expenses. They also revealed the selectivity of austerity: austerity cut social rights and entitlements, in front of labour market and welfare, but was not oriented towards big infrastructural public tenders. In this perspective, we can say that austerity is against people and not against capital.

The development of these NO movements constitutes one of the most important social conflicts and mass mobilisations in contemporary Italy (della Porta and Piazza 2008) and represents a field in which the relationship between radical politics and social movements is rapidly shifting. Although they appear as a local issue, the knowledge production inside these movements contributes towards transforming them into broader social facts, inspiring national debates and global political issues about progress and growth, and reifying the idea of global social phenomena (Robertson 1997). In order to provide some remarks about the relationship between politics and these types of social movements, we will briefly examine two paradigmatic cases: the *No Tav* and the *No Dal Molin* experiences.

No Tav (No High Speed Train) is a movement with a long trajectory. Born in 1991, nowadays it is still confronting, with positive results, the realisation of a new railway infrastructure, linking Italy to France, which will supposedly destroy a narrow valley and cause environmental damage to the local population. The planned investment was mainly based on EU funds[3] and was only supported by a bipartisan political coalition, joining post-social democrats on the left with right-wing parties. This was one of the main features of all these typologies of conflicts: on one side stood the big majority of the political system with the national and international economic corporations (industrial, trade…), on the other stood the local population. *No Tav* presented itself as a people's movement, crossing generations and unifying ordinary people against the *connubium* between immoral policies and immoral economics, whose effect was the destruction of a precarious environmental equilibrium in a local setting. *No Tav* acted as a movement against the system, because the system supported the waste of public resources without any concern for the social needs of the local population; in the accounts of activists, the system is concerned with just putting money inside the economy, inside banks, inside the financing (often corrupted) of politics, inside the web of companies supporting the political actors in power.[4] Indeed, the mainstream discourse and the media-scape, mainly against *No Tav*, was inflated with the argument of the NIMBY syndrome: a high speed train in Susa Valley is represented as a necessity for the economy, creating new jobs, and for the needs of the whole country, while inhabitants are represented as egoistic, primitives subjects refusing the obligations of social progress.

The *No Tav* movement, during its long history, with roots both in the workers' struggle in the cotton factories of the Valley in the 1970s (Accornero 2011) and in the fight against the construction of a highway in the 1980s, has revealed an impressive and long-standing capacity of mobilisation (hundreds of thousands of people in the demonstrations), as well as a radicalisation in the techniques of fight, shifting from demonstration to direct action in order to stop, interrupt or boycott the new railway and tunnel construction. The physical and permanent concentration in specific places, like the *indignados' acampadas*, was often experimented with the aim to prevent tunnel drilling. In these camps, like in *Puerta del Sol* in Madrid or in *Plaza Catalunya* in Barcelona, thousands of ordinary people and activists organised themselves and structured a common life devoted to the resistance and to success in the struggle. In other words, they materialised in a micro-dimension a new political arena where the conflict was staged. The state, in order to *liberate* the sites for drilling, applied massive repression with a huge deployment of police and military force, which drove to several legal indictments from resistance to terrorism. An example was to condemn one of the no-violent charismatic leaders of the movement Alberto Perino (who was 70 years old by that time) for resistance to a public officer in a demonstration in 2010. Recently, thousands of activists were incriminated under the terrorist law, several have been condemned to a total of 140 years in jail within a maxi-trial started by one of the most famous anti-mafia persecutors. In the speech for that trial in Turin, a State Procurator compared *No Tav* to Colombian FARC.[5] The military solution appeared to be the only one, in a context in which the State never tried seriously to negotiate with the movement. Indeed in this kind of conflict, the space for negotiation is narrow, because the activist just wants the withdrawal of the project. It is not a bargaining of a wage, it is just the measure of strength and determination between two actors, something that can be solved only in a yes/no dimension.

In the long run, *No Tav* mobilisation was able to build a large community across generations, with rituals, memories, popular institutions, sanctions against outsiders, recognition for insiders. Senaldi (2016) in his ethnography, reported accounts about the everyday boycotting of shop owners in the Susa Valley who supported the High Speed Project; elders reframed the state military intervention, evoking the memory of resistance against fascism. The use of violence as self-defence, direct action and sabotage against drilling were an important part of the local population and socially accepted as legitimate action, to make the fight more effective. Youth activists, applying their "body capital" in these forms of action, were supported by older generations.

The *No Tav* experience worked as a powerful imaginary device in the multiplication of local struggles all around Italy which progressively started to question the capitalistic way of development. For instance, the *No Tav* flag become the model for other NO movements.

Even if this movement was populated by many radical leftists, many of them coming from the autonomous and anarchist Italian squatting experience, the radical Left as a political subject in electoral competition was progressively displaced by the new M5S. The radical Left, as a political actor, lost social support as a result of being perceived as part of the power system of the Susa Valley. The Green and Communist parties (*Rifondazione Comunista*) had massive electoral wins in the Valley since the start of mobilisation. Nevertheless, their involvement in a government with Catholics and social democrats in 2006, strongly supporting the Tav project, undermined their credibility at a local level. Consequently, the M5S emerged as the main political subject in the social space of the movement; at the same time many local councils were progressively occupied by civic electoral coalitions supporting the *No Tav* movement.

In the *No Tav* sentiment, the State, due to the increasingly repressive management of social conflict, was progressively reframed as a "mafia conglomerate" which destroys the life and the territory of people for profit. The State and the Judicial System were perceived as a military force of occupation, with no evidence of a real difference between left- and right-wings. The participation of the radical electoral Left in the functioning of that system at a national level involved withdrawal and retrenchment from the electoral competition amongst activists of a social movement which clearly hegemonised the culture of a local setting.

The case of the *No Tav* was like the "foundational movement" of the "single issues" which arose in Italy during the last two decades. It is interesting, for this reason, to look at other "NO movements" so as to understand both the similarities and the differences.

The case on which we reflect is the *No Dal Molin* movement, which arose in 2006 in Vicenza, a small to medium city (113,000 inhabitants) of Northern-East Italy. The protest originated in the presentation from the city administration, ruled by centre-right, of the construction of a new US military base in the unused city airport "Dal Molin". The new base would have meant the arrival of 2,000 soldiers and their families, representing a further encroachment of US military presence in its territory which already included "Camp Ederle", one of the biggest US bases in Europe and two NATO military sites located inside, underground in the hillside above Vicenza where heavy weapons, including those with nuclear capabilities, have been stored.[6] Due to this foreign military concentration in its territory, the city has a long history of pacifist/anti-military movements, which were organised in the 1980s around social Catholicism and left-wing representation in the city. Although the cohabitation[7] with the American community was peaceful, several protests and demonstrations were carried out against their military presence. Nevertheless, the initial nucleus of protest around the construction of the new base arose from a coordination of different residents committees living in the neighbourhoods next to the area where the future base would have been built. These actors protested because they were fearful of the consequences for their territory in terms of the worsening quality of life and because of the environmental impact of the new base, which would have removed one of the few green areas of the city, would have put one of the biggest aquifers of the region in danger, and would have increased the vehicle traffic. For all these reasons and considering the fact that many people who joined the dissent were never political activists before, their protest mainly focused on the localisation of the base and the movement was suddenly labelled in the media–political discourse as a NIMBY movement. Nevertheless, this primordial formation of the movement was driven not only by chauvinism but also by a rebellion against an imposed decision coming from the top, excluding the people who lived in the territory, which showed the increasing distance between State and citizens and a crisis of "representativeness" (Privitera 2001), using words from the representative democratic system, which became wide-spread in Italy long before the beginning of the crisis. In the particular case of Vicenza, one of the main contested facts was the sale of the territory to a foreign State (Andrighetto and Bissoli 2007). In this moment, these committees recruited former militants from the pacifist movement in Vicenza, namely the members of the networks of leftist and Catholic activists who were mobilised during the era of Social Forums and the protest against the wars in Afghanistan and Iraq. The merger of these claims with the demands of sustainability and the respect of ter-ritory was also facilitated by the connection between anti-militarism and envi-ronmentalism, largely spread in Italy during the 1980s in the campaign against nuclear energy.

Nevertheless, the birth of the *No Dal Molin* movement happened at the end of 2006 when the city council approved the construction of the base. As Caruso affirmed (2010, 71) using a concept created by Piven and Cloward (1979), this was the "moment of madness" which took place when the actors who integrated a social movement reoriented their sense of belonging, displacing it from the single organisations to the movement, when new actors joined the movement and when the border between legal and illegal action became blurred.

In this circumstance, the movement became stronger and recruited a large number of Vicenza citizens and the mass initiative included people who took part in the Italian anti-globalist network and in other "*No* movements" (e.g. the *No Tav*). The protest was carried out along a double channel of both "institu-tional" and "street", which corresponds also with a sort of different role and competences within the *No Dal Molin* movement: the people of the committees and the more politicised activists. On the one hand, there was the organisation of a petition to stop the base project and later a local referendum. Moreover, there was institutional political action in trying to enter the local administration directly or indirectly through the local election (in 2008). On the other hand, there was the constitution of a Presidium located near the area of the future base, as well as that of the *No Tav* in Val di Susa. Here, self-financed by the activists, people started to meet every week to talk about the actions to take collectively against the Dal Molin project. Even if the Presidium was an open and horizontal space of discussion it was progressively hegemonised, little by little, by the most radical areas of the movement, which later broke with a progressive abandon-ment of the less politicised participants. This happened also because, in terms of organisation and leadership, the most experienced participants took action by displaying and disturbing, for example, the occupations of symbolic and institu-tional buildings of Vicenza and the interruption of the construction work. The Presidium *No Dal Molin* had the capacity to impose this question at a national level, appointing tactically mass-media coverage, which was obtained through different performances (e.g. they invited the Nobel prizewinner, Dario Fo, who spoke in support of the movement or they were protagonists on one of the most followed political talk shows).

In this sense, it is interesting to observe the position of the radical-left organ-isation in relation to the movement. *No Dal Molin* from the beginning refused being labelled politically in order to maintain the largest consensus. During the demonstration, the parties' and unions' flags were banned. Nevertheless, the leftist unions and parties tried constantly to visualise themselves inside the movement. The strong change in the relation between movement and governmental Left took place after the approval of the US base project by Prodi's Government, supported by *Rifondazione Comunista* in January 2007. Initially, the centre-left government, which won the general election in 2006 was seen as a hope for the *No Dal Molin* movement against the base project. This formalisation exacerbated the opposition inside the movement against the left parties' activists who were forced to choose a side. The ambiguity of the radical Left in declaring support for the *No Dal Molin* movement and in the practices supported by the government, was highlighted inside the parliament from other right parties, which started to create discontent within *Rifondazione*, contributing to the fall of the second Prodi government (Caruso 2010).

The governmental choice of *Rifondazione* marked the definitive break between radical-left and social movements in Italy. In the case of *No Dal Molin*, there were still some leaders who entered the political party at a regional level, including candidates for the Green party. On the other hand, also in this case, the role of a new actor emerged who jumped on the stage of Italian politics using another medium: the Internet. From the columns of his Blog, Beppe Grillo, in the case of *No Tav*, long before the foundation of the M5S, openly supported the referendum against Dal Molin, highlighting the betrayal of the traditional parties against the citizens.[8] The referendum was proposed by the Vicenza centre-left administration, which won the election mainly thanks to a clear position against the construction of the base. The new mayor promoted a local referendum, which was initially legally approved at a regional level but, afterwards, was blocked from a national court just four days before its celebration. Nevertheless, the referendum was symbolically celebrated thanks to the help of the activists, obtaining 30 per cent participation and 95 per cent of the decision against the base. After realising the impossibility of stopping the decision of building the base, which started in 2009, the *No Dal Molin* movement concentrated on stopping the construction work. Nevertheless, the required efforts became increasingly high and many people left, also because of the progressive split between the two souls of the movement. However, also if its action decreased, the Presidium resisted until 2013 and also started to foster other community initiatives (e.g. ethical consumption groups). In the beginning of 2017, the Presidium re-opened to celebrate the 10th year of its birth and to reflect on the experience of the movement. After the rejection of the referendum, the local administration started to negotiate with the national government for compensation to reduce the impact felt from the presence of the US base, obtaining the construction of a green area near the base, which would be named "Peace park".

The experience of the *No Dal Molin* movement, in comparison with *No Tav*, should be considered a defeat and the motivations, as Caruso (2010, 86–88) highlighted, must be attributed to the different history and duration of the protest, the different kind of works as well as the different actors in the two conflicting fields. Nevertheless, it is interesting to highlight what the two movements have in common. First, the two protests cut tangentially the political spectrum involving people with different (or no) political experiences, driven by the defence of commons good against global economic and political usurpation. Both bring the fight to the local doorsteps where the political actors become identifiable and nameable: citizens, activists, administrators, police forces … In this sense this fight is unlike the fights of other movements in other parts of the world in the last 30 years. Second, these movements are the re-materialisation of a fusion "in the street" of the two big social forces born in the Resistance against fascism which marked the post-war history of Italy: the communist movements and social Catholicism (which mostly acts in the silence of the Catholic hierarchies as in the case of the Dal Molin base). The bonding agent seems to be the environmental discourse that occurred in the 1980s.

Finally, in this brief overview, we can point out some elements in order to understand the low political capitalisation by the radical Left in the development of this new generation of social movements. First, the strategy of the electoral radical Left was always linked to a subaltern positioning: to stand as the leftist part in a coalition government, assuming the necessity to negotiate an electoral agreement with the majority party (the Democratic Party). The radical Left, at least this crucial subject – *Rifondazione Comunista* – never visualised a serious project of autonomy towards the idea of electoral coalition, both at local and national levels, something very different from the strategy of *Podemos* and SYRIZA, which built themselves against, respectively, PSOE and PASOK. In fact, PD, as PSOE, PASOK and other ancient social democrat parties all over Europe, have during the last decades completely interiorised the neo-liberal turn in politics, supporting capital-driven reforms in the labour market and in other social and economic spheres (Lavelle 2008). Economic interests prevail often on social concerns, as revealed in the case of big infrastructural public projects, neither discussed nor negotiated with the local population concerned.

From the Web to the street: the rise of the M5S

In the middle of the first decade of 2000, a new political player appeared in the Italian political arena that spoke outside the traditional political media of propaganda, such as newspapers and television. During these years, the Internet was already widespread within the general population and use of the Web permits generating messages without the mediation of expert message-makers (the journalists) as well as outside the control of the broadcasters. For this reason, the Internet has increasingly become the favourite media for activists of social movements because, on the one hand, it sets out a new form of organisation from a distance and, on the other, it has allowed for diffusion of messages practically for free, bypassing the politic and economic hegemonic gatekeepers (Castells 2015). Prior to the advent of Online Social Networks, the first decade of the new millennium was marked by a flourishing of personal and collective blogs where people started to express their ideas and opinions to a potentially unlimited audience who was also free to reply and comment. This change represents a huge step in terms of the creation of alternative sources of information.

In Italy, the blog that stood out for entering in the top ten of the most read blogs in the world was Beppe Grillo's (www.beppegrillo.it). Grillo is a famous Genoese comedian and political commentator from the 1980s. At the beginning of his career, he was banned from public television because of his biting satire against the corruption of the big Italian parties in the government, which would be swept away during the anti-corruption prosecution of the 1990s. After the television ban, he kept on with his ferocious critiques in the theatres and in the squares, attacking not only the political system but also global capitalism. His shows captured headlines when he denounced an Italian multinational company (Parmalat) for inflating its profits through financial tricks, a firm that went bankrupt that year pulling down with it hundreds of small investors who bought the shares of a "healthy" company that was not being investigated either by the press or by the justice system. This anti-establishment position converted Grillo and his blog to a legitimate public voice against the hegemonic political and economic powers in Italy.

The idea of creating a blog was proposed by an IT entrepreneur, Gianroberto Casaleggio, who shared Grillo's protest and understood the potentiality of the Web for conveying political communication. In other words, Casaleggio created the infrastructure of a new propaganda channel. In Grillo's blog, it was national and international experts (physics, biologists, economists, artists, philosophers, independent journalists) who granted authoritativeness and periodically posted their interventions, becoming both the sources and the senders of the message without intermediaries (Mosca *et al.* 2016). The legitimacy of these voices contributed to present Beppe Grillo's blog as a counter-information source within the galaxy of Italian media almost totally controlled by the broadcasts, the newspapers and the advertising empire of Berlusconi.

The main topics that mark the blog overlap the issues that the Italian social movement has brought to the public discourse since the GSF: opposition to global capitalism, environmentalism, pacifism, freedom of scientific research, defence of the common good, etc.

The proposals from the blog for achieving these aims were the realisation of a new "direct democracy", that returns power to the people excluded from the dynamic of globalisation (another GSF pillar), through the Internet. The Web-democracy in the discourse of the founders would break the bonds between economic power and the political system, that undergird representative democracy ruled by the traditional parties and which maintain control of information through traditional media.[9] In these directions, the blog began to promote the organisation of local groups (the "Friends of Beppe Grillo") that met together through the "Meet-up" Internet social platform. This platform, conceived for gathering together people with similar interests who lived nearby, became a medium of activism, to coordinate people who wanted to carry out local claims, for instance, promoting door-to-door waste collection instead of the construction of a polluting waste incinerator.

The creation of the Meet-ups, reified in practice a "real" movement in the streets, which was organised with a top-down model through the Web from a diarchy surrounded by scientific experts who boosted the formation of a galaxy of little local groups. The blog offered a post-ideological umbrella that permitted people of different political orientations to come together, to act on the level of local policies, where ideological conflict is reduced. These activists did not identify more with the old parties, which preferred to abandon the streets to create a simulacrum of conflict in the TV arenas (Baudrillard 1996). Furthermore, they could not accept their system of close hierarchies and clientelism, which configured them as "cast" far from "ordinary people" and substituted the modern class conflict between the richest oppressors and poorest oppressed (considering that Grillo himself is a billionaire).

At the same time, Beppe Grillo embraced the cause of the still existent local movement, as we mentioned before in the case of *No Tav* and *No Dal Molin*, offering them the opportunity for visibility and offering to the public an alternative narration to the one of the mainstream press. In this manner, Grillo acquired the legitimacy of being a speaker for these movements, within the media-political field (Mosca 2014).

Moreover, since the start of the economic crisis, the pages of Grillo's blog have carried a battle against the EU "austerity policies" that meant welfare expenditures and privatisation of common goods. The blog openly supported[10] one of the biggest Italian "anti-austerity protests" carried out by the committees, that of "water as a common good", which promoted the abrogative referendum against the privatisation of the distribution of potable water and the return to nuclear energy production, imposed by law during the Berlusconi government (2009). The battle of the committees won, due to the fact that the referendum had the largest participation since the 1990s and an overwhelming victory for the abrogation of the law (95 per cent).

The Grillo's "proto-movement" took to the street at a national level on 8 September (a symbolic date for the Italian history) of 2007 to organise the "V-day", where V stands for *Vendetta* and for *Vaffanculo* a popular insult that the comedian repeats persistently during his shows, as a *mantra* against the power abuse. This day, in 500 Italian squares, a petition for a popular law proposal "clean parliament" was proposed seeking to forbid people with criminal records to have the possibility to candidate for the parliament (a widespread practice within the main Italian parties). This initiative gathered in one day more than 300,000 firms and the support of important personalities from culture and showbiz. Practically, it was a way to test the potentialities of "real" political movements.

Therefore, Grillo recollected and amplified a discourse, which was already widespread within the Italian public sphere since GSF, thanks to the action of the different social movements at local and national levels. This discourse has been shared also by the radical Left parties until they chose a governmental alliance with the social-democratic ones, which was also one of the main causes of their almost complete disappearance from the parliament, obtaining a result slightly above 3 per cent in the elections of 2008 and 2013, losing two-thirds of the votes. On the other hand, he embraced the discourse on the justicialism which was a historical piece of resistance of the far-right, the *Lega Nord* (the separatist xenophobic party of Northern Italy), and the *Italia dei Valori* (Italy of the Values), the party founded at the end of the 1990s by Antonio di Pietro, an ex anti-corruption magistrate. Further, Grillo managed to expand the audience of the social movements translating their ideas in a message adapted to "ordinary people". In this sense, his showman abilities have been crucial: he managed to alternate rational thoughts with profanities, using the typical strategies of the populist leaders (Tronconi 2016).

When Italians began to feel the effects of the crisis, Grillo and his followers already became legitimate actors of the Italian political field. From his blog and in the street, Grillo spoke against the EU austerity policy, the hetero-direction and corruption of the Italian politicians obtaining an increasing consensus, especially among the young people who suffered most from the crisis,[11] who are informed through the Internet, and who feel abandoned by the parties and unions and cannot find a political subject at a national level with which they can identify.

This "conglomeration" of Grillo followers became a real political movement when, in 2008, the creation of a civil list at the local level for entering municipal administrations was proposed, like a "virus" which would infect the corrupted political system, starting from the bottom of the institutional organisation. For the European election in 2009, Grillo fostered the victory of a couple of candidates of the *Italia dei Valori*. In the same year he provocatively ran in the primary election for the leadership of the Democratic Party but he was banned from the run. Afterwards, he founded, together with Casaleggio, the M5S.

The five stars represent the principles that will drive the M5S: public goods (water), environment, connectivity, development and mobility. The M5S presents itself as a no-party with no leader, ruled by the citizens. Under this rhetoric there is, first, the attempt to not lose bonds with the social movements, reinforcing the complaint against the traditional parties in order to maintain a double nature of institutional and street movements. Second, this discourse is based on deliberative democracy (Graeber 2013), claiming equality in the political decision-making amongst all the citizens and it is summarised in the slogan: "One count one". The dream of the deliberative democracy relates the M5S to the anti-austerity movements in other countries. For this reason, they nominate "ordinary people" who do not have previous experience with political activism in the parties (who are not eligible as candidates) and can be nominated only for two terms. Within this rhetoric, the candidates are not professional politicians but only spokesmen: "citizens inside the institution". These restrictions are the expression of a utopia of purity that marks the M5S and presents it as radically different from the old dirty parties, claiming an idiosyncrasy between "the caste" (politic, economic, media establishment) and "the people" to whom they want to give a voice.

Drawing from Casaleggio, deliberative democracy can be achieved thanks to the Web, namely from an online platform (it is named *Rousseau*), where all the

M5S subscribers can present law proposals or discuss and vote for them, as well as nominate the candidate–spokesmen. Nevertheless, the Internet is not only the means for achieving the ends but it becomes an end in itself, a sacred object that makes real the utopia of a politics without the intermediation of the parties. This discourse hides the role of the charismatic leader and the creator of the infrastructure, who should only be warrantors of this transformation but in reality are the counsellors of the movement and they impose the political line and decide the expulsions for the elected dissidents, configuring de facto a theoretical horizontal movement as a top-down one (Dal Lago 2013).

The M5S has maintained a persistent ambiguity on its political orientation, which emerges as a contradiction in those issues that overcome the local level. For instance, in relation to the EU there is tension between Europeanism in order to avoid the threat of rising neo-nationalism/fascism and Anti-Europeanism, against an oppressive EU and asking for a referendum for quitting the Euro currency. Also the migration policy is a hot topic for the M5S that maintains a position that swings between reinforcing border control in order to stop "uncontrolled" migration, the abstention on the proposal of law for giving citizenship to migrants' children born in Italy and the creation of humanitarian corridors for refugees (Colloca and Corbetta 2016).

For all these features, the M5S is classified as a populist movement (Lanzone 2014). Despite Grillo continuing with an ambiguous political positioning, many of the 140,000 M5S activists of the meet-ups, and its representatives in municipal administrations and in the Parliament have a past history of activism in leftist social movement (Mosca 2014). In this sense, M5S represents a container and an umbrella for people who participate in different Italian social movements and see in the M5S another channel through which to pursue their own claims. Nevertheless, the ambiguity and the populism vocation risks hiding the claim of the social movements, which are the main force of the M5S. In this sense as remarked by the leftist cultural critic, the leftist activists inside M5S should get a cultural hegemony and not give in to compromise of accepting far-right discourses (Wu Ming-Giap 2013). Only in this sense can a movement adopt a populist strategy that can create a counter-hegemonic discourse (Laclau 2015).

In the last few years, the M5S has increasingly collected a series of excellent results and victories in the local, regional and general elections: it had the highest number of votes and ruled the government of middle cities and the capital. In this sense, it became the political reference of an anti-austerity protest during the economic crisis against the hegemonic system represented by the Troika, which de facto imposed the destitution of Berlusconi (2011) and imposed the technocratic government of Monti who was in charge of carrying out welfare expenditure (e.g. the reform of pensions). Furthermore, the centre-left supported Monti's government and until today is the political coalition in charge of applying austerity policies in Italy.

During the flourishing of the "European springs" and of the "Occupy movements" all over the world there was an attempt to build an anti-austerity movement among different institutional and extra-institutional subjects on the left.

The starting point of the movement would be the demonstration organised in Rome in autumn 2011 ("Occupy Rome") by the *indignati* the same day in which *Occupy* movements all over the world decided to demonstrate together. Despite 200,000 people participating in the demonstration in Rome, it was a failure. The most radical fringes assumed the leading role in the protest which turned violent, breaking away from the otherwise peaceful protest and the Italian *indignati* movement. On the one hand, the degeneration of the protest was due to disastrous police coordination that did not protect pacifists from the violent protesters. On the other hand, there was a lack of coordination amongst the anti-austerity forces who joined the demonstration but were more focused on the Berlusconi government falling than giving unity and autonomy to an Italian anti-austerity movement (Zamponi 2012).

Therefore, different from other Southern European countries, the anti-austerity protest displaced the fight from the street to the institutions. The M5S entered and legitimated itself as a new actor in a field of conflict that was abandoned by the Left and finally took that space. Despite this fact, in the cities where M5S won the government, it has not managed to take strong anti-austerity choices, nor act within the tracks of the *realpolitik*. However, the strong tradition of the Italian Left and its cultural hegemony were unable to let another political subject on the Left emerge, like *Podemos* in Spain.

Final considerations

Having explored nearly 17 years of the relationship between social movements and the radical Left in the Italian arena, one major point to highlight is the pervasiveness of the neo-liberal hegemony in politics. Indeed, left and right-wings share a lot of fundamentals in economics: market-driven reforms, privatisation, reduction of taxes and welfare provisions, flexibility of labour markets. They do not disagree on the direction, just on the intensity of a path, which is deemed the only one possible. For a major part of the observed period, austerity was actively managed and directed by a "soft leftist" coalition. In this frame, the radical Left renounced, or was not able to reimagine, itself, generating new discourses and visions of society; mainly it opted to represent a meaningless and powerless part in a democratic coalition. Social movements often acted in a frustrating relationship with the radical Left, which finally opened an empty space for political representation. Such an empty space was occupied by the M5S, claiming to be a coherent actor in the battle against austerity and the European cage of fiscal contracts, as well as against the bipartisan elite and their corrupted business. Nonetheless, its first experiences in government at the local level illustrate a growing gap between the rhetoric of horizontal democracy and social policies driven by the common good ideal, and reality, which features charismatic authoritarianism and the permeability of vested interests that mark the political line. The reflection we carry out suggests that the transformation of the Italian political system in its relationship with social constituencies, as for instance the social movements, is still in progress. The massive NO mobilisations that crossed Italy in the past decades and still continue (for instance in the case of the rejection of the last constitutional reform proposed by the government of the Democratic Party in 2016), clearly show that the refusal of the establishment and neo-liberal policies has not yet found the momentum for a new articulation between politics and social claims. As Gramsci taught us nearly 100 years ago, when fascism and communism fought to appear as a solution to the crisis of the bourgeois democracy, Italy in 2017 is still a context where the old is gone and the new is struggling to emerge.

Acknowledgement

We especially thank Sandro Mezzadra for sharing with us his reflections on the evolution of contemporary social movements and the radical Left in Italy. Thank you also to Francesco Bissoli and Luca Andrighetto for the interview and the materials on the *No Dal Molin* movement.

Notes

1 On the experience of Disobedients, it is interesting to consult the book, derived from the PhD thesis, of Iglesias Turrión (2011), the leader of *Podemos*.
2 For instance, retired workers are more than 50 per cent of those unionised in CGIL, the biggest Union in Italy (www.spi.cgil.it/quanti-siamo).
3 The project was part of the Mediterranean corridor of the EU Trans-European Transport Network (TEN-T).
4 For a narrative overview of the history of the *No Tav* movement, in its origins and claims, see Wu Ming 1 (2016).
5 Here there is the news release of the Italian news agency ANSA www.ansa.it/piemonte/notizie/2016/11/17/pg-condannate-no-tav-o-rischio-farc_56afc1aa-6453-4763-b0fc-c0645a863ffc.html.
6 The *No Dal Molin* Movement did a military "touristic" map of these sites www.nodalmolin.it/Disponibile-la-mappa-turistica#.WJDV0dLhDIU.
7 The military and their families have their own shops, pharmacy, hospitals, and schools inside the base and the opportunity of getting in contact with the autochthonous population has always been very limited.
8 www.beppegrillo.it/2008/10/reeferendum_on_line_per_la_base_militare_dal_molin.html www.beppegrillo.it/m/2011/12/person_of_the_y_1.html.
9 For a direct overview on how this concept has been shaped by Gianroberto Casaleggio, the co-founder and ideology of the movement, it is interesting to take a look at the book he wrote shortly before he passed away (Casaleggio 2016).
10 The referendum initiative was supported also by the radical Left and only at the very end by the Democratic Party.
11 Grillo (2007) edited the editorial success *Schiavi moderni* (Modern Slaves), in which he collected the stories of precarious people.

References

Aa.Vv. 2002. "La Primavera dei Movimenti". *Micromega*, no. 2.
Accornero, Aris. 2011. *Quando C'era la Classe Operaia. Storie di Vita e di Lotte al Cotonificio Valle Susa*. Bologna: Il Mulino.

Andrighetto, Luca, and Francesco Bissoli. 2007. "Nuovi Movimenti e Nuovi Strumenti di Democrazia: Vicenza e Il 'No Dal Molin.'" *Pace, Conflitti e Violenza* 4 (4): 9–14.

Baudrillard, Jean. 1996. *Il Delitto Perfetto. La Televisione Ha Ucciso la Realtà?* Milano: Cortina.

Borghi, Elisa. 2013. "The Impact of Anti-Crisis Measures and the Social and Employment Situation: Italy". *European Union*. Brussels.

Bosi, Lorenzo, and Lorenzo Zamponi. 2015. "Direct Social Actions and Economic Crises. The Relationship between Forms of Action and Socio-Economic Con-Text in Italy". *Patecipazione e Conflitto* 8 (2): 367–391.

Caruso, Loris. 2010. *Il Territorio della Politica. La Nuova Partecipazione di Massa nei Movimenti No Tav e No Dal Molin*. Milano: Franco Angeli.

Caruso, Loris, Alberta Giorgi, Alice Mattoni, and Gianni Piazza, eds. 2010. *Alla Ricerca dell'Onda. I Nuovi Conflitti nell'Istruzione Superiore*. Milano: Franco Angeli.

Casaleggio, Gianroberto. 2016. *Veni, Vidi, Web*. Milano: Adagio.

Castells, Manuel. 2015. *Networks of Outrage and Hope: Social Movements in the Internet Age*. 2nd edn. London & New York: Wiley & Sons.

Colloca, Pasquale, and Piergiorgio Corbetta. 2016. "Beyond Protest: Issues and Ideological Inconsistencies in the Voters of the Movimento 5 Stelle". In *Beppe Grillo's Five Star Movement. Organisation, Communication and Ideology*, edited by Filippo Tronconi, 195–212. Farnham: Ashgate.

Dal Lago, Alessandro. 2013. *Clic! Grillo, Casaleggio e la Demagogia Elettronica*. Napoli: Cronopio.

della Porta, Donatella. 1996. *Movimenti Collettivi e Sistema Politico in Italia, 1960–1995*. Bari: Laterza.

della Porta, Donatella, and Gianni Piazza. 2008. *Le Ragioni Del NO. Le Campagne Contro La Tav in Val Susa E Il Ponte Sullo Stretto*. Milano: Feltrinelli.

Eurostat. 2017. *Database Eurostat*. European Commission. http://ec.europa.eu/eurostat/data/database.

Ferrera, Maurizio. 1996. "The 'Southern Model' of Welfare in Social Europe". *Journal of European Social Policy* 6 (1): 17–37.

Gallino, Luciano. 2011. *Finanzcapitalismo*. Torino: Einaudi.

Gallino, Luciano. 2012. *La Lotta di Classe dopo la Lotta di Classe*. Bari: Laterza.

Giugni, Marco G. 1998. "Was It Worth the Effort? The Outcomes and Consequences of Social Movements". *Annual Review of Sociology* 24: 371–393.

Graeber, David. 2013. *The Democracy Project: A History, a Crisis, a Movement*. London: Allen Lane.

Grillo, Beppe, ed. 2007. *Schiavi Moderni. Il Precario nell'Italia Delle Meraviglie*. Casaleggio Associati.

GSF. 2002. *Genova – Il Libro Bianco*. Roma: Unità, Liberazione & manifesto libri.

Iglesias Turrión, Pablo. 2011. *Desobedientes. De Chiapas a Madrid*. Madrid: Editorial Popular.

Kitschelt, Herbert. 1986. "Political Opportunity Structures and Political Protest: Anti-Nuclear Movement in Four Democracies". *British Journal of Political Science* 16 (1): 57–85.

Kriesi, Hanspeter. 2007. "Political Context and Opportunity". In David A. Snow, Sarah A. Soule and Hanspeter Kriesi (eds), *The Blackwell Companion to Social Movements*, Oxford: Blackwell, 67–90.

Laclau, Ernesto. 2015. *Ernesto Laclau: Post-Marxism, Populism, and Critique*. Edited by David R Howarth. London & New York: Routledge.

Lanzone, Maria Elisabetta. 2014. "The 'Post-Modern' Populism in Italy: The Case of the Five Star Movement". In *The Many Faces of Populism: Current Perspectives*, edited by Dwayne Woods and Barbara Wejnert, 53–78. Bingley: Emerald Group Publishing Limited.

Lavelle, Ashley. 2008. *The Death of Social Democracy: Political Consequences in the 21st Century*. Aldershot: Ashgate.

Melucci, Alberto. 1996. *Challenging Codes: Collective Action in the Information Age*. Cambridge: Cambridge University Press.

Migliavacca, Mauro, Alessandro Rosina, and Emiliano Sironi. 2015. "Condizione lavorativa e mobilità internazionale delle nuove generazioni italiane". *Mondi Migranti*, 53–78.

Mosca, Lorenzo. 2014. "Il Movimento 5 Stelle E I Conflitti Locali". *Il Mulino*, no. 2: 223–230.

Mosca, Lorenzo, Cristian Vaccari, and Augusto Valeriani. 2016. "An Internet-Fuelled Party? The Movimento 5 Stelle and the Web". In *Beppe Grillo's Five Star Movement. Organisation, Communication and Ideology*, edited by Filippo Tronconi, 127–152. Farnham: Ashgate.

OECD. 2017. *OECD.stat*. http://stats.oecd.org/.

Piven, Frances Fox, and Richard A. Cloward. 1979. *Poor People's Movements: Why They Suceed, How They Fail*. New York: Vintage Book Editions.

Privitera, Walter. 2001. *Sfera Pubblica e Democratizzazione*. Roma-Bari: Laterza.

Robertson, Roland. 1997. "Glocalization: Time-Space and Homogeneity-Heterogeneity". In *Global Modernities*, edited by Mike Featherstone, Scott Lash, and Roland Robertson, 25–44. London: Sage.

Roca Martínez, Beltrán, Ibán Díaz Parra, and Emma Martín-Díaz, eds. 2017. *Challenging Austerity. Radical Left and Social Movements in the South of Europe*. London: Routledge.

Senaldi, Alessandro. 2016. *Cattivi e Primitivi. Il Movimento No Tav tra Discorso Pubblico, Controllo e Pratiche di Sottrazione*. Verona: Ombre corte.

Tarrow, Sidney. 1989. *Democracy and Disorder: Protest and Politics in Italy 1965–1975*. Oxford: Oxford University Press.

Tronconi, Filippo, ed. 2016. *Beppe Grillo's Five Star Movement. Organisation, Communication and Ideology*. Farnham: Ashgate.

Wu Ming-Giap. 2013. "Perché 'tifiamo Rivolta' nel Movimento 5 Stelle". www.wumingfoundation.com/giap/2013/02/piccola-storia-ignobile-con-lettera-aperta-al-movimento-5-stelle/.

Wu Ming 1. 2016. *Un Viaggio che non Promettiamo Breve. 25 Anni di Lotte NO TAV*. Torino: Einaudi.

Zamponi, Lorenzo. 2012. "'Why Don't Italians Occupy?' Hypotheses on a Failed Mobilisation". *Social Movement Studies* 11 (3–4): 416–426.

Conclusion

Learning from the economic crisis and the protest cycle in the South of Europe – implications for social movements and the Left

Emma Martín-Díaz, Ibán Díaz-Parra and Beltrán Roca

Throughout the different chapters of this book we have been able to distinguish two opposed and at the same time complementary tendencies: the first one refers to the importance of what, following Mercier, could be called "national colourings" in the configuration of social movements and the protagonist subjects of these movements. For this reason, in the approach of this book we decided to give space to the diachronic dimension and the historical background of these processes. As can be seen, although every country, with the exception of Italy, presents as common features a recent past of dictatorship in a post-war context, and a virtually simultaneous process of European convergence, the transition to a democratic context presents meaningful variations depending on the force interrelations among institutions and political groups that play a central role in such a transition. The cases of Spain and Portugal are good examples of this, since the army played a radically different role and the socialist parties opted for different strategies as a response to austerity policies: reinforcing the bi-party regime in the Spanish case, or reaffirming a Left coalition in the Portuguese case. The political crisis in Italy could not be understood without analysing the disappearance of the Communist Party in the context of the collapse of the Soviet regime and its area of influence. Neither could the situation of Greece be explained without paying attention to the PASOK crisis. It is demonstrated that these historical backgrounds are essential in order to explain the existing diversity in the analysed models.

But, together with the importance of the local level, we have demonstrated that there is also a common thread in all of these cases: the semi-peripheral position of these Nation-states within the EU, which is reflected in the form – common for all cases and different from the countries in the centre of the EU – in which the debt crisis affected them. In this sense, although the actors mobilized in order to give an alternative response from the Left to this situation of crisis are different, they have in common their ability to translate the discomfort of the population generating challenging discourses that, although do not have the quality of formulating alternative responses to austerity policies, provide delegitimizing and contesting elements before these policies and the powers that implement them.

This semi-peripheral character determines the political antagonism in its different configurations and scales, in grass-roots and social movements as well as in political institutions when this is taken by radical parties and electoral coalitions. On one hand, as we have shown in the case of Spain, the deep impact of the crisis in weak and highly speculative economies of Mediterranean Europe, raises the question of materialistic demands and the relation between movements and State institutions. The conception of social movements as strictly anti-conventional political and post-materialistic entities does not make sense in the crisis and post-crisis context in this region, as a result of the weakness of its position in the political and economic structure of Europe. On the other hand, the rise of radical governments has shown the weakness and limitations to autonomy and effective control on its national economy because of its peripheral position. The post-2008 crisis events have been especially significant in disciplining Nation-states, and have showed the extreme impotence of nation-state institutions against current centres of economic and political power in the European Union. Thus, the attempts in making a sovereign politics in the UK and Greece had a radically diverse political content and results. To what extent Portuguese, Spanish and Italian experience will follow the Greek path only political praxis in the next years would say.

The responses of labour, left parties and social movements

In the four countries, the first actors that gave the first response to austerity measures were trade unions. They tended to use general strikes as their main weapon before the imposition of public policies that undermine their sources of power and damaged the working class. In Portugal, social protest was initially (in the period 2010–2013) led by trade unions, *Confederação Geral dos Trabalhadores Portugueses* (CGTP) and the General Workers' Union or *União Geral de Trabalhadores* (UGT). The trade union movement, especially the CGTP, which has a more combative character, called five times for general strikes in order to contest austerity policies. In Spain, the major unions – Workers Commissions (*Comisiones Obreras-CCOO*) and General Workers Union (*Unión General de Trabajadores-UGT*) – called for three nationwide general strikes and the Basque majority unions ELA and LAB, supported by radical unions such as CGT, CNT and others, called for a general strike in 2011. In Greece, there has been large-scale use of the general strike. In the period 2009–2014 there took place approximately 30 general strikes, called by trade unions the Central Trade Unions Confederation of Greek Workers (GSEE) and Central Union of Civil Servants (ADEDY). In Italy, the Italian General Confederation of Labour (CGIL) called for a general strike against austerity on 6 September 2011. It also called for a strike of four hours on 14 November 2012, coinciding with the general strike in Spain. General strikes used to be combined with massive demonstrations in the four countries.

Left political parties had another key role in mobilizations. In Greece, KKE, Syriza and Antarsya supported social protest whereas PASOK (in power from 2009 to 2012), which had strong influence over major trade unions, used this influence to moderate and control labour opposition. In Spain, the socialist party (PSOE) also launched the first austerity policies with the Government of President Zapatero (2004–2011), although their historical links with the UGT did not impede the call for a general strike in 2010. In Portugal, the neo-liberal PSD (in office from 2011 to 2015) implemented the harder austerity policies, and Left parties PS, PCP and BE supported massive demonstrations and general strikes. In Italy, *Rifondazione* was integrated into a centre-left coalition from the 2006 elections, and left empty the political space of opposition to austerity.

Against this immediate background, 2011 marks the rise of a new political cycle, and the emergence of new political subjectivities that, in some cases, entered in contradiction with traditional Left parties and trade unions. The *indignados* massive protest in May 2011 in Spain spread to other countries in what has been called the "European spring". One of its characteristics was its initial distrust of political parties and trade unions. In Portugal, for example, the demonstration "Desperate Generation" on 12 March 2011 reflected the rise of this new pattern of mobilization (horizontal, Internet-based, autonomous from political parties, and with network form).

Nevertheless, as time went by, political parties and trade unions (especially those from the radical Left) began to cooperate with the new generations of activists. In Spain, the slogan "Trade unions, thanks for coming" in a demonstration in Madrid reflected this reconciliation. In the third chapter of this book, we suggest a materialist and electoral shift in social protest in Spain, with the collaboration between the *indignados* and the trade union movement after 2012, and the rise of Podemos and municipalist groups after 2014. As Estanque, Costa and Fonseca have stated, in Portugal, the support and affinity with these mobilizations from *Bloco de Esquerda* (which was created in 1999 and had strong links to NSMs in previous stages) was clearer than from trade unions and the PCP. The protests of 15 October 2011 after the signature of the Memorandum, was a part of a global protest, in which slogans reflected the representation crisis of traditional parties and State institutions ("Direct democracy now", "They don't represent us", and "We are the 99%"). Later, the protests "Screw the Troika!" in 2012 and 2013 deepened this popular opposition to austerity and representation crisis. The support of BE to general strikes and mobilizations in 2013 was essential. In Greece, the voice of the *indignados* movements grew louder and stronger. SYRIZA had a strategy of coalition and support with the *indignados*. However, KKE refused to support these mobilizations, which it regarded as apolitical and quasi-nationalist. In fact, KKE and trade unions used to march separately from SYRIZA, ANTARSYA and the *indignados*. In Italy, social protest did not become as radicalized and huge as in Portugal, Spain and Greece.

It must be added that social democratic parties were not only ambiguous or reluctant in regard to the new social movements, in some cases they were clear opponents. Those social democratic parties that implemented austerity policies –

Greek PASOK and Spanish PSOE – experienced a dramatic decline, setting the groundwork for the rise of alternative political forces. As Castellani and Queirolo Palma in Chapter 6 suggest, the political force that could occupy the empty space left by the neo-liberal turn of social democratic parties (PD in Italy), *Rifondazione Comunista*, opted for a strategy of forming coalition with the PD. This political space came to be occupied by the 5 Star Movement, which co-opted part of previous autonomous social movements, and had a clearly more ambivalent political position. M5S was the most voted party, with 25.5 per cent of the votes, in the Italian general elections of 2013. However, the coalitions of the other competing parties blocked any possibility of seizing power. In Greece, SYRIZA won enormous electoral support: from 4.5 per cent of the votes in 2009 to 16 per cent in May 2012 and 27 per cent in June 2012; in the 2015 elections it got 36 per cent of the votes and formed a government with a small Right party (ANEL). As Kanellopoulos points out in Chapter 4, SYRIZA seized power (instead of other Left parties, such as KKE and ANTARSYA (coalition of the anti-capitalist Left) which were bigger before the crisis and had a key role in anti-austerity protests, due to its "opportunistic" (populist) strategy in contrast with the more "ideologically coherent" strategy of KKE and ANTARSYA. In Spain, Podemos, created in 2014 for the European elections achieved in such elections more than one million votes (7.98 per cent) and five seats. In the 2015 Spanish elections, to which it concurred in coalition with United Left and other alternative political groups, they got 20.68 per cent of the votes (69 seats), getting closer to the 28.71 per cent of the Socialist Party, that was the second most voted for political party. In Portugal BE, in receiving 10.22 per cent of the votes in the general elections, opted to form a Government with the socialist and communist parties.

The old is dying and the new is to be born

Exhaustion of traditional Left institutions and a new path for political antagonism are the main topics in the current struggle against neo-liberalism and austerity in southern Europe. However, there are big differences between the four case studies in this book. Specifically, there seems to be major differences between Greece and Portugal on the one hand and Spain and Italy on the other. Political antagonism in Portugal and Greece is played out by traditional institutions of the working class: unions, communist parties. Whereas traditional working-class institutions in Spain and Italy, especially communist parties have shown a much bigger weakness. As result, new shapes have emerged with their own problems and contradictions.

The chapters in this book have discussed the crisis and obsolescence of traditional institutions of labour movement. Its limitations as the sole actor of political antagonism have been shown again and again in the last years, also during the economic crisis. However, in some sense, the 2008 economic crisis and 2011 political protest have shown the exhaustion and limitations of the classical *sixtyeighted* conception of social movements. Social movements have had a growing role in national politics and the relationship between social movements and political institutions has changed substantially, especially in Spain. Current social movements seem to be moving far from the political disaffection and post-materialism of New Social Movements born in the sixties. So, Spain shows the necessity in overcoming the limitations of the political disaffection and sole local and short-term action of social movements. In Italy, the increasing irrelevance of the radical Left set the groundwork for the rise of a post-political and opportunistic coalition such as the 5 Stars Movement. The rejection of state institutions and professional politics has driven the abandonment of state politics by social movements. This has been notorious in the disappearance of the left forces from Italian parliament. In Spain this topic was very similar to the situation in Italy, until the rise of Podemos and the recent local electoral coalitions. On the other hand, the model implemented by Podemos, as well as the action of Greek and Portuguese traditional left parties, still has a lot of the traditional state fetish. An alternative to this political reductionism is still to be found.

In every country of Southern Europe, both new political parties and social movements are prevented from reducing politics to a state-run institution. New relations between state institutions and social movements and the revitalization of the "party movement" formula, seem to be at the centre of the political debate now, even if the Greek situations seem to show a turning back to micro-politics after the SYRIZA deception. In any case, questions of state power, intervention in multiple scales and forms of organization (beyond communitarian and local scale) are unavoidable for antagonist politics nowadays and in Mediterranean Europe.

In his work *L'idéel et le matériel*, Godelier says that cultural transformations imply the substitution of the protagonist actors of each historical stage.[1] In the realm of ideas, these transformations go through three stages: the thinkable, the possible and the viable. For the social movements that have been analysed in this book there is a key date: the G8 meeting in Genoa in 2001, when the slogan "Another world is possible" got consolidated. However, the correct slogan would have been that another world was thinkable. The evolution of social movements in southern European countries present as a unifying thread evident signs that we are entering into the stage of the possible, although the resistance of hegemonic powers preserves the ability to impede to loom in a close horizon the stage of the viable. One could wonder if the wrestle between financial institutions and social movements can be sustained in the form and condition in which they currently take place without reaching a point of no return. In this respect, we must pay attention to the responses of the periphery in the following years, starting with Greece, where the disconnection seems to be becoming a real alternative to the austerity policies imposed by European powers.

Note

1 Godelier, Maurice, 1984, L'Idéel et le matériel. Pensée, économies, societés. Paris: Fayard.

Index

Page numbers in *italics* denote tables, those in **bold** denote figures.